The TROUBLE *with* TEXTBOOKS

The TROUBLE *with* TEXTBOOKS
Distorting History and Religion

GARY A. TOBIN
DENNIS R. YBARRA

LEXINGTON BOOKS
A division of
ROWMAN & LITTLEFIELD PUBLISHERS, INC.
Lanham • Boulder • New York • Toronto • Plymouth, UK

LEXINGTON BOOKS

A division of Rowman & Littlefield Publishers, Inc.
A wholly owned subsidiary of The Rowman &
Littlefield Publishing Group, Inc.
4501 Forbes Boulevard, Suite 200
Lanham, MD 20706

Estover Road
Plymouth PL6 7PY
United Kingdom

Copyright © 2008 by Lexington Books

British Library Cataloguing in Publication Information Available

Library of Congress Cataloging-in-Publication Data

Library of Congress Control Number: 2008931443

ISBN-13: 978-0-7391-3093-3 (cloth : alk. paper)
ISBN-10: 0-7391-3093-5 (cloth : alk. paper)
ISBN-13: 978-0-7391-3094-0 (pbk. : alk. paper)
ISBN-10: 0-7391-3094-3 (pbk. : alk. paper)
eISBN-13: 978-0-7391-3095-7
eISBN-10: 0-7391-3095-1

Printed in the United States of America

♾™ The paper used in this publication meets the minimum requirements
of American National Standard for Information Sciences—Permanence of
Paper for Printed Library Materials, ANSI/NISO Z39.48–1992.

CONTENTS

ACKNOWLEDGMENTS

This book is the product of many helpful hands. The research team at the Institute for Jewish & Community Research has contributed throughout the project. Beth Oelberger has been diligent in performing general research tasks, verifying citations and was involved in the survey of school districts. Thank you to Jenna Ferer for designing and implementing the survey of school districts and for her indispensable contribution to our supporting research. Rabbi Shlomo Zarchi reviewed the manuscript and was extremely helpful in fact checking sections relating to Jewish history, the bible, and history of the Middle East. Special thanks to Scott Rubin, who was instrumental in drafting the introduction and conclusion, and who contributed to the development of Chapter Two. We want to thank Josh Yoches for his valuable assistance in production and design.

CHAPTER ONE

TEXTBOOKS ARE IN TROUBLE

There is no substitute for a truly great textbook. Textbooks, whether they are lugged in a backpack or downloaded to a laptop, are vital components of American education. Almost every school in America uses some kind of textbook. They are portable, durable, and relatively economical, given their longevity in certain school districts. Additionally, studies have shown that having textbooks present in a classroom positively influences learning outcomes. Repeatedly, sociologists and educational researchers have found a strong positive correlation between the simple availability of textbooks in a school and higher student performance.[1] Clearly, then, if the books are present, even with quality limitations, students use them and learn from them.

Textbooks also carry the weight of their own weight. That is to say, because they are larger than ever and increasingly filled with impressive graphics, authoritative tables, and a booming authorial voice, students (and adults) tend to see their content as useful. The imprint of a respected publisher, even in an age of skepticism and distrust, gives textbooks authority. They are written or credentialed by people with advanced degrees, they have been purchased by the school system or the state, and therefore contain more sanctioned information than any single person, parent, or educator.

In some school districts, textbooks can be the sole source, or the predominant one, of information on a particular subject. Since teachers are not necessarily experts in the field they are teaching (and who could be, given that a single social studies class can range from ancient Japan to modern Spain to aboriginal Alaska?), both educators and students rely on textbooks for guidance. According to education researchers, teachers utilize textbooks to "provide structure for the course of study and the sequence of instruction. Many studies have shown that teachers adhere closely to texts, especially in mathematics, science, and reading instruction. Studies of teacher planning in these subjects have indicated that texts are the source of 85 percent to 95 percent of instructional activities."[2]

Even with the abundance of supplemental materials and the hyperavailability of information on the Internet, textbooks remain a primary source of classroom knowledge for American students (and, to a lesser extent, their teachers). The bottom line is that textbooks matter deeply. This is especially true of social studies textbooks, which have the task of teaching history, geography, and comparative religions that collectively tell the stories of American and world civilizations.

Our focus is on how textbooks deal with the history, sociology, and geography of the Jewish people, including lessons on the politics and history of Israel and the Middle East. We analyzed a sample of twenty-eight social studies, history, and geography textbooks. Many of them are widely distributed in public schools throughout the United States. (Religious and private schools often use the same textbooks as public schools.) We analyzed thousands of pages of text to determine how accurate and objective American textbooks are in this area. We also looked at some related supplemental materials and professional development teacher trainings.

Assessing how textbooks treat these topics provides telling insight into how textbooks approach complex subjects. What do students learn about Jews, Jewish history, and Judaism's relationship to Christianity? How does the ongoing challenging relationship between Jews and Muslims in the Middle East show up in the textbooks? What about the triangulation between Jews, Christians, and Muslims?

In each of our areas of study, we found a wide range of quality, from excellent models that demonstrated grade-level appropriate balance and impeccable facts to head-scratching mistakes, omissions, and mischaracterizations that bordered on propaganda. The situation is far from hopeless. The errors we found are easily fixable. We believe that naming them and explaining that only some words, passages, and lessons are wrong is the first step toward better materials. Our analysis did not find any single publisher's product or product line significantly more problematic than the others.

While the poor scholarship about Jews, Judaism, and Israel we uncovered are instructive, they are by no means the only examples that illustrate the need for reform in the way textbooks are developed, marketed, and distributed. Substitute another area—how we teach American history, Western civilization, and comparative religion—and we have another, equally intriguing case study. Our case study exemplifies what can go terribly wrong in discussing religion, geography, culture, or history—and in this case—all of them.

It would be parochial to read this book and dismiss it as being of concern only to Jews or only to those with a particular interest in the Middle East. This book is a case study of the information and messages in American classrooms: how factual they are, how inclusive, how balanced.

WHAT IS WRONG WITH THE TEXTBOOKS

K–12 education expert and textbook adoption process critic Chester Finn compared textbooks to junk food on the basis of the damage each does to schoolchildren in an op-ed piece in *USA Today*.

> It is hard to turn on the TV or open a newspaper these days without reading about the epidemic of obesity among Americans. The junk food industry, we are told, is at fault for peddling its high-calorie, nutrition-free products not only on supermarket shelves and in fast-food outlets, but also in school cafeterias.
>
> Yet, an equivalent threat to our national health has received scant attention: the steady diet of curricular junk being unloaded on students via the fat (and growing fatter) history books peddled by the multi-billion dollar, multinational textbook industry. These books— the products of committees of authors and editors closely watched and pressured by groups on the right and left—are overweight compilations of information, in which everything matters equally and nothing is truly important.[3]

Textbooks are flawed. Not every part of them, not every topic, not even all the titles from one particular publisher, but collectively, the twenty-eight history, geography, and social studies textbooks that we examined in our analysis could be much better than they are. (See Appendix A, Textbooks Reviewed by Publisher Parent Company.) Considering how vital textbooks are to the functioning and future of the United States, anything less than excellence is disappointing. In our research, we found that the problems we encountered are primarily a result of shoddy scholarship: assertions, illustrations, quizzes, and other lesson materials that are simply incorrect or are inconsistent with current and generally accepted knowledge of a particular topic. Shoddy scholarship—"flat-earth theories" and more subtle errors—are all too frequent.

Ignorance is just that: the writers about certain textbook topics do not know much about their subjects. Sometimes, the well-credentialed scholars whose names appear as authors of the textbooks have little if anything to do with the actual writing or content of the book. Those prestigious names may have at one point been associated with the publisher, they may have provided an initial outline, may provide a cursory read of the material, perhaps even an edit, or they may simply have leased the cachet of their renown to lend legitimacy to the textbooks. The workhorses, whether in-house writers or employees of a textbook development agency, who actually write the text may have a great deal or little expertise in their area of responsibility. According to William Bennetta, editor of *The Textbook Letter*, a newsletter that reviews middle and high school textbooks for accuracy and bias, of the hundreds of textbooks he has reviewed, "at least seventy-five percent have been so blatantly incompetent that I could say, with certainty, that the people who wrote them had no idea what they were writing about."[4] Of course, we found many examples of excellent passages, references, and analysis. They are tainted, however, often in the same textbook, by unnecessary mistakes and inferior work.

Sometimes information is just out of date. Of course, there are reasonable explanations for obsolete passages to appear in textbooks: it is prohibitively expensive to publish constant updates; there are no simple channels to distribute updates to the thousands of classrooms that may be using any given textbook; and the trend toward electronic publishing creates a disincentive for costly reprints. Nonetheless, millions of schoolchildren are given facts that may be out of date.[5]

The textbook marketplace is worth $3.7 billion,[6] yet the profit margins, as in much of publishing, are tight. It is a tough business, and often a thankless one. Creating a product that is not too expensive, is high quality, and makes everyone happy is no small challenge. Publishers must compete against each other for the limited number of consumers in their market. That means that textbooks must fulfill state educational requirements, keep up with the latest pedagogical advancements, and, for consumers with ever-decreasing attention spans, be flashy and quick. During the final development phase of a textbook, there comes a point when it is bad business to make sure that the product is perfect. A former employee of a large textbook development agency reported that he was sent to proof a science textbook just prior to publishing. "I was told that unless an expletive was printed on the page in large type, I should not change anything. I saw blatant errors, but I wasn't allowed to change them. It was too late and too expensive. The books went to print with mistakes that the publishers knew about."[7]

Sometimes shoddy scholarship comes from the general "dumbing down" that takes place in American textbooks. When a complex subject is simplified and the text that could explain the difficulties in controversial passages is instead replaced by brightly colored illustrations or amusing-but-not-edifying sidebars, the resulting lesson becomes weakened simply by the omissions. The responsibility for the eviscerated lessons lies in several places. While state standards mandate that students gain knowledge in specific and often far-ranging areas, the textbook publishers must devise some means of meeting those requirements. In some cases, the design is intended to entertain the students, to keep their attention long enough to satisfy the state testing requirements. Gilbert T. Sewall, director of the non-partisan American Textbook Council, reviewed, along with a team of historians and educators, the major history textbooks in use at American schools and concluded that the majority of textbooks "have abandoned narrative for a broken format of competing instructional activities." The pictures, sidebars, and exercises that abound in many history textbooks—and not just those for elementary and middle school children but for high school students as well—have squeezed out cogent writing about history, causing the books to be "overly detailed at points and superficial at others." In many cases, the compressed coverage "results in ambiguities and abstractions that fail to promote student understanding."[8] Some topics are covered so superficially as to be merely baffling, hardly the stuff to support the kind of critical thinking required in the prickly world outside the classroom. Other topics, like racism, slavery, and genocide, can be treated with the same light gloss as, say, the history of the ice cream cone, so that the horror the books *should* convey becomes yet another frothy reading assignment.

Shoddy scholarship also means the inclusion of false "facts," inaccurate generalizations, imprecise conclusions, repudiated theories, and, sometimes, rumors that have taken on the weight of truth without grounding in academic inquiry. Presenting competing and unresolved theories does not qualify as shoddy scholarship. Students who are old enough to learn about, say, speciation in island chains or the archaeological evidence of the ancient Kingdom of Israel, are also presumably sophisticated enough to read about different scholarly interpretations and theories surrounding those topics. The key is "scholarship."

Politically motivated propaganda may also wheedle its way into textbooks. Biased scholarship contains the stink of political or religious untruths. Biased scholarship means errors or misinformation in textbooks that denigrate one group in order to elevate another. We have no reason to believe that authors intentionally introduce their own prejudices into the writing, nor that editors are choosing one version of history over another because of personal bigotry. We can say that certain themes emerge in many textbooks that collectively comprise a bias. We attribute this outcome largely to shoddy scholarship rather than ill intent. We do not believe that textbook publishers are "out to get" anybody or any group. They are subject to all kinds of external pressures so that the higher pursuit of truth and accuracy can be sacrificed to narrow interests.

While it is sensible and logical that interest groups would want to have a say in the way their particular stories are told or their values represented, in many cases these groups have superceded the scholars charged with ensuring the accuracy of the textbooks. Bias may enter the textbooks, therefore, through the most effective lobbying groups wanting the narrative to say what they want. Biased scholarship is the unspoken lesson, the part that will not be on the test. It appears in passages about the history of the Middle East, in which the land that would become the state of Israel is referred to as "Palestine," centuries before the Romans would give it that name. It is the attempt to portray Muslim beliefs as historical fact while those of other religions are described in conditional terms. Biased scholarship is the sacrifice of the higher pursuit of truth and accuracy. It is the more pernicious of our two categories. It is less frequent, and nearly impossible to prove intent. The result is what matters anyway.

Some sort of bias in textbooks has been around as long as textbooks have existed. As Frances FitzGerald documents in *America Revised* and Kyle Ward illustrates in *History in the Making*,[9] his fascinating look at the way in which current political thought alters the details and descriptions of key events in American history textbooks, every generation—indeed every textbook writer—brings biases to the text. The role of textbooks as creators of civic values demands that a particular point of view, a specific set of ideals inform the lessons. Biased scholarship, or accusations of bias, lies at the heart of the political battles in public schools that have continued almost without a break since Europeans began living in North America. It has become commonplace to read conservative critics denounce the way in which social studies textbooks (and college curricula, for that matter) have moved away from a "Eurocentric" narrative of Western Civilization toward a "multicultural" approach. Similarly, critics from the left regularly denounce the evangelical Christian influence in public education. These fights are public and likely to continue as ongoing political discourse. Others are less well known such as the Council on Islamic Education (a Muslim group that provides consulting assistance to publishers' "content developers" on the treatment of Islam in textbooks).[10] Their views are often the ones we found in our analysis.

Sometimes remedies create their own biases. Multicultural education was developed as an attempt to correct a certain kind of bias; conservative groups rallied to reverse the excessive changes made by the multiculturalists. In the end, biased passages in textbooks proliferate because various groups, each entrenched in its particular world view, attempt to insure that only their view is presented in a textbook. Most groups are well-intentioned, but can be misguided. Others are more blatant in their desire to influence education to achieve their political goals while sacrificing accuracy. They tend to exploit a flawed process of publishing and distribution to serve their own needs. Bias plagues the textbooks by choosing one group's narrative over another—when that narrative is historically wrong and the facts are not facts. We will show this often to be the case in how textbooks discuss Israel.

"There is not a nation on earth," wrote education scholar Dr. A. E. Winship in 1915, "in which school books approach even faintly those of America."[11] But today, charges of censorship and banality in history textbooks reflect the struggles of a nation attempting description as one with common values and civic unity in the face of a loudly multi-faceted population. It is logical that textbooks would be implicated in the struggle to define the character and soul of America. They are, after all, repositories of widely digested national interpretations of ourselves.

Many of the social studies, history, and geography textbooks used in American schools are simply failing the public. While students, parents, and educators alike assume—indeed, count on—the authority of the textbooks in their classrooms, many of them are filled with misinformation. These problems cut across grades, where the highest level textbooks can sometimes contain the most detailed and therefore the most extensive errors. Lessons on world and United States history, ancient and modern civilizations, world religions, global geography, and politics are all prone to both minor and serious errors.

WHY TEXTBOOKS ARE TROUBLED

The causes of error in textbooks are complex and interrelated, and this perhaps accounts for the fact that, with so many years of complaints and (often partisan) criticism directed against the textbook publishing industry, the problems continue and have deepened. First, the *economic structure* of the textbook industry itself is partly responsible. An ongoing trend toward consolidation of the once diverse textbook publishing industry means that more and more titles are concentrated in fewer hands. (See Appendix B: Imprints of Major Textbook Publishing Corporations.)

In the last two decades, the elementary and high school publishing industry (known as "el-hi") has undergone a massive compression through acquisitions, mergers, and the withdrawal from certain segments of the market by publishers who have chosen no longer to compete in those areas. As of this writing, only three mega-publishers (down from nine in less than twenty years) control the el-hi textbook market. Those publishers—Pearson (British-based), Education Media and Publishing Group Limited (Irish/American-based), and McGraw-Hill (American-based)— are part of multi-national conglomerates and over the years have merged with or acquired many well-respected publishers such as Harcourt, Macmillan, and Prentice Hall, among many others. (A few boutique publishers, such as Teachers' Curriculum Institute [TCI] and Oxford, continue to put out social studies and history books, but they are small creatures scrambling for their footing among a three-headed herd of giants.) In

2006, the el-hi textbook market generated $3.7 billion in sales. The four major publishers at that time (in 2007 Houghton Mifflin and its parent company Education Media and Publishing Group Limited, acquired Harcourt Education from Dutch-based Reed Elsevier) achieved annual sales of around $2.6 billion or about 70 percent of all K–12 textbooks sold.[12]

Many of the formerly independent publishing companies now exist as imprints of their parent corporation or have been dissolved altogether. In 2006, sales of el-hi textbooks (the $3.7 billion mentioned above) in the United States was surpassed only by trade books[13] ($8.2 billion) among all books sold in the United States.[14] Unlike the trade publishing world, the textbook marketplace is a rarefied universe, in which the odd, quasi-governmental way by which the purchasers of the books make their decisions has made the development and marketing of textbooks so expensive that only a company with deeper pockets stands a chance to succeed. However, even the multinationals have to keep the costs of developing a textbook as low as possible.

Thus, in the first place, errors in one book now stand a greater chance of replicating themselves across other books because, even with different imprints on the spine, they may originate from the same source. In large part, this structure has arisen because only a large corporation with deep reserves of capital can afford to stay solvent during the long development cycle of a book and then float the high costs of distributing it into the classrooms.

Second, textbooks contain errors because of the *limitations of some of the writers themselves*. In many cases, those at the keyboards have little expertise in their assigned areas. They may work inside the publishing company; they may be contract writers; or they may be on staff at any number of textbook development agencies that hire young writers to produce less expensive volumes. (Again, the economics of the industry touches all aspects.)

Whatever their employment status, the true authors are not likely to be the academics whose names appear on the title pages of the textbooks. Without a deep and subtle knowledge of their topics, writers must rely on the outlines provided to them and their own independent research. The writers bring their own world views and personal experiences into the texts. If a writer believes that Israel is the primary culprit in the Middle East, the textbook will reflect that belief in its language and examples.

One of the ways that the publishers lower their development costs is to outsource the writing of the book. Since the publishing cycle is long and the time between purchase decisions even longer, it is not cost-effective for most publishers to maintain on their staff the writers, editors, and researchers needed to create a 1000-page manuscript on, say, ancient history. Instead, publishers sometimes hand over a section or an entire book to a textbook development agency, known in the industry as a "chop shop." Staffed mainly with educational specialists and writers, the textbook agencies follow the standards and guide-lines supplied by the publishers (to meet state standards) to create peda-gogically and statutorily correct textbooks. Notably absent from many of the chop shops are subject matter experts in history, religion, civics, and so on.

The chop shops cannot substitute for genuine scholarship. The man-agement of one such agency contains a senior editor whose credentials are listed as "Experienced editor of K–12 basal and supplementary materials. Developer of educational materials in both English and Spanish. Areas of special expertise include reading, language arts, technology, social stud-ies, and Spanish."[15] A well-rounded person, undoubtedly, but his list of achievements does not equal scholarly expertise in history. With such an emphasis on pedagogical expertise and so little on subject knowledge, it is no surprise that the textbook developers in such agencies would be sus-ceptible, for example, to the kind of information supplied by interest groups, such as the Council on Islamic Education, regarding the history and current state of Israel.

HOW TEXTBOOKS ARE SELECTED FOR THE CLASSROOM: ADOPTION, INTEREST GROUPS, AND SELF-CENSORSHIP

The third major reason that textbooks are flawed is due to the *political pressures* on the publishers that result from the adoption and review pro-cesses. California and Texas—strong exemplars of model blue and red states, respectively—partly determine the survival and lifespan of any given title. If a book can make it in either one of those states, as the song goes, it can make it anywhere.[16] (Florida rounds out the top three, repre-senting a coveted third prize to publishers in the adoption sweepstakes. California, Texas, and Florida together control about 25 percent of the nation's textbook market.[17]) During the course of the adoption process, in addition to professional and scholarly reviewers examining the proposed textbooks against a predetermined set of criteria (known as "educational content standards"), members of the public in both states have an opportunity to offer their comments and criticism.

And offer them they do. In Texas, for example, in 1961 Mel and Norma Gabler became concerned about the content of their son's textbooks, so they formed a non-profit organization called "Educational Research Analysts" to review all textbooks adopted in Texas. Their mission is clear in its viewpoint and its ambition: "We are a conservative Christian organization that reviews public school textbooks submitted for adoption in Texas. Our reviews have national relevance because Texas state-adopts textbooks and buys so many that publishers write them to Texas standards and sell them across the country." Among others, their "subject areas of concern" are "scientific weaknesses in evolutionary theories," "original intent of the U.S. Constitution," "respect for Judeo-Christian morals," "emphasis on abstinence in sex education," and "politically correct degradation of academics."[18] For more than forty years, the Gablers themselves reviewed textbooks submitted for adoption in Texas and "exerted an outsize influence on the textbooks that American elementary and secondary schools adopt." No book was published without "the unofficial Gabler seal of approval,"[19] yet Mel and Norma Gabler were not trained academics, historians, or educators. They simply worked the system, which is their right, of course. Others do so as well.

It would be a mistake to assign textbook troubles primarily to social conservatives like the Gablers. Conservative organizations are hardly the only active interest groups that often unabashedly peddle political views. For example, the National Organization for Women achieved considerable success during the 1970s in attacking some textbooks as sexist in California's adoption process.[20] The model created by Educational Research Analysts, while admittedly more powerful and influential than many, has been replicated by a host of other social, religious, and political groups from both sides of the spectrum. (The moderate middle ground rarely has passionate partisans. Who marches to advocate compromise and goodwill?) Publishers have come to fear any bad publicity about their products, so they submit—happily or begrudgingly—their manuscripts to anyone who might seem troublesome in the hope that they will allow the adoption processes in the two largest states, California and Texas, to proceed without interruption or surprises. Given the amount of money at risk in these two states, it is too expensive to do otherwise.

Every state in the country has its own policy regarding the purchase (which is not to say the actual deployment or usage in a classroom) of text-books. Twenty-one states, mainly in the West and South, use some form of textbook adoption in which the state compiles a list of the acceptable text-books that schools or districts may choose to purchase.[21] During the adop-tion cycle, textbooks are scrutinized by a review process of some sort (it differs from state to state), and if a book is rejected during that review, the publisher has lost what it invested during the book's development (unless, of course, it can sell the book to a different state with different review cri-teria). If a book is not adopted in either of the two biggest states, its chances of succeeding elsewhere are crippled. But having a book adopted in these states is expensive. Publishers typically spend millions just getting a book ready for submission to a major adoption state, and few boutique publish-ers can afford the outlay if their book is not guaranteed even a single sale.

Other states choose books at the county level, the district level, the school level, and sometimes at the level of the individual classroom. This uneven selection process means that publishers must satisfy the needs of an ever-changing and highly complicated set of purchasers. It is so expen-sive to get a book into a classroom that they will do their best not to offend various user groups along the way. The need to placate can translate to satisfying disparate and often contradictory expectations at the expense of accuracy and neutrality.

The state-level textbook adoption process necessitates textbook pub-lishers to heed potentially thousands of influential voices. The adoption process generally operates in the following way:

- The department of education or other governmental agency such as the state board of education drafts a detailed set of specifications or stan-dards for any textbook used in their state. (Some adoption states, like California, adopt textbooks for grades K–8; others, like Texas, adopt books at all levels.) Those standards also specify what the expected learning outcomes are for each grade level.[22]

- Next, textbook publishers create their materials to meet those specifica-tions. One former textbook writer said, "We were given a standard and had to show three instances where we thought we met that standard. If we satisfied those requirements, no one looked at the rest of what we wrote."[23] In other words, for the writers of the textbooks, expediency may trump thoroughness.

- Once a draft of a textbook is complete, it is submitted to the state for review. The review consists of two components: a) a check against standards to see if the educational framework is being addressed, and b) an overall review by educators and subject matter experts in the field covered by those books. The scholarly reviewers use objective criteria to assign a score to each submitted book, and all those texts that score high enough against the evaluation criteria move to the next phase of evaluation: public comment.

In most adoption states, once a book has been tentatively approved by the review boards, a period of public comment opens during which anyone—individuals or organizations—may offer criticism, support, suggestions, and editorial changes. It is during this time that many interest groups comb through the texts looking to change or excise any passages they deem unacceptable. This is a necessary function, given the way textbooks are produced. Interest groups find mistakes that *should* be changed. In a surprising number of instances, average citizens find errors that escaped the reviewers.

However, having many pairs of eyes read the textbooks during the evaluation period does not always translate into error-free products. It would be reasonable to assume that reviewers, in addition to looking for compliance with the state's criteria, would be looking for inaccuracies, misinformation, and outright propaganda as they read their assigned passages. But some reviewers add to the problem, not fix it. They let things go by on purpose, or add their own misinformation to the mix.

Interest groups have additional concerns of their own. Omission, or lack of inclusion, is the most common complaint, usually voiced by a minority group that finds itself underrepresented in the textbooks. Ethnic, racial, religious, social, and business groups, including representatives of certain industries like oil, timber, and big agriculture complain about the manner in which they are depicted in the books.[24] Some of these groups are highly organized. They may be part of larger organizations or may be wholly dedicated themselves to curriculum development, including lobbying for changes in textbooks in the adoption states.

Many of these groups also have representatives who regularly communicate with the publishers during the development of a book. At every step of the process, interest groups attempt to influence content. This can be positive, with advocacy groups adding to the quality and accuracy of the content they know best. Some of the changes requested by some groups might actually take on equal status to state-required standards in the minds of the publishers.

The most activist groups in this process lean toward censorship. Melissa N. Matusevich explains that even prior to submitting the books for review, publishers regularly censor themselves out of fear of losing a sale.

> The textbook publishing industry's self-censorship of books is little known by educators, yet has a dramatic impact in the history textbooks teachers and students use. It seems oxymoronic in a country whose constitution guarantees freedom of the press that publishers would choose to be an active partner in censorship due to pressures from outside groups.

She points out the ironic confluence between seemingly opposing groups in their attempts to exert excessive influence on textbook content:

> The result is that textbook creation is now controlled by extremists on both the left and the right, who have more in common than one might first suspect. While the particular issues they lobby for or against differ—the left is more concerned with how individuals and groups are presented while the right's issues relate to religion and morality—looking beneath the surface one can readily determine that the basis of their concerns is related to two main points: 1) the belief that textbooks have great power to impact children's minds, and 2) the further belief that children are gullible, so their thinking can be easily influenced. . . . These groups carry big sticks and publishers kowtow to them.[25]

In addition, as Gilbert Sewall of the American Textbook Council points out, "[a]ny company that plans to compete nationally in school publishing must be capital intensive and 'full service,' offering study guides, workbooks, and technology, along with discounts, premiums, and an array of teacher enticements. Spanish text versions, margins, texts, binders, and answer keys may determine which books are adopted."[26] The fear of financial loss has squelched much innovation, creativity, and risk-taking. From a business perspective, they reason it is better to create a textbook that offends no one (and perhaps instructs no one either).

As education historian Diane Ravitch notes in *The Language Police*, textbook publishers have been pummeled so thoroughly over the past two decades by any number of groups, including the education departments of many states, in an attempt to eliminate all bias that they reflexively cut out balanced treatments of many complex and sensitive subjects for fear of offending anyone. Publishers use "bias guidelines" that they developed initially (many in the 1980s) to meet state requirements (California is a notable and influential exporter of such anti-bias strictures) and subsequently at their own initiative to reduce the possibility of having a textbook rejected during an adoption or selection cycle. The purpose of the guidelines, according to Ravitch, "is to ensure that textbook writers to do not inadvertently use politically unacceptable language," but in essence "publishers have consented to a strict code of censorship."[27] The result is that textbooks adhere closely to "[a] cultural equivalence narrative" that is "so intent on shunning invidious comparisons that it elides hard questions. It celebrates everybody and omits many unpleasant historical facts."[28] Without hard questions, students—many of whom are too young to understand the larger cultural context in which complex contemporary and historical events take place—take at face value overly simplistic accounts of those events. Ironically, in an effort to avoid bias, the anti-bias guidelines can create more imbalanced learning.

TEXTBOOKS SHAPE THE NATIONAL SELF-IMAGE

Textbooks can help acculturate students into the multicultural salad that is American life. In every state in the country, education is compulsory for children until at least age sixteen. According to the United States Department of Education, in 2007 about 48 million American children, representing just over 88 percent of all K–12 students, were projected to be enrolled in *public* primary and secondary schools in the United States, with the number expected to rise to nearly 50 million by 2014.[29]

When the question of "What should be the content of schooling?" arises, parents, scholars, and educators have historically looked first to the textbooks to evaluate whether their content is aligned with the cultural messages and factual information they want to impart. In the mid-1800s, when the enormous increase of new Irish, German, and Catholic immigrants to the United States created the most multicultural and multi-religious nation since the fall of the Roman Empire, some of the first fights over textbook content began. Those early struggles were signs of a diverse nation finding its voice, but according to Frances FitzGerald, author of *America Revised: History Schoolbooks in the Twentieth Century,*

> [t]he first important outbreak of them occurred in the years following the First World War. In that period, the mayor of Chicago and the Hearst newspapers, using adjectives such as "unpatriotic" and "un-American," created an uproar over what they said was the pro-British bias of certain texts. . . . Simultaneously, the Daughters of the American Revolution attacked some of the texts for not putting enough stress on American military history. The Ku Klux Klan got into the act by complaining of pro-Jewish and pro-Catholic sentiments. Then a number of fundamentalist groups protested against the teaching of evolutionary theory, and eventually succeeded in purging some biology texts of references to evolution. Finally, and with no publicity at all, several utilities associations, including [gas, electric, and rail interests] put pressure on the publishers and school officials to doctor the texts in their favor.[30]

History, geography, and social studies textbooks are especially vulnerable to influence, because of the broad opportunities for subjectivity in the telling of historical narratives about the origins of civilizations, the births of nations, and the character of their people.

With the rise of multiculturalism, these textbooks receive a particularly hard look from critics, since they are repositories of how we think about who we are. Working within the model of multicultural education, professors of education Keith C. Barton and Linda Levstik dispel any notions that any single narrative—history, geography, civics—contains a single truth—facts—that could be encapsulated in a textbook and left alone for posterity. Arguing in favor of a multicultural approach to the teaching of history, they propose that "knowledge of the past depends on interpretation of evidence, that people disagree over such interpretations, and that history can be understood only by considering perspectives that differ from our own."[31]

Interpretation of evidence, by definition, must include personal interpretations of some sort, social, political, religious, or otherwise. In history textbooks, these views may influence the content to a much larger degree than most students, parents, and educators may realize. According to Diane Ravitch,

> every [history] textbook has a point of view, despite a façade of neutrality; the authors and editors select some interpretations and reject others, choose certain events as important and ignore others as unimportant. Even when they insert sidebars with point and counterpoint on a few issues, they give the false impression that all other issues are settled when they are not. The pretense of objectivity and authority is, at bottom, just that: a pretense.[32]

If they are flawed at their inception by the unavoidable fact of having been written by authors with their own perspectives, interpretations, and biases and with the growing trend toward electronic pedagogical materials and the greater access to primary sources that the internet provides, then why do textbooks still matter? Certainly in some school districts and in some states, paper textbooks seem to be diminishing in importance, yet they are unlikely to disappear altogether. Even if students switch to electronically delivered texts, which are (presumably) updated more frequently, the materials will still be subject to the same limitations in terms of interpretation and selective viewpoints.

THE ORGANIZATION OF THIS ANALYSIS

A Case Study of the Troubled Textbook: An Examination of Error

Innumerable pages have been—and continue to be—written, colloquia held, lectures delivered, and more in an attempt to understand and classify the persistent prejudice that is anti-Semitism, in both its ancient and contemporary forms. Research increasingly shows the relationship between anti-Semitism and anti-Israelism, and even more importantly, that anti-Israelism is often anti-Semitic in tone and substance. What is essential in this examination of American public education is an understanding of both *what* and *how* our elementary, middle, and high schools teach about Jews, Judaism, and Israel. Some of it is blatant prejudice, some is stereotypes, some is just plain inaccurate and wrong. The misstatements about Jewish theology, social structure, and the history of Israel, in aggregate, comprise an unsavory picture of Jews and Israel.

Chapter Two describes supplemental materials on Islam and the Middle East prepared by Muslim and Arab interest groups for teachers to use in classrooms. We profile the major providers of these materials and discuss their lesson plans and programs for teacher training. The materials are often more problematic than textbooks.

Chapters Three through Eight are devoted to the analysis of the textbooks themselves. They are organized by four major themes. Chapter Three looks at the way textbooks portray Jewish history and theology and the relationship to stereotypes of Jews. It examines the characterization of the Hebrew Bible and explanations of the relationship between the Jewish people and other peoples. The chapter explores textbook perspectives on the role of Jewish law in Jewish life and the concept of God in Judaism.

Chapter Four explores the representation of the relationship between Jews, Judaism, and Christianity. It includes the historical place of Judaism and Jewish law in the life of Jesus and the development of Christianity and the Jewish role in the crucifixion of Jesus. It analyzes the role of traditional Christian anti-Semitism in Western history.

Chapter Five examines the representation of the relationship between Jews, Judaism, and Islam as manifested in textbook differences in teaching about Judaism compared to the teaching about Islam. It looks at the devotional language about Islam and the idealized view of Muslim treatment of Jews found in supplemental materials.

Chapters Six through Eight discuss the narrative about the history and current state of the Middle East, including Israel. They encompass the history of the state of Israel and Palestine. They explore the role of Muslim terrorism in contemporary society, both in the West and in the Middle East; the question of refugees, both Jewish and Arab; and the depiction of current-day Israeli society.

These four subject areas span all twenty-eight textbooks, from ancient to modern history, from general social studies to geography. When we talk about anti-Semitism in instructional materials, we are referring, to some extent, to "classic" anti-Semitism such as blaming the Jews for the crucifixion of Jesus. Examples of this kind are less common in textbooks, although, as we show, they crop up here and there. Most misinformation is more subtle, such as introducing Jewish theological beliefs by saying "Jews claim . . . ," while presenting other religious traditions as historical fact. ("[Mary and Joseph's] status was undistinguished before the miraculous selection of the young Virgin Mary as the mother of the Messiah.") Additionally, in more advanced social studies textbooks as well as in geography books, an anti-Israel narrative appears throughout lessons on the Middle East.

Within each chapter, the analysis of textbooks and supplemental materials is organized by themes such as the role of Jews in the crucifixion or the omission of Jewish refugees created in Arab countries in response to the founding of Israel. Each section begins with passages that cover the theme particularly well with respect to historical accuracy. We then proceed to examine problematic items. The well constructed examples placed first serve as worthy models for emulation compared to the more numerous inaccuracies. They demonstrate that successful treatment of even challenging themes is possible.

The analysis of the twenty-eight textbooks found over 500 specific and notable problematic entries about Jews, Judaism, and Israel in at least one of the subject areas. An entry could be a review question in a teacher's guide, text for the students to read, maps, illustrations, a glossary entry, chapter summary quizzes, and so on. In each what emerged from the study was a set of beliefs and assertions about Jews, Judaism, and Israel, that, if unchallenged, could create a generation of misinformed or even bigoted American schoolchildren.

CHAPTER TWO

WHEN THE TEXTBOOK IS NOT ENOUGH: SUPPLEMENTAL MATERIALS, TEACHER TRAININGS, AND MORE

TEXTBOOKS ARE NOT THE ONLY PROBLEM

Over the years, textbooks have grown thicker with information, illustrations, tables, and activities. (The United States Consumer Project Safety Commission estimated that in 2003 there were over 21,000 back injuries among schoolchildren, many caused by the weight they lug in their backpacks.[1]) Yet, these enormous tomes often do not contain enough information for teachers who must cover vast and disparate social studies topics. For more, teachers turn to outside readings, DVDs, CDs, exercises, posters, brochures, or other non-textbook (and non-primary) sources. In some situations, these supplemental materials have become nearly as ubiquitous as the textbooks themselves, yet few critics and scholars can vouch for their factuality and message. They tend to pass below the official eyes of the state-sanctioned reviewers and rarely are examined by the many unapologetically partisan commentators and critics that scrutinize the textbooks.

The importance of supplemental materials could have passed us by as well. Our study began as an examination of textbooks only, but in interviews with teachers and school administrators, we learned that they counted on—and, more significantly, trusted—these supplemental materials to help them teach many of the more sensitive and complex subjects, especially those about which they had little training, knowledge, or personal experience. Many teachers, after all, hold a teaching certificate and B.A. in a multitude of fields, not necessarily in ancient history or world civilizations.

Our focus for this case study is how textbooks and other materials treat the topics of the Jewish people, Judaism, and Israel. Simply by glancing at the names of the organizations that provide supplemental materials about the Middle East (Saudi Aramco World and the Council on Islamic Education, to name just two) reveals the potential for abuse. Supplemental materials are rarely created by pedagogical institutions but rather by economic, political, cultural, racial, religious, or ethnic groups that have a vested interest in their stories being taught a certain way. Or being taught at all. (The Dairy Council generously donated materials and created lesson plans for schools to teach students about the "Milk Group" referenced in the "MyPyramid for Kids" dietary guidelines created by the USDA.[2] In 1956, the Council was so effective at propagating its message that "dairy" became its own food group, a framework later challenged by many nutrition experts.[3])

To encourage teachers to use their materials, the creators often provide them free or at nominal cost. At a time when educational budgets are under continuous pressure, grateful teachers are not likely to explore extensively their source or their underlying message. Many of the supplemental materials are sleek and brightly colored. They seem neutral and scholarly, which may account for their lack of scrutiny in the many vituperative debates about what our children are learning. Of the many fine books, articles, and op-eds that we consulted as part of our research, no other study comprehensively examined supplemental materials.

Teachers supplement their own knowledge in other ways. To upgrade their teaching credentials and salaries, teachers often attend some kind of on-going education. Many districts provide teachers with salary credits, bonuses, and the like for a certain number of hours of additional training. The opportunities for such professional development are wide and deep. State, regional, and national teachers' organizations such as the California Council for the Social Studies (CCSS), National Council for History Education (NCHE), and the National Council for the Social Studies (NCSS) organize massive annual conferences at which teachers may choose from hundreds of workshops in their teaching areas. It is at these conferences that teachers learn about, say, "American Gospels of Wealth, Civil Rights and Immigration," or "Ritual and Religion: Using Baseball and Sumo as Lenses into Japanese Culture."[4] Individual school districts also conduct teacher trainings or "in-services" on days that are specially set aside for that purpose. Some districts also provide funds for teachers to attend courses at local colleges or district-approved independent workshops on a subject of interest to the teacher.

As with the supplemental materials, social, political, and religious advocacy groups sponsor many of these workshops, and these groups see the gathering of teachers as their greatest opportunity to ensure that their message prevails over competing (and contradictory) messages from opposing groups. In our particular research focus, we found many such offerings for teachers. For example, the Council on Islamic Education (CIE), in addition to publishing a few of supplemental materials, organizes both its own workshops and sponsors others at teacher conferences. CIE, as well as other advocacy groups, supply the personnel, the materials, and the perspective on their particular topic which can be translated into a message of "truth" in the classroom. We have attended a sampling of such workshops and trainings, interviewed teachers who have attended them, and scrutinized the materials and messages—they comprise a specific narrative about Islam, Israel, and the Middle East.

Finally, we recognize that informal opportunities for learning take place every day in American schools. Field trips and guest speakers offer students a particular perspective, one that may or may not be accurate but that, by their very association with the school, carry a certain authority. We found that some teachers, when they were required to teach about religions other than their own, would look for outside speakers for help, inviting in a priest, pastor, imam, or rabbi. Sponsored by many of the same advocacy groups responsible for the supplemental materials and teacher trainings, speakers bureaus exist in many communities for the sole purpose of educating both children and adults in their particular area of interest. These speakers provide some of the richest and most interesting learning experiences many students have in their social studies classes. At the same time, speakers are not bound by the same rules that guide teachers. Sometimes they have been invited *because* they have a particular point of view. It is up to the teacher to offer balance, a different perspective, or correct factual errors. Of course, we could not, in the scope of our research, attend every, or even a representative number of field trips and presentations in individual classrooms across the country. If we did, what would we find? We cannot offer more than a recognition that such trips and presentations exist, and extrapolate from the rest of our findings that they are likely to be as problematic as the textbooks, supplemental materials, and teacher trainings we did analyze. Our best hope is that teachers are able to create a context in which students can understand the particular point of view of their guest speakers and that they do encourage students to listen, question, seek alternate points of view, and make their own informed decisions. Neither textbooks nor supplemental materials may be helping to achieve this most basic mission.

CLASSROOM MATERIALS

The punch line of an old joke goes, "The food is bad, and there's not enough of it." For teachers in American classrooms, the extra helping they serve their children often comes in the form of supplemental materials. These non-textbook learning resources include readings, films, posters, brochures, maps, and other materials brought into the classroom to enhance the learning experience of the students and to make up for what is lacking in the textbooks. Some of these materials are very good; some are decidedly not. Unlike textbooks, however, supplemental materials may not always have benign intentions, and their quality ranges from excellent to egregiously flawed. Nearly anyone can—and does—create supplemental materials, including groups with a political, social, or religious agenda to advance. Because these materials do not have to pass through any kind of state or district review, quality control exists only at the level of the educator who chooses to bring them into the classroom. This situation is especially problematic, given the reasons that teachers choose to use supplemental materials.

Teachers rely on the supplemental materials for several reasons. First, they make good pedagogical sense. Each student learns differently: some are visual, some aural, some kinesthetic, and so on. Adding something other than a textbook to the lesson increases the chances that more students will engage in some aspect of the learning. Second, supplemental materials provide a perspective and level of detail often unavailable in textbooks. They often have a singular focus and a particular intention, which can enrich the students' understanding of the topic they are covering.

Finally, teachers rely on supplemental materials because the teachers themselves often do not know enough about a particular subject and must borrow authority from outside the classroom. This statement is not a condemnation or criticism of teachers, who, amidst their many other pressing responsibilities, must seek quick solutions to the challenge of keeping up with the ever-changing flow of information outside of their classrooms. Rather, this is a long-standing problem in American education: educators routinely teach classes outside of their field, they do not have a field at all beyond a general education degree, or they have not kept pace with the subject matter they are teaching.

According to a report published by The Education Trust, a Washington-based K–12 advocacy group, "many states still grant generic teaching licenses that allow education majors to teach in grades all the way from kindergarten up through and including eighth grade." In the early grades, a lack of training in a particular subject area may not matter, but once students reach middle and high school, out-of-field teaching becomes more problematic.

> Nationwide 44% of middle-grade classes in core academic subjects are assigned to a teacher who lacks even a college minor in the subject being taught. . . . Nearly one fifth (18%) of high school classes in core academic subjects are assigned to someone lacking *even a college minor* in the subject or in a related field . . . When it comes to the more rigorous yet very reasonable expectation that high school teachers have an undergraduate major in a subject in order to teach it, the numbers get much bigger. Nearly one-fourth (24%) of all high school courses in core academic subjects are taught by someone lacking an undergraduate or graduate major in the field.[5]

The teachers themselves are not to blame: districts and individual schools make the assignments, and, given the choice, it is logical that teachers would always prefer to teach within their field rather than out of it. But, when they *are* facing a subject in which they have little or no formal training, they do what they hope their own students will do: they look to outside help. The supplemental materials are there waiting to fulfill their mission: they *supplement* the other available resources, including the teachers themselves.

HELPING HANDS: WHO IS CREATING THE SUPPLEMENTAL SALAD BAR?

Nearly everyone imaginable, it seems, creates a handout, a map, a booklet, or other material to use in American classrooms: the National Geographic Society, the Discovery Channel, the Washington State Beef Commission, and many others. While many of the materials available to teachers are unassailable in both their pedagogical approach and the accuracy and balance of their content, some are barely disguised propaganda pamphlets or are simply wrong. This is especially true of some materials designed for use in social studies classrooms. Because teachers employ supplemental materials to teach units in areas where either their own grasp of the subject or the textbooks is incomplete, it is not enough simply to evaluate the materials on their own. Context—that is, the source of the material and how it is used—can be as revealing as the content.

There are two main sources of materials: Some textbook publishers such as Teacher's Curriculum Institute (TCI) sell supplemental materials as part of their regular offerings. These are written and produced in much the same way as textbooks, although they are generally exempt from the same review processes applied to textbooks. The other, lesser-known sources of classroom materials are social, political, business, and religious groups with particular agendas and messages they would like to see students absorb. Our study focuses on the materials produced by these types of groups and in particular on those materials that address the topics we examine in our case study: the history of the Jewish people, Judaism and its relationship to Christianity and Islam, and the politics of the Middle East.

Using classroom materials prepared by outside groups is not, on its face, problematic. A civil rights group provides a poster with faces and data about important members of the civil rights movement. A local park district creates and distributes a geological map of the county. Mothers Against Drunk Driving makes available guidelines for safe driving for high school students. In many districts around the country, classrooms are richer for these free or low-cost materials available to teachers, most of whom are working with extremely limited budgets that often do not even cover essentials. Indeed, if there were not already a market for them, these additional materials would not have found such firm footing in American schools. Those who provide or sell such materials do so in part because they believe they are providing a service and in part because they see the opportunity to have millions of impressionable eyes absorbing their particular messages. Given the chance, who would NOT want their materials distributed in America's classrooms?

The problem, then, is not the existence of the supplemental materials nor even, in most cases, the origins of the materials, but rather how they are used and what they say. If the Dairy Council's learning activities about the food pyramid and the five food groups include "Graphing Favorite Dairy Foods" and otherwise extolling the virtues of consuming more milk and cheese for their high loads of "calcium for healthy bones and teeth," who can argue with that? You can be sure that high cholesterol, heart disease, and obesity appear nowhere near the enticing images of cheddar cheese. Only by having objective nutritionists and physicians offer a fuller perspective can students (or their parents) make their own well-informed decisions about their diet. And even if such a presentation were made, the poster on the wall remains as the last word on the subject long after the medical experts have departed (presumably not to go pick up a slice of pepperoni pizza). For all of the flaws of the textbooks, supplemental materials can be even more biased, *because that is often their mission*. Teachers should not—yet many well-intentioned ones do—use them as equivalents to or substitutes for textbooks, without a critical enough understanding of their points of view.

It is essential, then, to recognize who exactly is placing materials in our children's classrooms. Whose are the extra-textbook voices that our students listen to every day? For our study, we gathered readings, maps, exercises, and more from a range of religious, political, and social groups that have an interest in how schools portray Jews, Judaism, Christianity, Islam, and the Middle East. We found, not surprisingly, that since September 11, 2001, the interest in, and therefore the amount of material available about Islam and the Middle East has exploded. Schools have been charged with helping elementary, middle, and high school students understand the world of Islam, Arabs, and the Middle East in an effort to make sense of the attacks. This shift was a much-needed and important change: many K–12 materials, including some textbooks, in the past either ignored or did a poor job of presenting Islam, Arabs, and the Middle East. When it became apparent that Americans had to overcome their own ignorance about such an important faith, people, and region, many groups stepped up to provide resources, and many more teachers incorporated those materials into their classroom, often unquestioningly. They did so because they did not know any better or because they are fearful of appearing insensitive or bigoted by asking questions about peoples other than themselves. Such is the side effect of non-analytical or misunderstood multiculturalism. The results have not been good. The desire to learn more, teach more, and understand more has opened the door to some really bad materials.

In the following pages, we profile some of the more prolific and important providers of supplemental materials (and in many cases, as we note, of teacher trainings and guest speakers as well) regarding Islam and the Middle East. (While materials are also available for teaching about Christianity and Judaism in public schools, in our analysis we found that those that focused on Islam and the Middle East were both the most extensive and the most problematic.) The groups described below produce supplemental materials, help to train teachers, and provide speakers for the classroom about the Middle East.

The Council on Islamic Education (CIE)

Founded in 1990 by Shabbir Mansuri, a parent of a child in California public schools, the Council on Islamic Education is perhaps the most influential Muslim organization of its kind. In 2006, they also began focusing strongly on First Amendment guidelines regarding the teaching about religion in public schools. "Our mission of providing services, resources and research-based tools predicated upon the highest standards of historical and social science scholarship to K–12 school textbook publishers, state education officials and policymakers, curriculum developers, and teachers is now online and better than ever."[6] They have not always met the mission of the highest standards.

But they have been extremely successful in becoming an essential resource for publishers as well as a source of supplemental materials and teacher trainings. Publishers and teachers—including those without the expertise to evaluate the accuracy or bias of CIE's offerings—have come to count on them. "I would like to thank you for recommending the many Muslim scholars who share our mutual concerns. Their insight helps us achieve our goal of publishing accurate, fair, and unbiased material."[7] Their critics, however, charge them with undue influence. The American Textbook Council described them as "a content gatekeeper with virtually unchecked power over publishers."[8] Education historian and former assistant education secretary Diane Ravitch wrote "[t]hree publishers—Glencoe, Houghton Mifflin, and Prentice Hall—rely on the same individual from the Council on Islamic Education to review their Islamic content. This may account for the similarity of their material on Islam as well as the omission of anything that would enable students to understand conflicts between Islamic fundamentalism and Western liberalism."[9] And CIE's textbook advocacy extends well beyond Islamic content: for example, it has strong opinions about how to teach the relationship between Jesus and his fellow Jews. Examples are provided in Chapter Four. Mansuri himself told the *Orange County Weekly* that he is waging "a 'bloodless' revolution . . . inside American junior high and high school classrooms."[10]

In addition to influencing the content of textbooks, state and national curriculum standards and national curriculum dissemination organizations, CIE also conducts teacher training at teacher conferences and on-site in school districts. CIE has formed institutional partnerships with the First Amendment Center (an influential organization that advises schools on how they can best teach about religion); the Association for Supervision and Curriculum Development (a national organization representing and servicing school administrators and curriculum specialists); East-West Center (a federally funded educational research agency); and The Asia Society, (a national organization that fosters education about the Asia-Pacific region).

Arab World and Islamic Resources (AWAIR)

While the Council on Islamic Education concentrates largely on textbook publishers, Arab World and Islamic Resources focuses more intently upon teacher-training seminars, organized in conjunction with the Washington, D.C.-based Middle East Policy Council and made available to teachers at little or no charge on a nationwide basis. Their teacher training is supported by materials that they have developed—most prominently the 500-plus-page loose-leaf compendium, the *Arab World Studies Notebook*—as well as their extensive catalogue of materials for classroom use. The *Notebook* has been the subject of criticism from the American Jewish Committee and others for its tendency toward

> historical distortion as well as uncritical praise, whitewashing, and practically proselytizing. The result . . . is a text that appears largely designed to advance the anti-Israel and propagandistic views of the

Notebook's sponsors, the Middle East Policy Council (MEPC) and Arab World and Islamic Resources (AWAIR), to an audience of teachers who may not have the resources and knowledge to assess this text critically.[11]

Examples of the *Notebook's* treatment of the Six-Day War are analyzed in Chapter Seven.

Like the Council on Islamic Education, AWAIR has also been tremendously successful. According to Richard Wilson, executive director of the Middle East Policy Council, AWAIR has "made a tremendous impact on schools nationwide,"[12] an outcome consistent with AWAIR's goals:

> Recognizing that no work is of greater importance than the preparation of our young people for their roles as thoughtful and informed citizens of the twenty-first century, and recognizing too, that U.S. involvement with the Arab World and with the wider world of Islam is certain to remain close for many years, AWAIR's goal is to increase awareness and understanding of this world region and this world faith through educational outreach at the precollegiate level.[13]

Both AWAIR and the CIE are closely involved with the institutions and organizations associated with K–12 education. Audrey Shabbas, the executive director of AWAIR, has been an active member of the National Council for Social Studies (NCSS), the largest association in the country devoted to social studies education, with members in all fifty states, the District of Columbia, and sixty-nine other countries. She has served as its presidential appointee to its Equity and Social Justice Committee, and is a regular presenter at state, regional, and national social studies educator conferences.[14] Articles on the Middle East, 9/11 and the Iraq war in the NCSS official journal, *Social Education*, consistently refer educators to the CIE, AWAIR, and other Muslim/Arab interest groups as good resources for information.

Council on American Islamic Relations (CAIR)

The Council on American Islamic Relations has been active in textbook development and K–12 teacher training. In November 2002, CAIR announced that a "very dedicated member of CAIR-DFW's (Dallas Fort-Worth) board has been selected to serve as a community representative on the Textbook Review Committee for one of the largest school districts in the DFW area. . . . The importance of Muslim representatives on committees such as these was highlighted last week in Austin, when the Texas State Board of Education approved several changes to public school text-books that were clearly unfair representations of Islam and Muslims."[15] CAIR's efforts are not limited to Texas, however, as chapters around the country hold teacher-training seminars.

In addition, CAIR collaborates with CIE to handle complaints of mis-representation of Muslims in textbooks. CIE refers individual complaints to the Southern California chapter of CAIR, which is the "clearinghouse for lobbying efforts." In December 1999, for example, a publisher "decided to halt distribution of a college textbook that was deemed offensive to Islam . . . after a formal complaint was filed by the Council on American-Islamic Relations."[16]

In 2002, CAIR launched an initiative to "to put quality materials about Islam in all 17,000 public libraries in the United States."[17] The effort was launched with a $500,000 donation from Prince Alwaleed bin Talal bin Abdul Azziz al Saud, whose $10 million donation to the Twin Towers Fund was refused by then-Mayor of New York City Rudolph Giuliani because it came with a letter blaming the September 11, 2001, terrorist attacks on American support for Israel. For a $150 donation, an individual can sponsor a CAIR library package of eighteen books and tapes, which the organization will distribute to a local library. Titles include, *The Islamic Threat: Myth or Reality?*, *Gender Equity in Islam*, and *Reel Bad Arabs: How Hollywood Vilifies a People*, as well as the Council on Islamic Education's handbook, *Teaching About Islam and Muslims in the Public School Classroom*.

While CAIR works to combat prejudice, it has also been embroiled in its own controversies. In 2007, California Senator Barbara Boxer rescinded an award she had previously given to Sacramento-based CAIR official Basim Elkarra. "After directing her staff to look into CAIR, Boxer 'expressed concern' about some past statements and actions by the group, as well as assertions by some law enforcement officials that it 'gives aid to interna-tional terrorist groups,' according to Natalie Ravitz, the senator's press spokeswoman."[18]

The Middle East Policy Council

The Middle East Policy Council (MEPC) has been very active in influ-encing K–12 education through teacher-training workshops. MEPC puts on workshops in partnership with AWAIR (Arab World and Islamic

Resources). MEPC is a co-publisher of AWAIR's *Arab World Studies Notebook* (1998 edition) and co-sponsor of AWAIR's fully funded teacher-training seminars, which are aimed primarily at social studies teachers of grades seven through twelve. MPEC "was founded in 1981 to expand public discussion and understanding of issues affecting U.S. policy in the Middle East. The Council is a nonprofit, tax-exempt 501(c)3 educational organization whose activities extend throughout the United States."[19]

Amideast

Amideast is a private, Washington, D.C.-based nonprofit organization dedicated to strengthening "mutual understanding and cooperation between Americans and the peoples of the Middle East and North Africa."[20] They accomplish a large part of their goals through their work in classrooms:

> AMIDEAST's half century of experience indicates that the most effective way to improve Americans' understanding of the Arab world is through the educational system. . . . AMIDEAST works with thousands of educators in the United States. We exhibit educational materials and make presentations about the Arab world at the national conferences of teacher associations and at local teacher workshops across the country.[21]

Amideast distributes over 125 books, videos, posters, lesson plans, and student activities through their online catalogue. "Each year, we review scores of books and multimedia materials, and with input from area experts as well as teachers, we select for distribution those that are most accurate and objective, relevant to the social studies curriculum, and appropriate for various grade levels."[22]

Saudi Aramco World

The oil company Saudi Aramco distributes a free magazine, Saudi Aramco World, to teachers. The glossy, full color bimonthly magazine features articles about Arab and Muslim history, culture, society, and religion throughout the Arab world, including the Palestinian population. Saudi Aramco helps to fund AWAIR and Amideast. According to Amideast's 2006 annual report, Amideast also received donations from other oil companies as well, such as Occidental Petroleum and Chevron. "Anonymous" is included in the largest category of donors.[23]

Dar al Islam

Based in New Mexico, Dar al Islam works closely with other Islamic advocacy groups, including the Council on Islamic Education and AWAIR. Dar al Islam runs a Teachers Institute that trains secondary school teachers about Islam, as well as a Speakers Bureau that provides speakers on Islam to middle schools and high schools. (The summer Teachers Institute is discussed in detail later in this chapter.) It is the repository and distribution agency for AWAIR's materials. In addition, the organization maintains a presence at national and regional conferences of the National Council for the Social Studies.

While at first glance Dar al Islam seems to be focused solely upon raising educators' awareness about the religion of Islam, the organization also has an interest in Middle East politics. Dar al Islam runs a website, IslamAmerica,[24] which is linked to its homepage. IslamAmerica features numerous articles about the Israeli–Palestinian conflict, including essays excoriating Israel originally published in the Egyptian paper, *Al Ahram*. An essay by the late Columbia University professor Edward Said posted on the site accused Israel of launching an "all-out colonial assault on the Palestinian people," a "bullying, sadistic campaign of death and carnage," and called then-Prime Minister Sharon an "Arab-killer" with "homicidal instincts."[25]

Islamic Networks Group

The Islamic Networks Group (ING) is a national consortium of Islamic speakers bureaus. Like CIE and AWAIR, with which it is affiliated, ING works to "promote interfaith dialogue and education about world religions and their contributions to civilization by annually delivering thousands of presentations and other educational programs."[26] ING sends speakers to a broad range of venues, from churches and healthcare centers, to law enforcement agencies and public schools. "ING's goal in working with schools is to supplement education about Islam and Muslims in the context of social studies and world history, as well as give a human face to the fastest growing faith in America. Our strategy for achieving this goal is face-to-face interaction between trained and certified Muslim speakers and school children and teachers."[27]

Like many other groups of its kind, ING provides First Amendment-based guidelines on the teaching about religion in schools. It uses an image of the United States Constitution alongside a picture of an American postage stamp honoring the Muslim holiday of Eid as a banner at the top of its website. One of its guiding principles states: "We subscribe to the principles expressed in the religious clauses of the First Amendment of the U.S. Constitution; our products and services are therefore academic, informative, objective, neutral, but never devotional in nature." [28]

National Council on U.S.–Arab Relations— The Model Arab League

The National Council on U.S. Arab Relations, a nonprofit organization based in Washington, D.C., runs a national network called the Model Arab League, a program similar to the Model United Nations in which "high school students . . . (become) Arab diplomats . . . passionately debating political, economic, and social issues of a region half a world away . . . (gaining) an expanded perspective of Arab problems."[29] More than 25,000 students have participated in the program at both the college and high school levels.[30]

American–Arab Anti-Discrimination Committee

"The American–Arab Anti-Discrimination Committee, ADC, with its strong grass-roots national network of chapters, activists, parents and educators is committed to improve the quality of education about the Arab world."[31] ADC has a campaign called "Reaching the Teachers." It

> encourages Arab Americans to become more involved in their community schools, builds relationships with teachers associations, and sensitizes educators to the Arab American community and its concerns. While we have seen a steady improvement in increasing awareness of Arab-related issues, much needs to be done in spreading the word to the more than 300,000 Social Studies teachers and 12,000 school districts in the U.S.[32]

Their areas of work include:

• Build a national network of Arab Americans who are involved in their children's education and in their school systems.

• Advise, train and provide resources for education activities and ADC chapter Education Committees. Support their work as they give classroom presentations, provide educational materials to teachers and school libraries, organize teacher training workshops, monitor textbooks for bias and misrepresentation of the Arab world, take part in school Human Relations or Minority committees, and respond to incidents of insensitivity or discrimination in the schools.

• Develop lesson plans and bibliographies on Arab culture, anti-Arab discrimination, Arab women, religions of the Arab world, and Palestine.

• Supply teachers and school systems with good educational materials on the Arab world.

• Provide resources on Arabs and Americans to Schools of Education for use in multicultural teacher training.

• Place articles on Arab American concerns in national educational publications and professional journal(s) for educators.

• Sensitize key multicultural educators, whose work influences the education profession as a whole to the Arab-American community and its concerns.

• Cultivate a national network of Arab-American educators.

• Heighten the profile of Arab Americans and the Arab world in the multicultural curriculum. Put Arab Americans on the multicultural education agenda.[33]

Alternate Focus

According to their website, "Alternate Focus is a 501(c)(3) non-profit educational media group promoting an alternative view of Middle East issues. We use the web, cable and satellite television, and DVDs to showcase media not usually seen by American audiences."[34] Their programming includes, among others, the documentaries "Blue Gold," which discusses "the ethnic cleansing perpetrated on the Palestinians by the Israelis in 1948" through an exploration of "water use in the Holy Land"; and "Checkpoint," in which "gripping footage documents the daily struggles of Palestinians who face constant military, economic, political, civil, and religious oppression. While most Palestinians attempt to adapt to their tragic situation, others lash out against Israel and further perpetuate the conflict."[35] (In the mainstream media that Alternate Focus seeks to counteract, "lashing out against Israel" is usually described as a suicide bombing on civilian targets; here, such an attack seems the act of a petulant child.)

Middle East Cultural and Information Center

MECIC describes itself as

> an independent, non-partisan educational and cultural organization seeking to promote understanding of Middle Eastern Issues in general, and the Palestinian issue in particular. Formed initially in 1989 to support the Intifada and the Palestinian people in their historic struggle for self-determination and statehood, MECIC has continued its activities through the Gulf War of 1991, the Al Aqsa Intifadah, and the present tragedy in Iraq.[36]

At the 2007 California Council for Social Studies conference, MECIC distributed handouts to educate teachers about the Middle East, including one entitled, "The History of the Middle East Is Inseparable from Colonialism." This four-page brochure contained little text and instead featured a map of "depopulated Arab villages" in "Al Nakhba" ["the Catastrophe"], photos of Arabs brandishing keys from their "dispossession," and emotionally-charged photos of children in scenes of violence. Its message and point of view were unmistakable.

THE SALAD BAR: THEMES OF PROBLEMS WITH SUPPLEMENTAL MATERIALS

In many respects, the materials distributed by the groups listed above accomplish their stated objective: they teach non-Muslim students about Islam and the Muslim world. Sometimes, though, their lessons include what can only be described as devotional language about Islam (as opposed to neutral teaching) and a political bias in matters dealing with the Israeli–Palestinian conflict. Some of the information is blatant anti-Israel propaganda: Israel's right to exist is undermined or denied, and Israel is painted as the terrorist, the aggressor, and the obstacle to peace. Other materials present an image of an idyllic pre-1948 Middle East that was disrupted only by the creation of the state of Israel. "Jihad" is de-militarized, and terrorism against Israel is minimized, sometimes even defended. In addition, some materials present Islam as the one true faith, a successor to inherently flawed Christianity and Judaism. Specific examples of problematic sections of supplemental materials are integrated with the egregious textbook passages in the analysis chapters and organized thematically.

LOOKING FOR CURRICULAR RESOURCES

Few of the supplemental materials available to teachers arrive by themselves. They are often packaged together with lesson plans, curricula, and sometimes entire teaching modules or units so that educators know what to say and how to use the materials. In many cases, they are available for downloading on the Internet, a most attractive option for educators hard-pressed for the time to research the omnifarious topics they must teach. These resources range from high-level outlines and suggested discussion topics to scripted lessons and seat maps for teachers to arrange the chairs in their classrooms just so. They are available on almost any topic and from a sweeping array of sources, including business corporations, social group non-profits, science, art, and cultural museums, religious organizations, political groups, and others.

For many public school teachers, these lesson plans have become vital tools in their efforts to keep up with the standards and testing requirements of their states. Imagine a high school history teacher who needs to teach a unit about the Armenian genocide for the first time, a topic currently required by eleven states. (Most states require some teaching about the Holocaust of the Jews during World War II.) He types "teaching genocide" into his browser, and more than a million hits show up: the Armenian genocide at the top, the Holocaust, Rwanda, the Balkans, and more. Many of these sites have extensive discussions, definitions, bookstores, speakers bureaus, community events, and, of course, teacher resources. How is a teacher to choose among them? He clicks on one site.[37] It is professional, impressive, and filled with options, including podcasts, news, and a link to an "online campus."

The campus is "an online gathering place for Facing History's dynamic and dedicated network of educators." Teachers can share their favorite resources, lessons, and projects with each other, print study guides, and download complete lessons and units that "are designed to provide classroom activities based on the Facing History resources." The Armenian genocide, the first one on the alphabetical list of materials, contains eight options, divided into different interconnected units: "The Armenian Genocide: Analyzing Historical Evidence," "The Armenian Genocide: Denial, Free Speech, and Hate Speech," and so on. Clicking on the latter leads to an overview of the lesson, a list of the other lessons in this unit, historical context for the topic, a couple of activities for students, selected readings (including Facing History's own resource book on the topic), and a video that can be borrowed from the Facing History library for classroom use. There are statements to be written on the board, questions to ask students, and a directive to use the "Spontaneous Argumentation teaching strategy" to lead the discussion.[38]

Upon glancing at these pre-fabricated lessons, the teacher may look no further for alternatives nor question the accuracy or point of view of these materials. In an era when teachers constantly feel the pressure to teach to the test and when they have seen the amount of material they are expected to cover increase without a corresponding augmentation in their classroom or prep time, it would seem an obvious choice simply to adopt whole-cloth for their students lessons such as the ones available from Facing History. Over one million hits on the online search, and a relatively short time later, with whatever modifications in method and approach seem appropriate for his particular set of students, our high school teacher is prepared to face his class.

The lessons from Facing History happen to be well conceived. One curriculum developer we interviewed found the interactivity, the use of various media, and the inclusion of an assessment as part of the lesson structure to be praiseworthy from a purely pedagogical perspective.[39] She, like many people with teaching credentials and advanced education degrees, was unable to evaluate the content, because the Armenian genocide, or genocide in any of its tragic forms, fell far outside her area of expertise. If she were called upon to teach a lesson on the Armenian genocide, she—and many other fine educators, no doubt—would evaluate the worthiness of thousands of online, free curricula based upon what she knows: Is it well structured? Can I envision doing the activities suggested with my set of students? Does it seem to cover the topic or meet the standard I am teaching to? Can I afford it? Beyond questions like these (and certainly good teachers would ask a lot of questions), what other resources does a teacher have in selecting materials on unfamiliar topics? It is likely that the location on the search results page of a particular resource is as much a factor as any in a teacher's decision-making process. Facing History's website showed up near the top of our search results page. Once we clicked and began exploring, we had little need to return to the original list.

But what if the search terms were different? Or if the teacher looked elsewhere? Most materials are not as polished, well-researched, and expertly developed as those on the Facing History website. Or as disinterested in profit. Imagine a different social studies teacher preparing a lesson plan for the first time on Islam. The first two hits on her Internet search using the term "teaching Islam" brings up the websites for, respectively, Education World® ("The Educator's Best Friend") and Muslim Hope ("Teaching about Islam and Giving Muslims Hope through Jesus"). Most good teachers would instantly recognize the latter site as inappropriate for the classroom and potentially insulting to Muslims. (On its homepage, it address the "dear Muslim reader" directly, asking him to "see Islam for what it really is, a corruption and counterfeit of truth, and the Bible for what it really is, the Word of God that He is able to preserve."[40]) Education World, on the other hand, is geared for teachers, with articles, bulletin boards, virtual workshops, "teacher tunes," classroom strategies, and much more. This seems to be the kind of help our teacher is looking for.

The main article on the landing page (the page that showed up on the list of results of her Internet search) summarizes a workshop held in Connecticut in July, 2002, called the "Teachers' Institute on Middle Eastern Studies."[41] The article is bound on either side by columns jammed with links to other pages on the Education World website and—in blazing contrast with Facing History, which is non-commercial in every respect—scores of advertisements. In addition to ads for educational products and on-line universities offering advanced degrees in education, teachers can buy weight loss pills, outdoor furniture, used cars, low-cost insurance for that car, and many other unrelated items. There is also a small sidebar with links to outside resources for teaching about Islam and the Middle East. These resources include the websites IslamiCity; History in the News: The Middle East; A Brief Guide to Understanding Islam; Middle East History and Resources; and Islam 101. Our social studies teacher clicks on the first link: IslamiCity, which takes her to a page with articles, videos, and streaming audio devoted to Muslim life, prayer, and politics.[42] On IslamiCity, she can search the Quran, answer or place an ad seeking marriage to a Muslim, read complex articles on such topics as the punishment of apostasy in orthodox Islamic law, and learn to pray like a Muslim. There are no curricular resources, no state education frameworks on the teaching of religion, and no point of view other than that of a religious Muslim. Yet our teacher has arrived at this page by clicking on a link at Education World, a resource for teachers like her.

The second link in the list is the neutral sounding History in the News: The Middle East. The Department of History at State University of New York-Albany produces and maintains this website. It is free of commercial interests and cautions visitors that "the Middle East is a complex place with many religious ideas, colorful cultures, and a long history. Come with us on a journey to the Middle East through its amazing past and present."[43] It contains a simple site map, with links to History, Culture, Society, Religion, and more. Our teacher clicks on "Politics" and lands on a well-organized page divided into several sections: General Information, Peace and Conflicts, Organizations and Groups, and Water Crisis. Each of these sections itself contains links to other materials. Under Organizations and Groups, the teacher can jump to websites for the League of Arab States, the Peres Center for Peace (founded by Israeli Nobel laureate Shimon Peres), and the Islamic Resistance Support Association, among others. When the teacher opens the website for the Islamic Resistance Support Association, she sees first a page entirely in Arabic, with a button for an English version. Finally reaching her destination, the teacher can choose among daily news, articles, and statements issued by Sayyed Hassan Nasrallah, the Secretary General of Hizbullah [sic].[44] Each mention of Israel on these pages is set off by quotation marks to indicate the website's position that such a nation does not actually exist. Nowhere on the English version are the authors of the website mentioned, but it is apparent from its content that it is a Shi'a Islamist organization, sympathetic to, if not an apologist for, terrorist organizations like "Hizbullah."

In arriving at this page, our social studies teacher seems to have traveled far from her starting point of typing "teaching Islam" into her search engine. But in reality the journey has been frighteningly short: three clicks have taken her from a commercial provider of resources for teachers to propaganda disseminated by a terrorist group. To arrive at the Islamist homepage, she has passed through the gates of a respected university's history department, which implies that the State University of New York-Albany endorses its message and feels it on par with, say, that of the Peres Center for Peace. How is our social studies teacher—or any uninformed teacher wanting to be sensitive to the way she presents a topic as difficult and seemingly foreign as Islam and the Middle East—to distinguish the propaganda from the scholarship? How can she incorporate these complex issues into a classroom at a level that can help students learn to think and analyze on their own if she herself cannot?

It seems from the structure and tone of their website that Education World does not concern itself with such questions either. Most of their lesson plans, of which there are hundreds, are only superficially linked to teaching frameworks or standards. In addition to opportunities to purchase cars and spell-checking educational software, they mainly offer lists of ideas for teachers ("Read All About It! Ten Terrific Newspaper Lessons") rather than substance. Yet, Education World—"The Educator's Best Friend"—is the first portal through which a teacher seeking to learn more about teaching Islam may travel, depending on the vicissitudes of her Internet search and the specific terms she types in her browser.

Education World is not unique; Facing History seems to be. Many of the educational resources available online are as unsatisfactory or worse than Education World. In our research, we found that civil and human rights websites like Facing History offered supplemental materials and curricula that were, overall, of much higher quality and less likely to be tainted either by error or bias than most other such offerings. (We found a similar situation in the textbooks concerning the Holocaust of the Jews in World War II.) Few of the hundreds of other such sites are created for the sake of sharing scholarly knowledge. Some, like Education World, sustain themselves through ad revenues and must push as much new content as possible to keep teachers' eyeballs returning to their pages. Others rely on the support of larger organizations which may or may not hold expertise in the subject area or in pedagogy. And still others are sources of outright propaganda, created and maintained solely to insert their biases into classrooms.

Teachers need resources like Facing History. With limited time, decreasing budgets for materials or their own professional development, and the never-ending pressure to adhere to the standards for testing purposes, educators have come to rely on outside sources to assist them in their own classrooms. To facilitate the use of their materials, Facing History even helps teachers position their offerings to meet their own particular set of needs by a section on their website called "Standards and Frameworks." Accessible only to subscribers ("educators belonging to the Facing History Teacher Network" as well as those who have attended one of their many workshops, seminars, and courses), this resource contains "a collection of documents addressing the connections between Facing History and state and national learning standards." Teachers only need look here to feel comfortable that they are fulfilling their statutory obligations.

And indeed they may be. Or they may not. The problem with bringing materials into the classroom that do not undergo any review process by content matter experts or state standards review boards is that teachers cannot be counted on to evaluate them using the same criteria as these focused reviewers. It is beyond the scope of most teachers to fulfill all of their many daily responsibilities AND take on the evaluating tasks normally handled at the district or state level. While many providers of such materials anticipate this need and provide their own evaluations for teachers, there is no objective and knowledgeable oversight. The United States Department of Agriculture does not allow meat producers to inspect and grade their own product, because it would be bad for the consumer. Why should the consumers of classroom supplemental materials be offered any less protection?

TEACHING THE TEACHER

Facing History, like many other organizations that create and publish in-class materials and curricula, is much more than simply a resource for the classroom. They publish books (intended to be used as supplemental materials for students), provide a wide variety of materials for free through a multimedia lending library, sponsor community events such as lectures, and offer teachers a full range of professional development opportunities. Facing History is not alone in this; many providers of supplemental materials and curricula also invite teachers to learn from them in workshops, seminars, or summer courses. Any teacher enrolling in such classes would, of course, learn to use the materials offered by that same organization. The classes benefit both parties: In many states, teachers may earn credits toward pay increases based on the number and types of continuing education classes they take, and the organizations themselves guarantee that their message and materials are disseminated in classrooms.

Teacher trainings tend to take two different forms: shorter, information-sharing events such as those at teacher conferences like the annual meeting of the National Council for the Social Studies and more intense, district-approved courses that may be presented by the same organizations that publish supplemental materials. (Some of the shorter seminars at the conferences may also be offered by the publishers of supplemental material and curricula, but they usually do not meet the district or state requirements that would count toward an increase in compensation.) As might be expected, since the professional development courses are drawn from the same well as the supplemental materials and curricula, they have the potential to suffer from many of the same problems. They, too, have a particular point of view and are not subject to the same over-sight as textbooks, as problematic as that process has become. And teach-ers are similarly limited in their ability to evaluate the accuracy and bias of their content, perhaps even more so if the presenter is dynamic and convincing.

As part of our research, we attended seminars and workshops offered within the context of a teachers' conference as well as stand-alone classes that fulfill continuing education requirements and provide a teacher with the potential to earn more money. We paid particular attention to those classes that focused on the subject areas of our case study. We found that quality ranged from impeccable, balanced presentations of genuine use to teachers, all the way to propaganda sessions more appropriate for a polit-ical rally than a gathering of educators.

We observed two different teacher conferences: the annual meetings of the National Council for the Social Studies (NCSS) and the California Council for the Social Studies (CCSS). A single registration at each confer-ence allows the participant to choose from any number of workshops, seminars, and classes, each focused on a specialized aspect of social stud-ies pedagogy and content. The theme of the 2005 NCSS conference (held November 17–20, 2005, in Kansas City) was "Social Studies: The Heart of the Curriculum," chosen to reflect the increasing concern among social studies teachers that their field would become marginalized as a result of the federal focus (read: testing and funding) on the "core" skills of read-ing, math, and science prescribed by the No Child Left Behind Act. The conference presented teachers with hundreds of choices of workshops and seminars, most focused on the tactical aspects of teaching: "Research-ing Native American Heritage On-line," "Textiles Tell a Story," and so on. Most of the presenters were teachers themselves or college professors, and many of them provide participants with practical materials to use in their own classrooms, including curricula and supplemental materials. A minority of presenters were developers of such materials, such as the Teacher's Curriculum Institute, a small publisher that offered a workshop entitled, "Social Studies Alive! Build and Support Content Literacy in the Elementary Classroom."(It should be noted that "Social Studies Alive!" is also the name of one of their product series.) The last group of presenters were neither teachers nor textbook publishers but rather museums, consortia, and interest groups that were often exhibitors as well.

A note on the exhibitors: The NCSS conference is an opportunity for those who would like to market their materials or message to K–12 teachers. In 2005, textbook publishers outnumbered other exhibitors, who ranged from the History Channel Education Network and the Federal Reserve System, to more clearly partisan groups such as Historians Against the War and the Islamic Networks Group. At most booths, free materials, including textbooks, were available for the asking, and some organizations even paid for shipping. Free materials can be an important criterion in the decision to distribute materials to students. Accuracy and point-of-view can become secondary. Also, those organizations that offer for-credit teacher workshops tend to recruit at these large conferences. At their exhibitor's booths, they offer discounted registration fees and encourage teachers to attend by reminding them of their accreditation by the state.

The group Dar al Islam, often represented at conferences, invites teachers to a two-week-long summer Teacher's Institute to its site in New Mexico. Each summer, teachers live and learn on a 1,357-acre campus, at the center of which lie a North African-style mosque and madrassa (school). Teachers who would like three hours of "graduate-level academic credits" pay $120 per credit hour for the two-week session. Otherwise, they pay only their transportation and incidentals; Dar al Islam covers everything else. Why would an organization incur such expenses for teachers? Because they expect graduates of the program to further their agenda: Participation in the Teacher's Institute is by invitation only: "Participants are selected on the basis of effectiveness as a teacher, ability to influence school curriculum, and commitment to use the materials covered in the classroom."[45] In other words, teachers who attend the training are not only learning Islam as taught by "God-fearing" Muslims but are expected to influence their schools' curricula to reflect traditional Islam and perhaps even proselytize on behalf of Dar al Islam. Such an objective seems to flirt with violating First Amendment concerns over the establishment of religion, and perhaps even disregards the strict rules regarding the teaching about religion in public schools. How would the average non-Muslim teacher be able to discern the difference between proselytizing and teaching? Where does a high school student acquire the context in which to understand Dar al Islam's materials if they appear in his classroom? It would seem that such a teacher training would indeed extend the reach of the organization whose name, "House of Islam," historically refers to the lands under Muslim rule.

When we attended the California Council for the Social Studies annual meeting (held in Oakland on March 2–4, 2007), we focused on workshops and presenters that directly addressed the themes of our area of inquiry. They provided insight into the unavoidable danger of bias that informs such teacher trainings. Some of the presenters recognized the problem themselves and used it as a jumping off point for their own presentations. In a session entitled, "Middle East Nationalism: Arab–Israeli Conflict Analysis," Yitzhak Santis, Middle East Project Director of the San Francisco Jewish Community Relations Council (JCRC), opened his session with the following disclaimer: "I am Jewish and my wife is Israeli. I represent a Jewish organization. While I believe this to be a balanced presentation, I am stating my perspective up front. Be careful if you hear another presentation on the subject and the presenter says they are unbiased."[46]

This framework was especially important in the context of the CCSS meeting, where, similar to the NCSS conference, teachers demonstrated a deep hunger for information and help in teaching about non-Christian religions and about the Middle East. Among the exhibitors were two blatantly anti-Israel groups: Alternate Focus and the Middle East Cultural and Information Center (MECIC), both described earlier in this chapter. The Middle East Cultural and Information Center shared the same table as Alternate Focus.

Neither Alternate Focus nor MECIC are specifically in the field of education. They are not providers of supplemental materials designed for classroom use; they have no obligation to conform with state standards regarding the teaching about religion or history; nor are they neutral regarding one of the more difficult issues facing contemporary society. Their presence at the California Council for the Social Studies annual meeting indicates their desire not to peddle, say, a textbook like so many of the publishers in attendance, but rather to sell their ideas in the hope that teachers will incorporate them into the classroom. They are by no means the only such non-pedagogical group who regularly pay the exhibitor's fees to set up a table among the throngs of educators. They are just two among many organizations with a deep bias that want their perspectives to be presented to students. It is their right to do so, and in an ideal marketplace of ideas, their point of view would be debated in the context of other competing or opposing positions. It would be examined in a historical and religious context, and students would understand how such passionately held opinions reflect the current struggles in the Middle East.

But that is rarely the case.

Teachers are overworked. As we have seen, they are often underinformed and may be teaching so far out of their field that they do not have even the vocabulary to understand the long and difficult historical path that has led to the current conflict. An organization with the impartial name, "The Middle East Cultural and Information Center" would appear to be a kind of clearinghouse for the curious, like the San Francisco Visitor's Desk in the heart of the tourist center or the concierge in a good hotel. Without training, without the benefit of Yitzhak Santis' tip-of-the-hat to his inherent bias, how is a well-intentioned teacher to distinguish fact from fabrication, opinion from documented history? Photos can be cropped, stories can be edited, and materials that do not even feign compliance with state standards or the norms of curriculum development can find their way into classrooms as unbiased truth, as solid teaching matter.

When a teacher—the conduit through which so much information flows to students—picks up a flawed handout or attends a workshop promoting ideology in the context of a social studies conference, there is no way to ensure a responsible dialogue around such materials and trainings. When one considers the duty of public education to create informed citizens, the dissemination of propaganda in the guise of didactic truth becomes more than simply a bad lesson; it approaches the tragic.

CHAPTER THREE

LEARNING ABOUT JEWISH ORIGINS: STEREOTYPES OF JEWS

Contemporary societies often base socio-political claims on their collective memory, gathered in textbooks as definitive history, enshrining tradition or faith as fact. This is especially true in lessons that deal with the origins of Jews and Judaism. Both are represented well in some textbooks while others do a particularly bad job of presenting Jewish history, culture, and theology.

The problematic passages in some textbooks' coverage of Jewish origins contain stereotypes of Jews that have often been used to foster classical anti-Semitism. Jews are described as legalistic and Judaism is portrayed as merely an overlong list of arcane rules, devoid of any spirituality. Jews are depicted as intolerant of non-Jews and as looking down upon others with an attitude of superiority. Jews are even represented as unsophisticated in the arts and sciences. *World Civilizations*, a product of Thomson Wadsworth, states "Jewish arts and sciences were relatively underdeveloped compared with those of their more sophisticated and richer neighbors. Excepting the Old Testament's poetry, the Jews produced very little of note in any of the art forms. . . . There is no record of any important Jewish contributions to the sciences."[1] The overall perspective that comes through from these textbooks is that Judaism is outdated and obsolete, lacking in value compared to those faiths which came later.

JEWS AND JEWISH LAW

Harcourt/Holt's *Harcourt Horizons World History* offers an elegant and positive description of Jewish law. "Judaism teaches that God is just and that God's virtues must be imitated. In Judaism, a person's service to God is measured by how many good deeds he or she has done for other people."[2] However, other textbooks foster the familiar stereotypical notion that Jews are overly concerned about the letter of Jewish law and not its spirit. Jewish law is seen as harsh and retributional, the Jewish God as cruel and unforgiving. By extension, so are Jews.

In large part this distortion arises from unsophisticated and narrow views of certain Torah passages, isolated and without the context and perspective of the later prophetic books in the Jewish Bible. Nor does this misreading of Torah texts consider the development of the oral tradition, later set down in the Talmud, of how the laws should be interpreted. In large part, the practical application of Jewish law contains large measures of justice, and origins of the jurisprudence tradition to prevent the punishment of an accused who may be innocent are found many times in the Torah.

For example, several textbooks heavily emphasize the well known "an eye for an eye" passage from Exodus 21 as reflecting a lack of legal development and compassion and portray it as an uncritical Hebrew incorporation of the rule of "retaliation in kind" originating with the Babylonians. McGraw-Hill's *Traditions and Encounters* says "Hebrew law, for example, borrowed the principle of *lex talionis* from Hammurabi's code" and later, in a discussion of Christianity, characterizes the Exodus text as "moral and legal principles that southwest Asian peoples had followed since the third millennium B.C.E."[3] The expression "an eye for an eye" was never meant to be taken literally and every textbook that quotes it should acknowledge that fact.

World History: Continuity and Change by Holt gets it completely backwards and wrong. "Like the code of Hammurabi, Mosaic Law demanded 'an eye for an eye'—though unlike Hammurabi's Code it did not allow for the substitution of a money payment for those who could afford it."[4] The whole point of "an eye for an eye" in Jewish legal tradition is the requirement of monetary damages in proportion to the offense. The expression was designed as an innovation to introduce proportionality into legal punishment. Its interpretation by the oral tradition was understood to require monetary damages in proportion to the injury. Biblical scholar

James L. Kugel explains the interplay between the "two canons, the biblical one and the great corpus of writings included under the Oral Torah. Although these two bodies of writing were, and are, said to be of equal importance, the Oral Torah always wins. The written Torah may say 'an eye for an eye,' but what these words mean is what the Oral Torah says they mean, namely, monetary compensation for any such injury (*b. Baba Qamma* 83b–84a)."[5] The lack of understanding of Jewish law reflected here has the direct result of fostering stereotypes of Jewish law as negative from its inception.

McDougal Littell's *Ancient World History*, so eloquent in describing the ethical monotheism of the Hebrews, features a page that highlights "Development of Law" which compares excerpts from three ancient legal traditions. The headings are "Hammurabi's Code," "Confucius," and the unhelpful label "Old Testament." The Torah excerpts seem selected intentionally for their harshness. Neither of the other sources contains the death penalty, yet here is the death penalty levied in two cases of childhood disobedience, from Exodus 21:16–17.

What would school children think of Jewish law when they read the passage without context or interpretation or the explanation of hyperbole and literary exaggeration? "Whoever strikes his father or his mother will be put to death. Whoever curses his father or mother will be put to death." There seems to be no record in Jewish history of any child being executed for these offenses. And why choose these from the hundreds of laws in the Torah?

The Torah passage, complete with the authoritative looking illustration of a Torah scroll, includes punishments that seem brutal to modern sensibilities. In fact, the "Document-Based Question" at the end of the passage asks "What principle underlies these laws? How would you describe the punishments in these laws?" The suggested answers lead us to the conclusion apparently desired by the textbook. "The severity of a punishment must match the seriousness of the crime. Some punishments—including death for disrespecting parents—are very harsh."[6] It would be hard to conceive of a stronger indictment of Jewish law.

Why choose passages that require sophisticated exegesis instead of those that would provide a balanced perspective on Jewish law? Chapter 22 of Exodus, which follows the Chapter 21 passage quoted in the textbook, contains an alternative: the often repeated Torah admonition "You shall not molest or oppress an alien for you were once aliens in the land of Egypt. You shall not wrong any widow or orphan. If ever you wrong them and they cry out to me, I will surely hear their cry." Certainly this or many other legal passages could serve the purpose better. And why are no capital offenses included for Hammurabi?

McGraw-Hill's *Humanities in Western Culture* echoes the other textbooks' unsophisticated and uncritical stereotype of the Mosaic Law as indistinguishable from Babylonian justice. "In common with earlier codes, the basic principle [of Hammurabi's Code] was 'retaliation in kind' or, as expressed by the Hebrews, 'an eye for an eye, a tooth for a tooth.'"[7]

The Earth and Its Peoples by Houghton Mifflin reinforces the idea that Judaism was only concerned with many rigid rules, to the exclusion of divinely mandated concern for one's fellow or the weakest members of society. "Jews lived by a rigid set of rules. Dietary restrictions . . . Ritual baths . . . The Jews venerated the Sabbath . . . These strictures . . . tended to isolate the Jews from other peoples . . ."[8] The Jewish code is not only considered overly legalistic by this textbook's authors; it also serves as justification for another stereotype that is often used to perpetuate anti-Semitism: that Jews are clannish and seek to isolate themselves from other peoples.

An advanced-level high school text, *World Civilizations,* by Thomson Wadsworth offers an elaboration of this line of thinking: "The faith that Yahweh desired was supported by a set of rigid rules . . ."[9] which resulted in the Jews' "preoccupation with the finer points of the Law laid down by Moses and his successors . . ."[10]

Houghton Mifflin *Earth and Its Peoples* adds the associated stereotype that the Israelites' God was harsh and unforgiving. "During their reported forty years in the desert, the Israelites became devoted to a stern and warlike god."[11] Also in *World Civilizations* by Thomson Wadsworth, the Israelite God is seen as a warrior deity devoid of the merciful aspects that the Torah also attributes to him. "Whether or not the Gentiles worshipped him, he was their all-powerful judge and would reward or punish them (mostly the latter) as they conformed or not to the demands of conscience."[12] The focus on only the punishing and stern side of the Jewish God comports well with the accusation of legalism.

Finally, as we move forward in time from the Exodus toward the birth of Christianity, two textbooks set the stage for the advent of Jesus by taking parting jabs at the Judaism of the period. *World Civilizations: The Global*

Experience, by Pearson Longman characterizes late biblical Judaism as legalistic, in need of reform, even obsolete. "Christianity began in reaction to rigidities that had developed in the Jewish priesthood two centuries before the birth of Jesus Christ."[13] Along the same lines Holt's *World History: The Human Journey* asserts that, in contrast with the soulless legalistic Judaism of his day, "[Jesus] also taught that God cares more for people, especially those who are suffering, than he does for laws and rituals."[14]

Whether against the backdrop of Jesus' message or during biblical times, overemphasizing the idea of Judaism as solely a strict conformity to a code of commandments and observances denigrates modern Judaism, reduces its historical form to a one dimensional spiritual system, and robs it of the very value touted by some of the textbooks. The full panoply and richness of Israelite ethical monotheism as a major contribution to world civilization gets lost if characterized as simply an endless set of rules.

JEWS ARE INTOLERANT

Several of the textbooks portray Jews as intolerant of other ethnic and religious groups, stating that they look down upon non-Jews. This view contends that Jews harbor an attitude of elitism and snobbery, even superiority toward others. The charge that Jews are intolerant is explained as having a foundation in Jewish scripture and belief. These stereotypes of intolerant Jews are particularly inappropriate and egregious in textbook chapters dealing with the origins of Judaism. If aspects of Jewish origins and fundamental beliefs consist of stereotypes that have been used to foster classic anti-Semitism, how can the textbooks be relied upon to portray Jews fairly in later history of Christian and Muslim origins, or the modern Middle East?

Probably the most misused concept in Jewish religion and history is the concept of Jews as the "chosen people." Non-Jews and some Jews themselves alike have erroneously attributed chauvinistic qualities to the biblical and religious notion of election, being chosen. This is especially true through some interpretations of the Christian scriptures that reflect an uncritical acceptance of the triumphalist perspective of Christianity.

Triumphalism embraces the viewpoint that only the more universalist Christianity is the path to a life of holiness and God, is the logical and only fulfillment of Judaism, and deserves to triumph over a Judaism which contains unappealing arrogance and particularism. Some textbook authors and their scholarly consultants continue to include this perspective, now rejected by Christian leaders.

Both the textbook focus on the Jews as the chosen people and text-book phrasing which talks about the degree to which Jews *saw themselves* as God's chosen have the effect of undermining modern Christian under-standing of Jews as participants in their enduring covenant with God. Affirmation of the special *continuing* relationship between the Jewish peo-ple and God is a hallmark of contemporary Christian teaching. Rather than saying "the Jews thought they were chosen" textbooks should explain that Jews believe they have a special responsibility to improve the world.

The tension between particularism and universalism in Judaism is complex. It is the struggle between an inward focus and the relationship to the larger world. In discussing the idea that Jews look down on others, one Christian scholar put it this way. In biblical times

> on the one hand, Judaism tended to draw apart from the world and turn inward on itself, exhibiting at times an attitude that was narrow and even intolerant. On the other hand, one observes evidences of a warm and lively concern for the salvation of the nations, something approaching a true missionary spirit . . . The Salvation of the Nations: Universalistic Tendencies in Judaism. . . . Prophets of the restoration period . . . awaited the time when foreigners would flock to Zion. . . . Moreover, the law, far from placing any barrier in the way of this, provided for the reception of proselytes and accorded them equality of treatment. . . . This is witnessed by the fact that proselytes *were* made. Before New Testament times they were to be found every-where.[15] [emphasis from original]

The word proselyte comes from the Greek meaning "one who has been converted from one religious faith to another . . . , specifically a convert to Judaism who performs all the religious duties required of Jews and enjoys all the privileges."[16]

Indeed, most Jewish communities today do not pro-actively seek con-verts. Judaism developed an abhorrence to missionary activities in the Middle Ages when faced by stringent prohibitions against proselytizing by the ruling Christian and Muslim authorities. Encouraging conversions to Judaism could result in torture or death. Jews were forced out of the conversion process; they did not abdicate from it.

However, conversion and missionary activity took place at other times in Jewish history. During the first century, which included Jesus' lifetime, the substantial Jewish population of the Roman Empire demonstrates that the growth in the size of the community could not have been due to natural increase alone. Matthew's Gospel describes the zeal of Pharisees who "traverse sea and land to make one convert . . ."[17] Jewish outreach to non-Jews was widespread and reflected the vibrancy and diversity of Judaism of the time.[18]

One textbook recognizes this fact explicitly. McGraw-Hill/Glencoe's *Human Heritage: A World History* reports the number of Jews in the empire in a teacher sidebar: "Did You Know? During the time Jesus preached, there were about 2.5 million Jews in Palestine and another 4 million elsewhere in the Roman Empire."[19] The total of 6.5 million compares to an estimated population of the Roman Empire as a whole of 57 million during the reign of Augustus (27 B.C.E.–14 C.E.), for an approximate proportion of 11 percent.[20] Converts to Judaism figure prominently in the Christian Pentecost story, adding further evidence of widespread Jewish proselytizing at this time. The Acts of the Apostles recounts that at Pentecost (the Jewish festival of Shavuot) "there were devout Jews from every nation under heaven staying in Jerusalem. . . . [They said] 'We are . . . both Jews and *converts* to Judaism . . .'" [21] [emphasis added] The large proportion of Jews in the empire and their distribution in lands far from Judea shows the effects of both efforts at proselytization and the intermarriage with neighboring peoples that has been a hallmark of Jewish existence through the centuries.

One textbook in particular alleges Jews' aversion to conversion of non-Jews in biblical times. Pearson Longman's *World Civilizations: The Global Experience* reads "because Judaism stressed God's special compact with the chosen people, there was no premium placed on converting non-Jews."[22] The two concepts paired in this sentence are not related. The Jewish covenant with God, if anything, is meant by its nature to be something of value to be shared with others, and is not exclusionary.

Two exercises from *Ancient World History*, published by McDougal Littell reflect the allegations of Jewish intolerance and lack of understanding of a Judaism that in fact actively sought converts. The first example is a teacher's sidebar that reads "Christianity Spreads Through the Empire: Critical Thinking. Q. Why was the apostle Paul so important to the spread of Christianity? A. Paul traveled widely and interpreted Christ's teachings in ways that further distinguished them from Jewish law." Of critical importance, the text offers two explanations of exactly how Paul distanced his teachings from Judaism, one correct, the other problematic. One of the two explanations offered is "Paul stressed that Jesus was the son of God who died for people's sins." But the second reflects a subtle jab at Judaism. "He also declared that Christianity should welcome all converts, Jew or Gentile (non-Jew). It was this universality that enabled Christianity to become more than just a *local* religion."[23] [emphasis added] The description of Judaism as only "local" is inaccurate and somewhat demeaning, given Judaism's wide reach at that time.

The second exercise from *Ancient World History* is similar in content and serves to reinforce the overdrawn distinction between Christians and Jews in the text, without proper context. The lesson is entitled "Comparing Religions" and is meant to compare and contrast Judaism and Christianity at a point in the text when the separation between the two religions occurred. If executed properly, the exercise could serve a useful pedagogical purpose, as it is important that students be familiar with the differences between the two religions in light of the substantial Jewish content in Christianity. Unfortunately, the dimensions of comparisons in the lesson's suggested answer reflect the same classic stereotype that Jews are intolerant.

The exercise reads as follows. "Recall with students that Christianity arose from Jewish teachings. . . . To help students recognize similarities and differences between the religions, work with students to complete a Venn diagram. Here is an example." The suggested answer lists the following items in the three areas of the diagram:

Christian only:
• Belief that Jesus is the Messiah
• *Acceptance of Gentiles and Jews alike*

Jewish only:
• *Belief that Jews are the chosen people*
• Adherence to Jewish law

Both [points of overlap, in the intersection region in the center of the diagram]:
• Belief in one God
• Belief in the Ten Commandments.[24] [emphasis added]

The implication of the exercise's overemphasis on Jewish belief that Jews are the chosen people is that Jews are not accepting of others, that they are intolerant and chauvinistic. Rather than focus on the Jews as chosen, which is not really an effective point of differentiation because Christianity has adopted the concept, the exercise should focus on Christian belief in the divinity of Jesus and his role as messiah. A better exercise would be two columns: What beliefs do Judaism and Christianity share? What beliefs distinguish them? For example, the "Differences" section could read:

- God became human in the form of Jesus of Nazareth
- Jesus is the fulfillment of the messianic prophecies in the Jewish scriptures
- Jesus had to die on the cross for the sins of mankind

In reality, the notion of the Jews as the "chosen people" means that in the divine scheme of things, God chose the Jewish people to be a vehicle for God's revelation to be transmitted to the world. The prophets best articulated the meaning of chosenness and its implications. Isaiah says it means to be "a light of nations"[25] while in Amos, God states clearly "[y]ou alone have I singled out [o]f all the families of the earth—[t]hat is why I will call you to account [f]or all your iniquities."[26] The prophets establish the connection between the Jews' receipt of God's revelation and a call to a higher standard of ethical behavior. This is a responsibility, an obligation, a religious mission, rather than a self-appointed superior status over others. Beyond displaying a fundamental misunderstanding of the meaning of "chosen," the phraseology of several of the textbooks compounds the portrayal of Jews as harboring a haughty self-image by saying "Jews looked upon themselves as chosen." Textbook passages which ascribe to Jews an attitude of superiority and intolerance can tend to generate negative feelings against Jews. For example, *The World and Its People*, published by McGraw-Hill/Glencoe, puts it "[i]f Abraham moved to the land of Canaan . . . all nations would be blessed through him. Because of this covenant, Abraham's Israelite descendants believed that they were God's 'chosen people' and would remain so as long as they followed God's laws."[27] Similarly, Prentice Hall's *World Cultures: A Global Mosaic*, states "[t]he Hebrews believed that God had made a covenant, or binding agreement with Moses. Under this agreement the Hebrews accepted God as the ruler of heaven and Earth. In return, God made the Hebrews the chosen people on earth."[28] The problem with the passage's third sentence is that it leaves hanging what the Jews were chosen *for*, with no further elaboration. If God is the ruler of the universe, then it must hold that Jews are to rule other peoples on the earth—that Jews thought they were to be masters of other people. The Bible's commission to propagate biblical ethical monotheism to the peoples of the world gets lost entirely.

At the most egregious extreme of textbooks, *World Civilizations*, a product of Thomson Wadsworth, imposes no filter in its wholesale disdain for the notion of Jews as the chosen people. *World Civilizations* illustrates the danger of perpetuating stereotypes of Jews taken to their logical conclusion. The scorn which Jews are alleged to hold toward others is evident, and this is alleged to be a unique feature of Jews. "*More than most*, the Jews divided humanity into *we* and *they*. This was undoubtedly the result of their religious tradition whereby they had been selected as the Chosen. Jews looked upon non-Jews as distinctly *lesser breeds*, whose main function in the divine plan was to act as tempters and obstacles that the pious must overcome."[29] [emphasis added]

The overemphasis on the Jews as a chosen people as well as the terms some textbooks used to characterize Jews as haughty is a misinterpretation of the concept of the Jews as a chosen people. The rationale used by virtually every textbook to study the origins of Judaism is the Jewish contribution of ethical monotheism to world civilization. It is indeed ironic that, instead of connecting this mission to civilization with the Bible's call to be a light unto the nations, the concept of chosenness is used to disparage Jews as intolerant of others.

Common practice in academic writing about history is to avoid the term "Old Testament" when referring to the Jewish Bible. The preferred scholarly terms include "Hebrew Bible" "Jewish Scriptures" or variations of these terms. Old Testament is an outmoded expression that connotes the supercessionist view that the Jewish Bible, though incorporated into the canon of the Christian Bible, serves primarily to foreshadow and serve as the foundation for Christianity, rather than retaining intrinsic value on its own. It is merely old, replaced by something new—and better.

Today's Christian denominations, especially clergy and scholars in the United States, have reaffirmed a special relationship between Jews and God, a covenant that did not pass away with the advent of the New

Testament. The theology that embraces Jesus as the Messiah does not negate the importance or validity of the Hebrew Bible in the view of contemporary Christian thought. Christian leaders have adopted a much more respectful approach to Judaism, avoiding highlighting the "new" to connote "improved" and "better" compared to "old" which carries the meaning of "obsolete" or "stale" or "in need of reform." Nearly all Christian denominations have apologized for this former way of looking at Jews and moved on toward richer interfaith relationships with Jews. Many Christian churches now go out of their way to use objective terms such as "Hebrew Scriptures" within their own flocks, especially those churches heavily involved in interfaith dialogue.

In a similar way, most scholars and a few textbooks in our list of those reviewed eschew the familiar but Christocentric dating system "B.C.," "Before Christ" and "A.D.," "Anno Domini," "The year of the Lord," in favor of the analogous "B.C.E." "Before the Common Era" and "C.E." "Common Era." The goal is the same as in avoiding "Old Testament": to achieve a more universal, less restrictive terminology in our educational systems.

We tabulated the terminology used for the Hebrew Scriptures *within each textbook's discussion of Judaism and its origins, irrespective of the wording used in the sections on Christian origins.* We noted the avoidance of "Old Testament" in sections covering pre-Christian times in favor of more neutral terms such as "Torah" or "the Bible." Figure 3.1 displays the results of the tabulation by number of textbooks.

The majority of the texts, 64 percent (16), used outdated terminology. Thirty-six percent (9) met the neutral terminology test. (Three textbooks were geography or world cultures texts not dealing with religious history.)

Glencoe World History is among the texts which use mixed terminology that is not ideal. "Much of

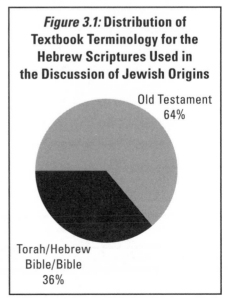

Figure 3.1: Distribution of Textbook Terminology for the Hebrew Scriptures Used in the Discussion of Jewish Origins

Old Testament
64%

Torah/Hebrew
Bible/Bible
36%

the history and religious beliefs of the Israelites were eventually recorded in written form in the Hebrew Bible, parts of which are known to Christians as the Old Testament." "According to the Bible, [God] gave these Commandments to Moses . . ." "Scribes in ancient Israel carefully copied the Torah by hand." "[God's will] was open to anyone who could read the Torah."[30] On the other hand, Holt's *World History: Continuity & Change* uses uniformly neutral expressions. "These [Hebrew] writings later formed the foundation for the Bible." "The word Torah . . . includes all Jewish religious writings, consisting of the 39 books of the Hebrew Bible, as well as the oral Torah . . ."[31]

We found more examples of "traditional" terminology, such as in Holt's *World History: The Human Journey, Modern World*. The following "Interdisciplinary Connection" appears in a teacher sidebar: "Literature. The Torah, Hebrew for 'law' or 'doctrine,' consists of the first five books of the Old Testament, also called the Pentateuch."[32] Another example comes from *Modern World History* by McDougal Littell. It notes the Christian connection, "the Hebrew Bible (the Old Testament, to Christians)," and later continues, after this introduction but still well within the Judaism and Jewish history section, "The [Jewish] prophets attacked war, oppression, and greed in statements such as these from the Old Testament."[33] In the same section the terms "Torah," "Bible," "Hebrew Scriptures" are used appropriately.

A teacher's sidebar in *Harcourt Horizons World History*, by Harcourt/ Holt, supplies additional information on scripture terminology to supplement the student text, but the information is misleading. "Background: The Hebrew Bible. The Bible is divided into the Old Testament and the New Testament. Jewish people call the Old Testament the Hebrew Bible."[34] This passage in a lesson on Jewish history and the ancient Israelites should reflect a Jewish frame of reference and proper chronology. The Jewish Bible was written well before the Christian scriptures came into existence, so it should be listed first. The Old Testament terminology is not appropriate until the textbook discusses Christian origins in later chapters.

These representative positive and negative examples serve to show: 1) some textbooks, although a minority, successfully avoid the "Old Testament" terminology in an embrace of practices of scholarly writers and; 2) the remainder of textbooks reflect outdated terminology that does not reflect current scholarship or today's positive interfaith relations between Christians and Jews.

The picture of Jews and Judaism that emerges from some textbooks' units about Jewish origins is problematic. Judaism comes across as an outdated, legalistic faith practiced by Jews who are intolerant of others. In the next chapter we will examine the narrative textbooks use to describe the beginnings of Christianity and the teachings of Jesus. Do the stereotypes we found in the discussion of Jewish origins continue into lessons on the Christian era? How do textbooks approach the difficult separation of Christianity from Judaism?

CHAPTER FOUR

JEWS, JUDAISM, AND CHRISTIANITY

INTRODUCTION: TEXTBOOKS SHOULD REFLECT
CURRENT SCHOLARSHIP AND CHRISTIAN THINKING

Some textbooks recognize the contribution of Jewish "ethical mono-theism" and its worldwide influence. They portray Judaism and Jewish culture as a robust way of life, a sophisticated theology, a life of faith, an ethical system, and a world view that has evolved and endured for thousands of years. Others teach students in a way that causes them to wonder why they should even study this small people who spent most of their history dwarfed by more powerful neighboring empires, and then as a small minority in countries around the globe. Others are even less flattering, especially in how they describe the interactions with Christians.

Textbook treatment of Jews and Christianity has to be examined within the context of contemporary multiculturalism and the increased sensitivity to the place of minorities in our society. Racial and religious tolerance are now accepted norms in many societies today, particularly in the West (but of course not all). Textbooks pride themselves on sensitive treatment of minorities.

Recent writings by scholars of religion and historians as well as theological statements by most major Christian denominations have taken pains to reflect an appreciation of the Jewishness of Jesus and the inherent and substantial Jewish content of his teachings. All this is an effort to reverse the tradition of most Christian churches (now modified and rejected by these very same churches) which minimized the Jewish connection to Jesus. Of course, both Jews and Christians have had their reasons over the centuries to deny common ground. As the two branches of Judaism became separate they became more hostile, and both had their arguments to proclaim that Jesus had nothing to do with the other. Christians de-emphasized that Jesus was a Jew, as were all the apostles and early followers of Jesus and Jews, feeling that Jesus was a false Messiah, wanted to distance themselves as much as possible. This history became ugly over time, beginning to heal only in the last two generations.

The healing is so profound and important in the history of religion, to say nothing of the actual relationship between Jews and Christians, that it should pervade textbook awareness and commentary. It is unfortunate that textbooks have not captured the scholarly, theological and social leaps of the last sixty years, and instead still repeat the telling of history and descriptions of religious belief as if they were writing in 1707 instead of the twenty-first century. But old perspectives and outdated approaches still sprinkle over textbooks in describing the interactions of Jews and Christians, Judaism and Christianity.

Recognizing the extent of Jesus' Jewish background and that his teachings were rooted in the rich and diverse Judaism of his day is now seen by nearly all Christian denominations as deepening their own faith, fostering appreciation of their Jewish co-religionists and combating anti-Semitism.

Judaism is the mother of Christianity, a point that seems obvious to most of today's Christians and Jews in America. The Jewish content in Christianity is so pervasive it would seem almost superfluous to have to emphasize Christianity's Jewish origins and the connections between the religions. Early Christians were Jews themselves, and certainly the Roman rulers saw Christians as a sect within Judaism. Jesus was considered a Jewish teacher, a rabbi like many others of his day in Judea and Galilee. The Jews who were receptive found his teachings familiar within the context of Jewish thought and culture.

Indeed, modern academic (non-devotional, non-sectarian) scholarship would even support the assertion in one textbook that Jesus and his initial disciples did not intend to found a new religion at all but saw themselves as a Jewish sect: "Initially, there seems to have been no intent on [Jesus'] or his followers' part to found a new religion."[1] A Catholic edition of the Bible makes plain, in a footnote to Acts 2:46, "[T]he chief characteristics of the Jerusalem [followers of Jesus were] . . . continued attendance at the temple, since in this initial stage [at the first Pentecost,] there was little or no thought of any dividing line between Christianity and Judaism."[2] Pope John Paul II likened the Jewish–Christian relationship to siblings when he said "You [the Jews] are our dearly beloved brothers and, in a certain way, it could be said that you are our elder brothers."[3] Therefore, it is deeply puzzling why textbook writers continue to include concepts rejected by scholars and Christian denominations alike.

Textbooks do a good job in their coverage of historical Christian anti-Semitism during eras in which attitudes toward Jews were not nearly so enlightened as current Christian thinking. Virtually every text amply and objectively describes anti-Semitism in various European eras, particularly the anti-Semitism of the Dreyfus era in France and the Holocaust throughout Europe. Moreover the anti-Semitic persecution of Jews is often described as having its origins among the Christian majority. One good example comes from *The Earth and Its Peoples* by Houghton Mifflin in the preamble to an elaborate two-page spread containing Christian primary source documents. "Because they did not belong to the dominant Latin Christian faith, Jews suffered from periodic discrimination and persecution. For the most part, religious and secular authorities tried to curb such anti-Semitism. Jews, after all, were useful citizens who worshipped the same God as their Christian neighbors."[4] Unfortunately, beyond the coverage of Christian anti-Semitism much of the rest of textbook treatment is more uneven.

As textbooks struggle to find points of theological distinction between Judaism and the Christianity which developed from it, they frequently offer inaccurate ideas. There are two broad themes in the negative narrative about Jews that appear in the textbooks' discussion of Christian origins.

First, supersessionism or replacement theology (the terms will be used interchangeably) supports the idea that the Christian church has displaced and replaced Judaism theologically, and therefore Judaism is outdated and no longer has any validity. Replacement theology has two major components: 1) Jesus reformed the legalism inherent in Jewish theology and 2) Jews were responsible for the crucifixion. Judaism is characterized by empty legalism and ritualism devoid of feeling or compassion. As this narrative goes, Jesus arrived and offered a radically new perspective to a Jewish tradition that was stale and hidebound. According to this telling, Jesus ridiculed and even condemned Jewish law, especially as personified by the Pharisees.

Second, textbooks use language that collectively serves to claim that Jesus was not Jewish, but something else. This distortion applies to the teachings of Jesus, and his religious and national origins. The incorrect notions that love of God and neighbor are not Jewish concepts and that Jews do not believe in the coming of God's kingdom are concepts that deny Jesus' Jewishness.

THE THEOLOGICAL RELATIONSHIP BETWEEN JUDAISM AND CHRISTIANITY (SUPERSESSIONISM)

The logical underpinnings of the concept of supersessionism or replacement theology, until recently a mainstay of Christian views about the post-Jesus validity of Judaism, have been described by Catholic theologian Mary Boys as summarized by Padraic O'Hare in *The Enduring Covenant: The Education of Christians and the End of Antisemitism*. O'Hare writes that Boys "points to the etymology of the term *supersessionism* . . . , noting that it derives from the Latin verb *supersedere*, 'to sit upon.' Boys identifies eight tenets that define supersessionism." Her list ties together in a logical order several of the problematic themes about Jews and Christianity that appear in textbooks and provides an understanding of both the context of past Christian theology as well as a contemporary Christian view.

(1) revelation in Jesus Christ supersedes the revelation to Israel;
(2) the New Testament fulfills the Old Testament;
(3) the Church replaces the Jews as God's people;
(4) Judaism is obsolete; its covenant abrogated;
(5) post-exilic Judaism was legalistic;
(6) the Jews did not heed the warnings of the prophets;
(7) the Jews did not understand the prophesies about Jesus;
(8) the Jews were Christ killers.[5]

Much of the anti-Semitic effects of historical Christian teaching are neatly encompassed in this logical schema. The line of causation from dry theology to preaching in churches and popular belief among rank and file

Christians to anti-Semitic persecutions is clear. The supposedly deserved divine disinheritance of Israel and the Jewish people has historically been used to justify punishment of the Jews.

The early Christian church's self-understanding as replacing the Jews is described by scholar James L. Kugel:

> The fact that [Joshua as the] "Old Testament Jesus" took over for Moses was understood to symbolize Christianity's taking over for the religion of Moses, its "new covenant" mediated by Jesus replacing the old covenant that had been mediated through Moses at Mount Sinai. This was, for ancient Christians, one of those extremely significant ties between Old and New: it not only said something about Jesus, it also showed something profound about the Bible itself, a book brimming with hidden meanings and half-concealed correspondences. Indeed, thanks in part to this equation of Joshua and Jesus, the new church came to think of itself as verus Israel, the "true Israel" (as opposed to the Jews, who were the people of Israel only in the genetic, "fleshly sense"—see 1 Cor. 10:18; Rom. 2:28–29; Phil. 3:3).[6]

The persecution of Jews by Christians is directly linked to claims of supersessionism. As a result, one of the most universal themes in the recent statements of the Christian denominations is that Judaism and Jews remain in covenant with God despite their ancestors' opposition to the spreading of the Gospel and the Jewish people not accepting Jesus as Messiah. Modern Christian leaders have understood that undoing supersessionism was a key ingredient in making right their post-Holocaust relationships with Jews. An Evangelical commentator wrote, in an acknowledgement of the damage done by the doctrine, "The replacement teaching indicates a distinctive motivation for Christian treatment of the Jewish people with contempt, suspicion, and hatred. It points out the reasons why Christians committed sins of violence, oppression, injustice, and untruth against the Jews."[7]

Some Christian statements disavowing supersessionism are listed below.

Catholic: "Nevertheless, God holds the Jews most dear for the sake of their Fathers; He does not repent of the gifts He makes or of the calls He issues—such is the witness of the Apostle. . . . Although the Church is the new people of God, the Jews should not be presented as rejected or accursed by God, as if this followed from the Holy Scriptures."[8]

Methodist:

> Christians and Jews are bound to God through biblical covenants that are eternally valid. As Christians, we stand firm in our belief that Jesus was sent by God as the Christ to redeem all people, and that in Christ the biblical covenant has been made radically new. While church tradition has taught that Judaism has been superseded by Christianity as the "new Israel," we do not believe that earlier covenantal relationships have been invalidated or that God has abandoned Jewish partners in covenant. . . . As Christians, we are clearly called to witness to the gospel of Jesus Christ in every age and place. At the same time, we believe that God has continued, and continues today, to work through Judaism and the Jewish people.[9]

Presbyterian: "[W]e here present to the church . . . theological affirmations . . . [including] an acknowledgement by Christians that Jews are in covenant relationship with God and the consideration of the implications of this reality for evangelism and witness . . ."[10]

Evangelical: "There is a heresy . . . [whose] generic name is supersessionism, or as it is more commonly known, replacement theology. . . . If God is God, then it is human arrogance to suggest that God made a mistake in an earlier expression of the Divine word."[11]

Supersessionism asserts that the Jews were responsible for the crucifixion of Jesus, at the time it happened and subsequently therefore through history. While this blame has been part of Christian thinking in various forms as late as the 1960s, Christian churches have repudiated the attribution of responsibility to Jews as a people. Textbook treatment of the subject shows some carelessness in language that does not reflect current Christian attitudes.

One textbook effectively discusses the implications of supersessionism. Glencoe's *World History: The Human Experience* is one of the few texts to mention the deicide charge as the main cause of anti-Semitism. "The most powerful source of anti-Semitism, or hatred of the Jews, came from interpretations of Christian doctrine. Many church leaders and laity blamed the Jews for Jesus' death and resented Jews' refusal to become Christians. . . . Beginning in the late 1200s, rulers in England, France, and certain parts of central Europe even expelled their Jewish subjects. Many of the expelled Jews settled in eastern Europe, especially Poland, where they received protection."[12]

Some textbooks get it perfectly correct about the unique ideas of Jesus. For example, in *World History: Connections to Today* by Prentice Hall, the distinction is made that "at the same time, Jesus preached new [as distinguished from Judaism] beliefs. According to his followers, he called himself the Son of God. Many people believed he was the messiah whose appearance Jews had long predicted."[13]

Harcourt Horizons World History correctly avoids agreement with the tenet of supersessionism that blames Jews for the crucifixion and instead assigns responsibility to the Romans. In a teacher sidebar and again in the student material it reads "Pontius Pilate was concerned that conflicts over Jesus would stir rebellion against Rome and so had Jesus put to death."[14] The nature of the threat Jesus represented to the good order of Roman authority over the restive and fractious Jews, the Romans holding the reins of power in Judea in issues great and small, and Rome's response in executing him are properly presented. This textbook stands as a model for others of how to objectively represent this history.

The disavowal of supersessionism and its assumptions by the major denominations is a key ingredient in Christian reassessment of their persecution of Jews, supported by scholarly opinion on Jesus and Jewish law, the Jewish power to crucify someone, and the Jewish content of Jesus' teachings. Therefore, textbooks should get this right. Sadly, some of them fail badly. In the most egregious cases, they offer wording that directly affirms the conclusions of discredited replacement theology. Christian churches have realized their characterization of Jesus' contemporaries overlooks the richness of Jewish practice and have moved on. Why not textbooks?

Two textbooks stand out as advancing supersessionist arguments. McGraw-Hill's *Humanities in Western Culture* boldly restates supersessionist ideas when it describes the evolution of Christianity.

> Paul argued (and Peter later agreed) that the Law was no longer valid, even for Jews; it could only bring people to an understanding of their dependence on Christ in a new covenant with Christ the Savior. Sweeping aside Jewish rituals and practices, Paul, the "apostle to the Gentiles," carried the message of salvation through faith in Christ throughout the eastern Mediterranean and into Rome itself.[15]

First, the idea that the Law was no longer valid "even for Jews" is an assertion that disparages Judaism. Second, the injury is compounded by the wording "sweeping aside Jewish rituals and practices," which in harsh terms states directly that observances in Judaism are of no value. This passage represents the basis for historical Christian anti-Semitism and is unreflective of post-Holocaust Christian revision of attitudes toward Jews.

The same text goes on to set Jesus' teachings completely against Judaism using problematic language to boot.

> Literary Selection 26: The Sermon on the Mount . . . The basic ethical teachings of Christ are presented in the Sermon on the Mount, in which the Ten Commandments of Moses are compared with a new ethic. Beginning with the statement "You have heard that it was said to the men of old," Jesus takes each commandment in turn and contrasts it with his own commandment. As presented by Matthew, Jesus is the new Moses expounding a new Torah, which commands a higher righteousness than that found *even in the best of Judaism*.[16] [emphasis added]

"Higher righteousness" asserts Christian superiority and triumph over Judaism.

World Civilizations by Thomson Wadsworth reduces Judaism to a mere precursor of Christianity, devoid of intrinsic value. "The mold for the evolution of Christianity had been formed. All that was needed was the appearance of the long-rumored messiah who would fulfill the promise that the Chosen would enter glory, someday."[17] Moreover, after the Jewish exile, the only purpose of Judaism is to provide breeding grounds for Christianity. "One result of this [Roman] forced eviction from Judaea was the establishment of Jewish exile colonies that became breeding grounds for Christianity throughout the eastern Mediterranean basin and soon in Italy itself."[18]

In its summary of Christian origins, *World Civilizations* even uses the word "supersede." "By the second century, a written New Testament had appeared that was accepted by all Christians and largely superseded the Old Testament of the Jews in their eyes."[19] In *World Civilizations* and *Humanities in Western Culture* Judaism's value has been eradicated.

THE CLAIM THAT JESUS SET HIMSELF AGAINST JEWISH LAW

Many textbooks repeat discredited canards that Jesus set himself against Jewish law, even as they extol the profound effect of Jewish concepts of ethical monotheism (read "moral laws") on western civilization and Islam as the whole rationale for studying Jewish history in the first place. Jesus' Messiahship or his followers' belief that he was the son of God should be used to distinguish Christianity from Judaism, rather than his debatable opposition to Jewish legal codes, so heavily emphasized in textbooks.

People, Places, and Change by Holt, Rinehart & Winston reduces Christianity to opposition to Jewish law. "During the era of Roman Control, a Jewish man named Jesus . . . taught that faith and love were more important than Judaism's many laws."[20] Houghton Mifflin's *The Earth and Its Peoples* commendably defines Jesus as a rabbi but then associates him with opposition to rituals based on Jewish law. "[Jesus] was essentially a rabbi, or teacher, and that, offended . . . *by the perfunctory nature of mainstream Jewish religious practice in his time*, he prescribed a return to the personal faith and spirituality of an earlier age."[21] [emphasis added]

The danger of this stereotype of Jews as overridingly legalistic is illustrated by one textbook which takes the concept to its logical conclusion: intolerance of Jews. The most egregious distortion of Jesus' attitude toward the laws of his own people can be found in Thomson Wadsworth's *World Civilizations* which claims that

> [t]o the Sadducees and Pharisees, Jesus's admonition to stop confusing the letter of the law with its spirit was an attempt to seduce the Jews, who had survived and remained a distinct nation only because of their unbending adherence to their Mosaic laws. Zealots wished to fight the Romans and had no empathy with a prophet who asked them to "render unto Caesar the things that are Caesar's"—that is, to accept the legitimate demands of their Roman overlords.[22]

Terminology like "seduce," "unbending," and "confusing the letter and spirit of the law" is inflammatory. And to imply that Roman demands for submission were legitimate compounds even more the textbook perspective of Jews as inflexible and unreasonable.

Much is made in textbooks of the confrontations of Jesus with the Pharisees as reported in the Gospels. It is characterized as conflict over Jewish law, minus the subtleties and sophistication of modern Christian scholarship. James Carroll sets this relationship in the correct context when he writes, in his landmark work, *Constantine's Sword: The Church and the Jews,*

> In fact, Jesus' movement had more in common with that of the Pharisees than perhaps any other Jewish sect. . . . Of all the characters in the Jesus story, none are more vilified by the Christian imagination than the Pharisees, and not because they would have so opposed what Jesus represented, or because they actually challenged him during his lifetime.[23]

Judaism throughout its history has embraced pluralistic debate and disputations among its rabbis. The Talmud records debates among the rabbis on various legal points, with minority opinions often recorded. In this context, therefore, the legal discussions recorded in the Gospels between Jesus and the scribes, Pharisees, and priests on theological and legal points would have raised no eyebrows. It was normal for Jews to debate such questions as "what is the greatest commandment?" None of the following textbook examples from Harcourt/Holt reflect any understanding of this normative Jewish practice, which is essential to understand the implications of the amazing diversity of Jewish thought and philosophical streams in the Judaism of Jesus' day.

"Some Jewish leaders argued that Jesus and his disciples did not strictly follow Jewish laws. Often the teachings of Jesus caused great debate among the Jewish people and concern among the Roman leaders in Judaea."[24] reads *Harcourt Horizons World History*. Debate was the hallmark of Jewish thought. *The World* (Harcourt Horizons) also incorrectly states, "some Jewish leaders argued that Jesus and his disciples did not strictly follow Jewish law."[25] Jesus was a teacher like others and Jewish teachers discuss and disagree. For example, Hillel and Shammai, who lived during the reign of King Herod (37–4 BCE), were "friendly adversaries" of each other. Jesus, like other teachers, debated with other Jews.

World History: Continuity & Change by Holt declares "Jesus began to attack many Jewish practices openly."[26] All rabbis were self-critical. For example the Pharisees, Essenes, Sadducees, and others interpreted Jewish practices within Judaism. Jesus was asking difficult questions and challenging ideas and practices as Jewish leaders had always done, and continue to do today.

Thomson Wadsworth's *World Civilizations* claims that Jesus' teachings "cast him in a dubious light among the tradition-bound rabbis" who thought of Jesus as an enemy *"of the Mosaic Law."*[27] [emphasis added] Setting up Jesus as the "enemy" of the foundation of Judaism, the Mosaic Law, whose agents were "tradition-bound" is historically inaccurate and disparaging of Jews.

In the 2005 California History-Social Science adoption, the Council on Islamic Education opposed edits proposed and later adopted by the California Department of Education's Content Review Panel (CRP) and Instructional Materials Advisory Panel (IMAP) designed to clarify the relationship between Jesus and Jewish authorities. The draft version of the Houghton Mifflin sixth grade history text *World History: Ancient Civilizations* as submitted to the California Department of Education stated "However, [Jesus] taught certain ideas and practices that seemed to have put him at odds with some Jewish leaders." The state's edits changed this to "However, [Jesus] also taught certain ideas and practices that differed from what others were teaching." CIE claimed in its objections that the changes would "sanitize the issue by avoiding known facts."[28]

THE JEWISH ROLE IN THE CRUCIFIXION

"At that moment, I sensed a kind of Pontius Pilate feeling, for I was free of all guilt," said Adolf Eichmann, in testimony at his Jerusalem trial for crimes against humanity. The problematic figure of Pontius Pilate as a blameless bystander to the crucifixion has passed from some Christian teachings into the literature and consciousness of the West. The myth of Roman innocence in the crucifixion combined with Jewish culpability resonates into our own times in vehicles such as the film *Passion of the Christ*.

Good Friday services, passion plays, Christian sermons, and theological works have incited Jew-hatred for centuries. They are filled with the charge of deicide, the killing of God. In medieval Europe, Jewish communities would brace themselves as Christian worshippers, fresh from hearing about the "perfidious Jews," attacked the Jews with cries of "Christ killers" ringing in their ears. The Gospel passage "his blood be on us and on our children" was both popularly and theologically understood as divine sanction that all Jews for all ages mystically inherited collective guilt for the crucifixion. The church taught that Jews were forever condemned to wander the earth and be persecuted for their great crime of "crucifying the Lord." This teaching passed from early Christianity into the Orthodox and Protestant branches of Christian churches. For example, the standard Orthodox Christian liturgy used throughout the world implores, "the Jewish tribe which condemned you to crucifixion, repay them, Oh Lord."[29]

Historians agree, however, that crucifixion was a uniquely Roman punishment and Jews in Roman Judea did not have the authority to put anyone to death. Some Jewish leaders may have approved, applauded, and prodded for the punishment of other Jews. Perhaps they succeeded sometimes, and other times not. The Romans decided.

Precisely because of the disastrous results of the charge of deicide, the most explicit and strongest denominational statements of reassessment of views on Jews are the repudiation of this guilt and its implications. The Catholic Church's is the strongest on this point: "what happened in [Jesus'] passion cannot be charged against all the Jews, without distinction, then alive, nor against the Jews of today."[30]

Due to the extreme sensitivity of this issue, textbooks should studiously avoid mentioning Jews in connection to the crucifixion, without a thorough and sophisticated explanation reflecting current scholarship and Christian thinking. Unfortunately, there are too many examples in textbooks that imply Jewish culpability.

World History: Continuity & Change, a product of Holt, has it that "[a]fter hearing that he claimed to be the son of God, [leading priests of the Temple] condemned him and convinced the Roman authorities in Judaea to put him to death."[31] This places culpability for Jesus' death squarely on the Jewish religious leadership. Another publisher's product, *The Earth and Its Peoples*, by Houghton Mifflin echoes this approach when it says "the Jewish authorities in Jerusalem . . . turned him over to the Roman governor, Pontius Pilate. . . . Jesus was . . . executed by crucifixion . . ."[32] Roman concerns about rebellion are transferred to the Jewish religious leaders. *The World*, by Pearson/Scott Foresman also blames the Jews: "Though the Romans found [Jesus] innocent, they wanted to please local leaders. So they sentenced Jesus to be crucified . . ."[33] While acknowledging that the Romans held the legal authority in the land and not singling out the local leaders as Jews per se, this version still casts Rome as a reluctant actor in a play choreographed by the religious leaders historians say it had installed.

Thomson Wadsworth's *World Civilizations* is the worst example of the syndrome of blaming the Jews. Jews are definitely the villains in their version of history:

> Jesus's challenges to the traditionalist rabbis did create difficulties in governing. In the most literal sense, Jesus was "stirring things up." As a result, when the Jewish leaders demanded that the Roman procurator, Pontius Pilate, allow them to punish this disturber of the peace, he reluctantly agreed, and Jesus was crucified on Golgotha near Jerusalem. . . . [T]he high-placed [rabbis] . . . induced [Pontius Pilate] to let them crucify Christ as an enemy of Roman rule . . .[34]

World Civilizations assigns responsibility for the crucifixion solely to the rabbis. The Romans are merely an afterthought.

Most textbooks do not ascribe direct blame for the crucifixion to Jews or Jewish leaders. But enough textbook examples of wording reflecting the culpability of Jews stand as lingering vestiges of outdated and discredited theology. Given the key historical role of the deicide charge in fomenting anti-Semitism, it is a subject that requires the utmost accuracy. The charge of killing Jesus represents some of the most dangerous material to be found in textbooks.

Despite this danger, in the 2005 California History–Social Science adoption, the Council on Islamic Education opposed edits proposed and later adopted by the California Department of Education's Content Review Panel (CRP) and Instructional Materials Advisory Panel (IMAP) intended to avoid any support of the deicide charge against Jews. The draft version of the Houghton Mifflin sixth grade history text *World History: Ancient Civilizations* as submitted to the California Department of Education asserted

> Jesus had made enemies among the Roman rulers as well as among his fellow Jews. . . . These public challenges to Rome and Jewish authorities appointed by Rome sealed his fate. Jewish leaders arrested Jesus and turned him over to the Romans for punishment. . . . [Review question:] How did Jewish and Roman leaders view Jesus when he came to Jerusalem? [Possible answers:] Both groups found Jesus a threat. The Jews because certain ideas of Jesus put him at odds with Jewish leaders.[35]

The California Department of Education amended these sentences to read: "Jesus had made enemies among the Roman rulers. . . . These public challenges to Rome sealed his fate. Jesus was arrested and turned over to the Roman authorities for punishment. . . . [Review question:] How did Roman leaders view Jesus when he came to Jerusalem? [Possible answer:] They considered Jesus a threat because the claim that he was the Messiah threatened their political rule."[36]

The Council on Islamic Education, an acknowledged "content consultant" to Houghton Mifflin, argued that to make the changes California ultimately required be made was "distorting history by overstating the relationship between Jesus and the Roman authorities" and "occludes the particular historical actors in the situation. Despite the sensitivity of the subject for Christian–Jewish relations it is important to present a historical narrative that is careful, accurate, and in keeping with the criteria to provide a story well told. . . . The suggested change is an utterly unhistoric approach to this sensitive issue."[37] One could ask why a Muslim advocacy group would be arguing so strenuously for the retention of ideas that have historically been used to promote anti-Semitism, but are now rejected by many churches.

DENYING JESUS' JEWISHNESS

Today's consensus of the scholarly and religious opinion of virtually all Christians and Jews alike is that Jesus was born Jewish, of Jewish parents, and especially a Jewish mother, which places him indisputably in the category of Jewish according to Halacha (Jewish law). The Gospels portray him and his family observing Jewish lifecycle rituals: circumcision, Pidyon Haben (redemption of the first born), teaching in the Temple when he reached Bar Mitzvah age, and so on. Virtually everybody in the Gospels is Jewish, certainly all the main characters are with the exception of the Romans. The idea that Jesus came from a thoroughly Jewish milieu is hardly controversial. In fact, the Catholic Church has this to say on the subject: "[Jews] are the fathers and from them is the Christ according to the flesh (Rom. 9:4–5), the Son of the Virgin Mary. [The church] also recalls that the Apostles, the Church's main-stay and pillars, as well as most of the early disciples who proclaimed Christ's Gospel to the world, sprang from the Jewish people."[38]

The notion that Jesus was both the Son of God and the Messiah indeed are fundamental differentiating beliefs of the two religions. This is the chief theological divergence between Judaism and Christianity. In the Acts of the Apostles Peter states, "Let all Israel then accept as certain that God has made this same Jesus . . . both Lord and Messiah."[39] A family feud resulted from the fact that, in Christian eyes, "[Jesus] came to his own, and his own people would not accept him."[40] McDougal Littell's *Ancient World History: Patterns of Interaction* seems conflicted whether the teachings of Jesus were Jewish or not. 1) "The chief priests of the Jews . . . said [Jesus'] teachings were blasphemy, or contempt for God." 2) "Jesus' teachings did not contradict Jewish law, and his first followers were Jews."[41] This textbook appears to contradict itself on a single page. The early Christians (all originally Jews themselves) felt dismay that the masses of their fellow Jews did not accept Jesus as the Messiah, which resulted in recriminations between the two faiths that lasted almost two thousand years. The complicated history of Christianity emerging from its Jewish base requires more subtle and thorough discussion than most textbooks include.

LOVE OF GOD AND NEIGHBOR ARE VALUES SHARED BY CHRISTIANITY AND JUDAISM

Jews daily recite the Ve'ahavta prayer, part of the Shema, the fundamental Jewish statement of faith. "You will love the Lord your God with all your heart, with all your soul and with all your strength." Indeed, the evangelist Mark has Jesus and a scribe strongly in agreement on this point as the scribe asks "'Which is the first of all the commandments?' He answered, '. . . you must love the Lord your God with all your heart, with all your soul, with all your mind, and with all your strength. The second is this: You must love your neighbor as yourself. No other commandment is greater than these.' The scribe said to him, 'Well said, teacher. You are right in saying . . . .'"[42] In fact Jesus is quoting directly from Deuteronomy (6:4–5) and Leviticus (19:8) of the Hebrew scriptures, not inventing something new from scratch. Jesus embraces and reflects his own Judaism. Love of God and neighbor are key concepts in Judaism, a fact highlighted in current Christian theology.

But some textbooks present the erroneous notion that Jesus originated the idea that humanity should love God and neighbor. In McDougal Littell's *Modern World History: Patterns of Interaction*, "Jesus' ideas went beyond traditional [i.e., Jewish] morality. He stressed the importance of people's love for God, their neighbors, their enemies, and themselves."[43] Of this passage, only "enemies" did not come from the Jewish mainstream of then and now, the Hebrew scriptures and Jewish tradition. *World History: Continuity & Change* by Holt asserts that "Jesus laid down two primary rules for his followers: they must love God above all else and they must love others as they loved themselves. . . . Such teachings . . . alarmed Jewish religious authorities."[44] The two primary rules cited come directly from the Torah as quoted by Jesus, hardly alarming.

THE JEWISH MESSIANIC AGE AND "THY KINGDOM COME"

The coming of the messianic age, "the world to come," is so important in Judaism that its major concept of the messiah was adapted to serve as the foundation of Christianity.[45] A cornerstone of Jewish belief is that "all nations of the world have a share in the world to come." Actually, the Jewish idea of the messianic era of universal peace in which God will reign came into Jesus' consciousness via his Judaic upbringing. Jesus' lifetime was a time of fervent messianism in the Jewish world.

Textbooks' use of Jesus' emphasis on the coming of the "kingdom of God" is inaccurate as a point of differentiation between Jesus and Judaism, because at the simplest level both Judaism and Christianity share this belief. *Harcourt Horizons World History* asserts "yet in some ways [Jesus'] teachings were very different from [other Jewish teachers']. Jesus told of the coming of what he called the kingdom of God. He called on the Jewish people to turn away from sin, or going against the word of God, so that they could be part of God's kingdom. Jesus explained that God loved them and would forgive those who were sorry for their sins."[46] None of the listed teachings differentiated Jesus from mainstream Jewish thought of the time. An exercise provided for teachers by *Harcourt Horizons World History* to have students compare and contrast Jewish and Christian beliefs reinforces the error when it says Christianity "believes in the coming of the kingdom of God" while Judaism "does not believe in the coming of the kingdom of God." This misrepresentation of Jewish belief is particularly egregious considering Jews invented the idea of the messianic coming, but did not accept Jesus as the Messiah. These are two completely different points. The same problem is found in McDougal Littell's *Modern World*

History: Patterns of Interaction, "Jesus' ideas went beyond traditional morality. . . . He also taught that God would eventually end wickedness in the world and would establish an eternal kingdom in which he would reign."[47]

Houghton Mifflin's *The Earth and Its Peoples* sets Jesus in opposition to Jewish leaders using some of the worst stereotypes of Jews as justification. Jesus was "offended by what he perceived as Jewish religious and political leaders' excessive concern with money and power . . ."[48] Jews as preoccupied with accumulating wealth and aggrandizing their power is a staple of centuries of anti-Semitism.

Similarly, in Thomson's *Ancient Civilizations*, a direct indictment of Jesus' Jewish listeners is leveled. "In this manner, the message of the Lord speaking through the great prophets was distorted into a promise of *earthly grandeur* rather than a promise of immortal salvation for those who believed."[49] [emphasis added] This passage indicates that misguided Jews "distorted" their own teachings in favor of "earthly grandeur" which caused them to stubbornly reject those teachings' fulfillment in Jesus. This wording denies flatly the spiritual component of Judaism.

TEXTBOOKS ARE OUT OF STEP WITH CHRISTIAN THINKING AND CURRENT SCHOLARSHIP

Textbooks can fall into the trap of promulgating stereotypes and misconceptions, with too many textbooks repeating discredited ideas. For example, the discussion of Christian origins in some textbooks elaborates on the legalistic image of Judaism presented in their narratives about Jewish origins, now elevated further to teach the religions' presumed different approaches to law. While Christian churches are forging ahead into new dimensions of appreciation and scholarly research is delving into the richness of Jesus' Jewish milieu, many textbooks lag behind. Textbooks continue to present narratives about the life of Jesus, the belief system of the Jewish religion, and the relationship between the two faiths that depict Jews and Judaism as inferior to Christians—views rejected by Christians and Jews alike. The passages in some textbooks read as if the Second Vatican Council, in which the Catholic Church disavowed collective Jewish responsibility for the crucifixion, never took place.

In a time when philo-Semitism (positive attitudes and beliefs about Jews) is high in the United States, as evidenced by a recent survey of the

Anti-Defamation League, which showed that 86 percent of Americans showed no anti-Semitic propensities,[50] the existence of disparaging passages in the textbooks indicates a deep dysfunction and disconnect between the books and the American public. Intentionally or not, textbooks are teaching against the positive strides made toward warm Christian-Jewish relations in the last forty years.

In the following chapter we will examine the narrative about Jews used to teach about the origins of the other great monotheistic religion, Islam.

CHAPTER FIVE

DOUBLE STANDARDS IN TEACHING ABOUT JUDAISM COMPARED TO ISLAM

The wording used to describe the content of the Hebrew scriptures in some textbooks is unusually conditional in ways not applied to the sacred writings of Christianity and especially of Islam. Most often the words "stories" or "legends" or even "tales" appear which give the reader the impression that the Jewish biblical content being described is akin to fable. The same effect is achieved by an indefinite passive voice such as "it is told that . . ." or "the Israelites are said to . . ." This approach would be less problematic if it were taken across the board in discussing other religions, but it is not. Either all religions should be framed this way or none.

Islam is treated with a devotional tone in some textbooks, less detached and analytical than it ought to be. Muslim beliefs are described in several instances as fact, without any clear qualifier such as "Muslims believe . . ." This is in remarkable contrast to the much more critical treatment of Judaism compared to the treatment of other major religions. In effect, many textbooks serve as apologists for Islam in a way that they do not for Christianity, Judaism, or any other major religion. No religion should be presented in history textbooks as absolute truth, either on its own or compared to any other, or they all should be. Supplemental materials go even further in their unqualified praise for all things Islamic.

A majority of textbooks use a more evenhanded approach. Phrases such as "according to the Bible . . ." or "Muslims believe that . . ." are not uncommon. "Jesus taught . . ." "according to the Gospels . . ." "the Torah states . . ." "Jewish tradition holds . . ." are some analogues typically used for most textbook discussions of Christianity and Judaism, for example, to avoid partisanship and endorsement of these religions. Some textbooks, unfortunately, tend to hold Judaism to a different standard of documented history than other religions.

The favored treatment Islam receives in textbooks extends well beyond the discussion of Muslim scripture. For example, Muslim restrictions on women's freedom are described in favorable terms in Prentice Hall's *World Cultures: A Global Mosaic* in a section entitled "Lives of Women":

> Among Muslims, traditions and customs made women subordinate to men. . . . During childhood, a girl had to obey her father. After marriage, she had to obey her husband and her husband's father. . . . In some Muslim homes, women used separate entrances and ate their meals only in the company of other women.
>
>   The system gave women security. Women in Islamic societies knew that their fathers, brothers, or husbands would protect and provide for them. Also, within their homes and with their children, many women exercised considerable influence.[1]

Issues such as the role of women in Islam are beyond the scope of this analysis. The American Textbook Council has published *Islam In The Classroom: What The Textbooks Tell Us* that analyzes how textbooks handle Islam in greater depth.[2]

TEACHING ABOUT RELIGION

Why is it so hard to teach about religion without violating the precepts of academic rigorousness and neutrality? In many ways, the answer is obvious: religion is personal. In poll after poll, most Americans (85 percent or more) state that religion is an important part of their lives, and many say that it is very important.[3] How we teach about religion or if we teach about it at all matters to many Americans. Since *Abington v. Schempp* disallowed Bible reading in public schools in 1963, the courts have been called upon repeatedly to mediate in cases involving the separation of church and state in public schools.[4] Religion is personal, yet some Americans, as part of the passionate nature of their religious beliefs, want to increase its public profile. (A minority of Americans holds this desire: Only 27 percent of the American public believes that organized religion should have "more influence in this nation,"[5] referring to their own personal religion.) Many fewer parents are likely to want to know how their children's textbooks explain the Pythagorean theorem than how they handle their family's particular religious faith. After all, the Council on Islamic Education was born of a parent's concern about how textbooks and public schools were representing Islam, as was Mel and Norma Gabler's Educational Research Analysts to change textbooks to reflect their conservative Christian values.

The teaching of religion is problematic because we have not resolved the tension between the need to present religion factually, as any other subject within the history curriculum subjected to a test of verifiability, or to present religion as those of a particular faith believe it. Our national desire to provide a broad, multicultural education reflective of the changing nature of our population brings with it our fear of offending anyone. In an attempt to resolve these tensions, publishers have been inconsistent in their approach. Many textbooks are lenient in applying verifiability tests to Muslim beliefs, while they are stringent in attempting to distinguish faith from fact when depicting Jewish beliefs. The treatment of Christian beliefs lies somewhere in between. Scholars, teachers, textbook publishers, and the public itself have succumbed to the fallacy proposed by the late Columbia University English professor Edward Said in his book, *Orientalism*.[6] Said claimed that only those from a particular culture were qualified to write about that culture. While he was specifically referring to the supposed inability of the West to understand Islam, some who design the teaching of religion in American public schools seem to be following Said as well.

Religion is different. Many religious groups consider their beliefs an unassailable set of truths. According to Muslims, for example, the Qur'an is the direct word of God.[7] In Muslim practice, no one, and especially a non-Muslim, may interpret or represent it. If only a Muslim can write about or review the sections on Islam in the textbooks, then it is logical that the Muslim worldview of the Qur'an will prevail. The publishers do not want to risk offending Muslims, and the states have a legal and moral obligation to teach religion in a way that does not denigrate any group.

One instructive case is Modesto, California's mandated world religions course, first introduced in 2000. The course guidelines go to great lengths to maintain impartiality. For example,

> [f]or the sake of neutrality, teachers aren't allowed to share their own faith backgrounds during the semester, nor are outside speakers welcome. Every class in the district . . . follows the same scripted lesson plans. "It can almost feel prescribed," [teacher Sherry] Sheppard said, "but it prevents teachers from sliding in their own biases." Students, though, are encouraged to share their own beliefs and ask questions.[8]

The Modesto course has been successful in producing students who ". . . had become more tolerant of other religions and more willing to protect the rights of people of other faiths. In their own words, students say the course broadened their views and empowered them to fight back against faith-based bullying."[9] The key principle cited by students is the maintenance of neutrality. " 'It made a big difference that teachers didn't take sides,' says [Jewish student] Edward Zeiden. . . . Added [Buddhist] classmate Amy Boudsady, 'It made me feel safe to share my own beliefs. I didn't feel like someone was judging me.' "[10]

While it may seem a wise approach on the part of the publishers and the states to defer to members of a particular religious group on all matters related to that religion, the result is often an unscholarly treatise better suited to Sunday school or a madrassah than to a public school social studies classroom.

The World by Pearson/Scott Foresman opens its discussion of Islam by talking about its pilgrimage requirement. "The pilgrimage, or hajj (haj), to Mecca is an essential part of Islam, the religion *revealed* to Muhammad. . . . "[11] [emphasis added] The direct language "revealed" is not qualified by customary critical expressions of neutrality such as "Muslim belief is . . ." or "According to the Qur'an . . ." which appear in most textbooks when they introduce key beliefs of world religions. In this particular case, the phrase "according to Muslim beliefs an angel visited [Muhammad]" is present in the discussion, but appears later and away from the main point. The qualifying phrase should be present at the first mention of major beliefs, giving it high priority and visibility. Otherwise, its impact is lost in the jumble of other details of belief or religious history.

In contrast, in its discussion of Judaism, *The World* uses more dispassionate language. In the caption of a picture of the Passover seder plate used by Jews it reads "foods on the seder plate are symbolic of an ancient Hebrew *story*."[12] The word "story" places the Exodus on a par with legend. Perhaps it is–but then all religious "stories" need to be qualified as such. If this is the mode of presentation, then every reference to Jesus, Muhammad, and Moses should have qualifiers that include myth, legend, oral history, or some other language that consistently connotes "maybe it happened, maybe it did not."

Glossary entries are often the most egregious in their unqualified depictions of Islam. Space is at a premium and explanations and qualifiers must be brief, making it easier for them to be wrong. The wording of entries on Islam relies heavily on a devotional approach, especially compared to Christianity and Judaism. Two textbooks are especially problematic. *World History: Continuity & Change* by Holt defines the Qur'an in its glossary as the "Holy Book of Islam containing revelations *received by* Muhammad from God."[13] [emphasis added] The direct language leaves no doubt that Muhammad's receipt of revelations is a historical fact.

As a reality check, it is helpful to compare a similar entry in the same book that pertains to a different religion. The entry for the Ten Commandments is instructive. *World History*'s definition is "Moral laws Moses *claimed to have received* from the Hebrew God Yahweh on Mount Sinai."[14] [emphasis added] Both the Qur'an and the Ten Commandments from the Torah are of equivalent importance to each faith tradition. The Ten Commandments are central to Christianity as well. Yet the contrast in language is stark. Both the lack of any qualifier in the Qur'an definition and the particularly qualified wording for Moses, going beyond the usual "Jews believe . . ." are troublesome. That Moses "claimed to have received" the Commandments sounds as if he made the whole thing up. The lack of uniformity in standards of wording about the two religions is indicative of a kind of kid-glove treatment that characterizes some textbook writing about Muslims.

The second textbook that contains problematic glossary entries is *World Civilizations: The Global Experience*, published by Pearson Longman.

The glossary entry for Muhammad reads "Muhammad Prophet of Islam; . . . *received revelations from Allah* in 610 C.E. and thereafter; . . . " In contrast, the entry for "Jesus of Nazareth" reads in part, "prophet and teacher among the Jews; *believed* by Christians to be the Messiah; . . ."[15]

McDougal Littell's *Modern World History: Patterns of Interaction* asserts "Muhammad's teachings, which *are the revealed word of God . . .* , are found in the holy book called the Qur'an."[16] But *Modern World History* prefaces its description of Jesus' birth and resurrection with the appropriate qualifiers: "*According to the New Testament,* Jesus of Nazareth was born around 6 to 4 B.C." "*According to Jesus' followers,* he rose from the dead. . . ."[17] In these cases, the Muslim belief is stated as fact, while the Jewish and Christian beliefs are characterized as something less . . . verifiable?

World Cultures and Geography: Eastern Hemisphere and Europe by McDougal Littell, presents on a single page a summary of beliefs of three major religions: Christianity, Islam, and Judaism. In a unit overview for the teacher, "Key Ideas" for the section "Birthplace of Three Religions" are summarized as follows. "Judaism, Christianity, and Islam all share common traits. Judaism is a *story* of exile. Christians *believe* that Jesus was the promised Messiah. The Qur'an is the collection of God's *revelations* to Muhammad."[18] [emphasis added] The description of Muslim beliefs is expressed as historical fact; the Muslim scriptures simply are revelations. As if descending on the scale of historical certainty we come to Christianity. Jesus' role is less certain; Christians believe he was the Messiah. And Judaism occupies the lowest rung, its theology reduced to a story of exile, and no more.

McGraw-Hill's *Glencoe World History* asserts archaeological evidence does not support the biblical Exodus account, a test it does not apply to the scriptures of other religions. Perhaps these are all stories and legends. Perhaps all religious histories are myths. Consistency is all that is required, a standard way of approaching religious testaments and scriptures that distinguishes faith from fact. (See Table 5.1.)

Other textbooks repeat the error so neatly displayed in *World Cultures and Geography.* In *The Earth and Its Peoples,* published by Houghton Mifflin, Muhammad's spiritual experience is described as follows. "During one night vigil, known to later tradition as the 'Night of Power and Excellence,' *a being whom Muhammad later understood to be the angel Gabriel (Jibra'il in Arabic) spoke to him . . .*"[19] [emphasis added] Although the wording com-

Table 5.1: Comparison of Language Used for Beliefs of the Three Major Religions in Selected Textbooks

Textbook	Judaism	Christianity	Islam
The World (Pearson/Scott Foresman)	Caption to a picture of a seder plate: "Foods on the seder plate are symbolic of an ancient Hebrew *story*."		"The pilgrimage, or hajj (haj), to Mecca is an essential part of Islam, the religion *revealed* to Muhammad. . . ."
World History: Continuity & Change (Holt)	Glossary entry: "Ten Commandments: Moral laws Moses *claimed* to have received from the Hebrew God Yahweh on Mount Sinai."		Glossary entry: "Qur'an: Holy Book of Islam containing *revelations received by Muhammad from God*."
World Civilizations: The Global Experience (Pearson)		Glossary entry: "Jesus of Nazareth" reads in part, "prophet and teacher among the Jews; *believed* by Christians to be the Messiah . . ."	Glossary entry: "Muhammad Prophet of Islam . . . ; *received revelations from Allah* in 610 C.E. and thereafter. . . ."
Modern World History: Patterns of Interaction (McDougal Littell)		"*According to the New Testament*, Jesus of Nazareth was born around 6 to 4 B.C." "*According to Jesus' followers*, he rose from the dead. . . ."	"Muhammad's teachings, which *are the revealed word of God* . . . , are found in the holy book called the Qur'an."
World Cultures and Geography: Eastern Hemisphere and Europe (McDougal Littell)	Teacher's Planning Guide: "[Section] Overview: Key Ideas Birthplace of Three Religions . . . Judaism, Christianity, and Islam all share common traits."		
	"Judaism is a *story* of exile."	"Christians *believe* that Jesus was the promised Messiah."	"The Qur'an is the collection of *God's revelations* to Muhammad"
Glencoe World History (McGraw-Hill)	"Then, because of drought, the Israelites migrated to Egypt, where they were enslaved until Moses led them out of Egypt. . . . Some interpretations of recent archaeological evidence *contradict* details of the biblical account."		

municates that Muhammad *understood* it to be an angel who spoke to him, the basic sentence structure still reads declaratively "a being spoke to him." It still needs the more direct qualifier "Muslims believe . . ." that covers all the thoughts in the sentence.

Islam Is the True Religion

Supplemental materials produced for public schools by Muslim groups go even beyond the textbooks' use of devotional language about Islam. These materials make no pretense of neutrality. They extol Islam as the perfection of Judaism and Christianity. The language waxes nostalgic for the glory days of Islamic power and influence at its height. Muslim rule is presented as an idyllic time of inter-religious harmony in which Jews and Christians were well-treated. The primary themes in the supplemental materials are discussed below.

Teaching materials by Muslim groups often posit Islam as the one "true" faith, while depicting Judaism and Christianity as inherently flawed. Amideast's *Islam: A Primer* states that Muhammad's "aim was not to found a new religion, but to correct and complete the message of his predecessors, [Jesus and Moses]."[20] Furthermore, Amideast's *Primer* states that "Muslims venerate the Quran with an intensity hardly known to Jews or Christians."[21] CIE's "Glossary of Terms Associated with Islam and Muslim History" defines "Torah" as the "Arabic name for the holy book revealed to Prophet Moses thousands of years ago. For Muslims, the *Torah* was a scriptural precursor to the *Qur'an*, just as Moses was a predecessor of Muhammad in the history of divinely revealed monotheism."[22]

This definition is inconsistent with the accepted etymology of the word *Torah*. *The American Heritage Dictionary* identifies the origin of *Torah* as Hebrew and defines it as: "1. The first five books of the Hebrew Scriptures. . . . 2. A scroll of parchment containing the first five books of the Hebrew Scriptures, used in a synagogue during services. 3. The entire body of religious law and learning including both sacred literature and oral tradition."[23] While the Qur'an certainly does borrow from the Torah, to describe the Torah only as a scriptural precursor of the Qur'an is worse than the textbooks' problematic use of the Christian term Old Testament for the Jewish Bible.

A suggested lesson plan in the *Arab World Studies Notebook* states, "To understand the Muslim world view, it is important to understand how

God-centered Islam really is. And to understand how Islam requires of Muslims that they put God at the center of their lives, everyday, all the time, is perhaps best *experienced*."[24] The lesson then suggests that teachers ask their students to "practice" phrases such as *"alhamdu-lillah,"* which means, "the praise belongs to God."[25] The *Notebook* also recommends that "the phrase, *'alhamdu-lillah,'* is a very appropriate one to attach to students' good work . . . " and offers for sale a self-inking stamp of the word in Arabic calligraphy for classroom use.[26] It is an unsubtle form of proselytizing for Islam.

The Islamic Empire Was a Time of Glory

Nostalgia for the lost Islamic empire is a frequent theme in these teaching materials. The glorification of Islamic imperialism stands in stark contrast to the materials' condemnation of Western colonialism and of Israel. The materials encourage teachers to spend more classroom time and attention on the glories of Islamic civilization than on European accomplishments, which are presented as lesser than, and inherently indebted to, Muslim society. The *Arab World Studies Notebook* offers for sale a video entitled, *The Challenge of the Past*, the description of which states: "The nostalgia for lost glory still affects many Muslims . . . the expulsion of the Muslims from Islamic Spain [is] still viewed as a gaping wound in Islam."[27] It does not attempt to ask whether this is positive or negative, but leaves the impression that the gaping wound needs to be healed by a return to glory, rather than letting go of the past.

Islam Has Always Tolerated the Jews

The Arab and Islamic groups' curricula and supplemental teaching materials present an image of an idyllic, multicultural and tolerant Arab world—a harmonious place that was only disrupted by the creation of the state of Israel. The Council on Islamic Education's curriculum explains that "forced conversion to Islam is a historical myth" and that "Islam advocates positive relations and designates Christians and Jews as *Ahl al-Kitab,* or 'People of the Book . . . .' "[28] "Historically, Muslims accepted Jews and Christians as *dhimmis*, or protected communities . . . ."[29] The Saudi Arabian Ministry of Education's *Understanding Islam* webpage claims that "racism is incomprehensible to Muslims . . . ."[30] The *Arab World Studies Notebook* concurs: "Islam is an inclusivist religion . . . ."[31]

The term dhimmitude was coined by author Bat Ye'or for the conditions and status of the dhimmis, protected non-Muslims under Muslim rule. But these supplementary materials do not address the negative aspects of the second-class status of dhimmis. The idealization of dhimmitude contained in materials developed by the Arab interest groups negates the fact that, as Ye'or writes, "dhimmitude can only be understood in the context of *jihad* . . . infidels who submit without fighting to the Islamic armies, are granted a pledge of security. . . . Peace and security for non-Muslims are recognised only after their submission."[32]

For example, the *Arab World Studies Notebook* features a profile of Maimonides, the preeminent Jewish theologian. "Under the Almohads, the intellectual life of Córdoba was not what it had been, and [Maimonides] and many other intellectuals . . . preferred to live in the other regions . . . ruled by Muslims of not such a 'puritanical' persuasion."[33]

However, scholars disagree. "Maimonides and his family fled Muslim fundamentalism in Córdoba in 1148 when he was barely in his teens."[34] According to the *Jewish Virtual Library*, "To avoid persecution by the [Almohades] Muslim sect—which was wont to offer Jews and Christians the choice of conversion to Islam or death—Maimonides fled with his family. . . ."[35]

On the other hand, there were periods of history in which Jews were comfortable—and even flourished—in Muslim lands. According to an article in the *New York Times* entitled "Was the Islam of Old Spain Truly Tolerant?," one reason for "the impulse to idealize Anadalusia . . . may be that it looks so good given what followed." Compared to the Inquisition in Spain and Portugal, "many societies might resemble paradise." This does not change, however, the fact that in *Al-Andalus*, "Christians and Jews . . . had the status of . . . alien minorities. They rose high but remained second-class citizens; one 11th-century legal text called them members of 'the devil's party.' . . . Violence also erupted, including a massacre of thousands of Jews in Grenada in 1066 and the forced exile of many Christians in 1126."[36]

The Muslim narrative about the historic place of Jews and Christians under Islamic rule and about the current state of affairs in the Middle East does not reflect much enlightened Muslim thinking and scholarship. Where are the voices that reject extremism? Where is the teaching about moderate countries like Jordan and Morocco? Why are Muslim opponents of Islamist policies like Irshad Manji and Ayaan Hirsii Ali seemingly not consulted to contribute their knowledge and wisdom to the vetting and adoption process?

If neither contemporary Christian thinking nor moderate Muslim scholarship is informing textbook content, then those groups suffer as well. Students and other readers will come away from their schooling with an unfair and unrepresentative depiction of these two exceedingly important religious and cultural traditions. Enlightened Muslims do not find their own viewpoints represented in the public schools. Jews, Christians, and Muslims, and have a joint interest in ensuring not only the accuracy but the neutrality of the textbooks, both for their own self-interest and for the larger goal of building a stronger, more inclusive society. Correcting the textbooks is the beginning of returning their birthright to the children of a democracy.

The following three chapters turn from classroom discussions of religious origins to various aspects of the history and politics of the modern Middle East. If teaching about religion in an accurate and neutral way is difficult, then the complexities and controversies of the Arab–Israeli conflict present an even greater challenge.

CHAPTER SIX

THE ANCIENT HISTORY OF ISRAEL

INTRODUCTION TO MIDDLE EAST ANALYSIS: HISTORICAL NARRATIVES VERSUS HISTORICAL ACCURACY

The coverage of Middle East history and the Arab–Israeli dispute in textbooks and supplemental materials contains significant elements of the Arab narrative. The Arab narrative is the framing of the Arab–Israeli dispute from Arab and Palestinian points of view. It encompasses a view of ancient Middle Eastern history as well as interpretations of more modern history. The outline of the Arab narrative discussed in the chapters that follow can be seen in Appendix D.

Many of the textbooks we examined, regardless of how well they might deal with the origins of Judaism, Christianity, and Islam, usually discard their reasonable scholarship when they present the Israeli–Arab conflict. Indeed, some textbooks have adopted wholesale Arab narratives about the modern Middle East. Textbooks should strive for historical accuracy rather than language that misleads the reader.

In this chapter and the two that follow, we have thoroughly examined the Arab and Palestinian points of view in total and within each theme covered by textbooks. We understand the Arab and Palestinian position and acknowledge it represents their deeply held beliefs. We present the best defense of their line of reasoning. We show the instances in which, after conducting our analysis, we came to the conclusion that the Arab and Palestinian reasoning is often not correct. Their conclusions represent a simplistic view of the complex reality of the modern Middle East.

A terminology of victimization pervades the Palestinian narrative and the majority of textbooks that have adopted it. Palestinian suffering squeezes out the coverage of anything positive about Palestinian society. Palestinians as victims is the major defining theme that underlies much of the lessons on the Middle East in textbooks and supplemental materials.

Perhaps the most flagrant violation of historical accuracy in textbook coverage of the Middle East is found in *World History: The Human Journey, Modern World*, published by Holt. An introductory activity begins the teacher's introduction to the section entitled "War, Revolution, and Oil in the Middle East and North Africa," the first subject of which is "The Arab–Israel Confrontation."

> [Bellringer symbol] LET'S GET STARTED! As students enter the classroom, ask them to imagine that the United States was structured so that only members of a certain religion could hold leadership positions in government and that all laws were based on that religion's beliefs. Call on class members to suggest social and political problems that might arise from such an arrangement. Ask students if they would like to live in such a society and to explain why or why not they feel as they do.[1]

At first glance one must ask oneself what possible connection this teacher-led classroom exercise has to the subject of the section it introduces, "The Arab–Israeli Confrontation." When it becomes clear that Israel is the only possible country to which the authors' could be referring, the intent of the activity is laid bare: to discredit the idea of Israel as a Jewish state.

The free exercise of religion is guaranteed to all the citizens of Israel beginning with its Declaration of Independence proclaimed May 14, 1948 and reinforced and expanded by parliamentary legislation and Supreme Court decisions over the years. Non-Jewish citizens enjoy the same rights as their Jewish counterparts. The Arab and Druze minorities are represented in parliament, the judiciary and in all sectors of the civil society. The inaccurate picture of religious freedom in this example is part of a pattern that includes references all the way back to ancient times. The delegitimization of Israel begins by labeling Israel as something—giving it a name that does not belong. Israel is called Palestine at times in history before the name Palestine existed.

IT'S ALL IN A NAME: ANACHRONISTIC REFERENCES TO PALESTINE

The use of the word "Palestine" as opposed to "Israel" or "Judea" at various points in history can be historically misleading. This is far more than simple semantics. For all intents and purposes, the name Palestine was not in use by the inhabitants of the region until after the second Jewish revolt in 135 C.E. Yet, many textbooks exhibit a strong tendency to project the word "Palestine" well backward into history when its use is inappropriate and anachronistic, not to mention confusing to students.[2] Textbooks' misuse of the name Palestine before it was appropriate discredits the historical roots of Jews in the land of Israel.

The same textbooks assiduously avoid the name "Israel" even for the ancient monarchies that bore this official name. Textbooks need to exercise greater care in their use of these labels in the classroom in light of the present conflict. Inaccurate land terminology can distort students' understanding. For example, the commonly held belief that the roots of the Israeli–Palestinian conflict go back centuries or millennia is erroneous. Its origins are much more recent—the late nineteenth and early twentieth century during the rise of the nationalism of other peoples.

The Palestinian perspective holds that their roots extend back into pre-Islamic times, to the Canaanites and Philistines, for whom Palestine was named. They see the ability to trace historical links thousands of years into the past enhances their sense of peoplehood, lends legitimacy to their nationalist aspirations, and strengthens their claim to the land. Palestinians fervently believe these ideas about their origins as the truth. There are aspects of Palestinian culture that relate to these earlier roots such as the architecture of houses that resemble Canaanite architecture. The Latin Palaestina was in fact derived by the Romans from what is Philistia in English.

On the other hand, scholars say that the Philistines were an Indo-European people not related to the Semitic Palestinians. Neither is there any evidence of a racial link between the Canaanites and the Palestinians. Most importantly, there is a critical difference between the modern political identity that evolved following the rise of general Arab nationalism and the creation of independent Arab nations.

The Council on Islamic Education, a content consultant to many publishers, ascribes considerable importance to the terminology used by the textbooks. For example, the organization explains its philosophy in its comments on draft versions of Holt and Ballard & Tighe textbooks submitted for the 2005 California History-Social Science adoption.

> The [state's proposed] change from "Canaan" to "Israel and Judah" [in a particular sentence in the draft Holt textbook] is correct, given the time period in question. . . . However, given the common teleological problem (exacerbated by advocacy groups) of conflating ancient Israel with the modern state in order to buttress absolute territorial claims, it would be appropriate from a historical standpoint to insert the word "ancient" in front of "Israel and Judah" in the sentence.

CIE says, in discussing the "issue of the anachronistic use of Palestine" in the draft Ballard & Tighe textbook,

> [t]he fact that this is a sensitive topic should not preclude a historiographically sound treatment. In any case, the narrative should not be driven by partisan interests. A corollary matter on the issue of anachronism about this subject (in keeping with the desire for chronological and historical accuracy), is to avoid conflating the ancient kingdom of Israel with the modern nation-state. Moreover, it is important to avoid treating the name "Israel" as the normative designation for territory whose boundaries and claimants have shifted throughout human history. Of course, through proper attribution of their perspectives, textbooks can discuss the importance of this region to various groups in time. Interest groups may seek to advance nationalist or ideological claims about natural or de facto "ownership" of land, but the state [of California] must ensure that educational materials do not do so.[3]

The powerful Romans who ruled the land in question during the critical first century when Christianity was born and rabbinic Judaism evolved were not ones to consider names and terminology as trivial. On the contrary, as Middle East scholar Bernard Lewis writes,

After the revolt of Bar-Kokhba in 135 CE, the Romans decided once and for all to rid themselves of this troublesome [Jewish] people. Like the Babylonians before them, they sent a large part of the Jewish population into captivity and exile, and this time there was no Cyrus to restore them. Even the historic nomenclature of the Jews was to be obliterated. Jerusalem was renamed Aelia Capitolina, and a temple to Jupiter built on the site of the destroyed Jewish Temple. The names Judaea and Samaria were abolished, and the country renamed Palestine, after the long-forgotten Philistines.[4]

So the name Palestine was imposed on Judea, Galilee and Samaria as a punishment against the Jews for their many revolts, as the Roman overlords lost patience. Surely this historical turning point would be significant enough to fix the point in time when the name of the land changed. Some textbooks highlight this connection, but others ignore it.

The Hebrew scriptures, as noted and given weight by some textbooks, never speak of "Palestine" because the term was not in use when they were written. These scriptures speak of "Canaan," which is the only period-appropriate term when describing the call of Abraham and the Exodus, until the time of the Israelite monarchy, at which time the name clearly became "Israel." For example, in the first book of Kings the name of the country is clear. "The other events of Jeroboam's reign . . . are recorded in the Annals of the Kings of Israel."[5] Outside of the Hebrew Bible, according to James L. Kugel in *How to Read the Bible*, the first mention of the name "Israel" in non-Israelite sources, "known to us is found (in passing) on a victory stele attributed to the Egyptian king Merneptah . . . in the late thirteenth century [B.C.E.]. . . ."[6]

Marching ahead in time from the Hebrew scriptures, neither is there any reference to Palestine in the Christian Scriptures. Containing both Jewish and Gentile influences, the Christian scriptures offer evidence that no one referred to the land as "Palestine" at the time they were written. The Gospels and the Acts of the Apostles are the most comprehensive and widely known portrait of life in the western Mediterranean in the first century, a critical period from the perspective of both the religious and political history of the Middle East and its influence on the wider world.

Luke's Gospel, for example, offers a comprehensive ". . . situating [of] the call of John the Baptist in terms of the civil rulers of the period. . . ."[7] He writes, of the beginnings of the Christian era, "In the fifteenth year of the reign of Tiberius Caesar, when Pontius Pilate was governor of Judea, and

Herod was Tetrarch of Galilee, and his brother Philip tetrarch of the region of Ituraea and Trachonitis, and Lysanias was tetrarch of Abilene, during the high priesthood of Annas and Caiaphas, the word of God came to John, the son of Zechariah in the desert."[8] If there had been any political or geographical entity called "Palestine" at that time, surely this enumeration of civil administration would have included mention of it. Matthew places Jesus' birth "at Bethlehem in Judea," not Palestine, as several textbooks would have it.[9] The apostles asked Jesus, before his ascension from the Mt. of Olives, "Lord, are you at this time going to restore the kingdom to Israel?" signifying that the collective name for the provinces was Israel.[10] Similarly, the ministry of Jesus is summed up after his death as follows. "You know the word that [God] sent to the Israelites as he proclaimed peace through Jesus Christ, who is Lord of all, what has happened all over Judea, beginning in Galilee after the baptism that John preached, how God anointed Jesus of Nazareth with the holy Spirit and power."[11]

Among the more accurate texts are those who recount the Roman renaming of the land. *Harcourt Horizons World History* describes the renaming in a straightforward manner. "The Jews continued to revolt against Roman rule until A.D. 135, when the Romans drove many of the Jews out of Jerusalem. At about this time, the Romans renamed the area Palaestina, or Philistia. The name Palaestina became Palestine in English." The textbook's activity book reinforces this point in a chronology exercise. "The Romans drive the Jews from Jerusalem and rename the land Palestina, or Palestine."[12]

Harcourt Horizons World History's sister textbook, *The World*, also published by Harcourt/Holt, make the reason for the renaming of the land even more clear, even though they attribute it to an earlier rebellion. "Around A.D. 70 the Jews were forced to leave Judaea. The Romans changed the region's name to Palestine to remove all connection of the land to the Jews." This passage makes it plain the Romans renamed the land as a punishment designed to erase Jews' connection to Israel. This is a critical historical concept because it rebuts the historically inaccurate claim that current day Jews have no connection to the land.

Later in the same textbook, the idea is repeated and connected to the Jews' longing for Israel throughout history.

> In A.D. 70, however, the Romans destroyed the Jewish capital of Jerusalem. . . . The Romans then referred to the region as Palestine, removing the Jewish people's connection with the land they had once

controlled. . . . [Jews] who left never forgot their homeland, however. Jews around the world end their Passover Seder . . . with these words: "Next year in Jerusalem."[13]

Similarly, *World Cultures: A Global Mosaic* states clearly, "During the late 1800s, persecution of Jews led to the modern form of Zionism. This movement sought to reestablish a Jewish state in Palestine. As you read in Chapter 25, the Romans had expelled the Jews from Palestine in A.D. 70. Since then, Jews had dreamed of returning."[14] *World History: Continuity and Change* puts it this way: "Jewish settlement had been known in Palestine since ancient times."[15] Finally, the idea of the existence of Israel as based in historical continuity is ably summarized by Glencoe's *World History: The Human Experience*. In describing competing Jewish and Arab nationalism, it says of Jewish nationalism "[t]he Jews claimed the land [of Palestine] on the basis of their biblical heritage and the continuing presence of Jews in the area since ancient times."[16]

World History: The Human Journey, published by Holt, uses "Canaan" for the land appropriately to place various early key events in the biblical period. "[Abraham] led his people through the desert to the borders of northern Canaan. . . . Moses announced that Canaan was a land promised to his ancestors." During the period of the monarchy, it does not shy away from the name "Israel." "The first king of this united kingdom called Israel was Saul."[17]

A Houghton Mifflin offering, *The Earth and Its Peoples*, argues for choosing a name or names for the land with care to avoid confusing students. "The land and the people at the heart of this story have gone by various names: Canaan, Israel, Palestine; Hebrews, *Israelites*, Jews. For the sake of consistency, the people are referred to here as Israelites, the land they occupied in antiquity as **Israel**."[18] [emphasis from original] The point made by this high school level textbook is convincing. The textbooks which attempt to impose a concept of "ancient Palestine" over the top of the names used by the historical sources, both in the body of the text as well as in accompanying maps, are pushing past historical accuracy. Is it in the pursuit of a political agenda?

Other texts also get it right. In its entire discussion of the history of the Hebrews, *Human Heritage: A World History* published by McGraw-Hill/ Glencoe, uses Canaan or Israel, as appropriate to the time period, never Palestine. For example "In exchange, Yahweh promised that they and their descendants . . . could always live in Canaan."[19] This is another demonstration that a clear and complete picture of the ancient Hebrews can be constructed without the introduction of the muddling term Palestine when it is historically inappropriate.

Similarly, *World History: The Human Experience* by Glencoe uses Canaan and Israel consistently and accurately. "According to the Bible, once in the land of Canaan, the descendants of Abraham shared the land with other peoples such as the Phoenicians and Philistines." This correct terminology facilitates discussion of the Canaanites and their interaction with the Israelites much better than if the land were also simultaneously called Palestine. "The Canaanites settled in Canaan . . . [and] some Canaanites settled along the coast and became known as Phoenicians."[20]

Finally, Prentice Hall's *World Civilizations: The Global Experience* makes use of the term "Israel" to represent the two provinces of Judea and Galilee mentioned in the Gospels. "Jesus preached widely in Israel . . . ,"[21] illustrating that the term Palestine is still anachronistic during this time period.

Their presentation of the material demonstrates that Palestine is an unnecessary descriptor before the renaming of the land by the Romans and rewrites history in a way that discredits the Jewish connection to ancient Israel. It is evident from these examples that some textbooks do just fine and provide a clear historical narrative without introducing the term Palestine before it is historically appropriate.

Examples of the problems with inconsistent land terminology start with Holt's *World History: The Human Journey, Modern World*. In its map of "Egypt: The New Kingdom, c. 1450 B.C." it uses the inaccurate label "Palestine" for the western Mediterranean coastal plain. But the accompanying text only speaks of Canaan, making this lesson a confusing one for students.[22]

People, Places, and Change by Holt asserts that the official Roman nomenclature was Palestine at the time they conquered it. "In the 60s B.C. the Roman Empire conquered the region, which they called Palestine."[23] The assertion is false. The Romans called it "Judea and Galilee" until the second century and this convention is reflected in the Christian Scriptures.

World Geography Today by Harcourt/Holt describes the Jewish–Roman political situation as follows. "Many Jews resented Roman rule of Palestine." It should read "Judea." The textbook goes on to explain, somewhat erroneously, that "Palestine is an old Greek name for the eastern . . . Mediterranean."[24] While appearing in a few isolated sources, mostly as Syria–Palestina ["Philistia," after the Philistines], the name was not in common use until after 135 C.E.

Holt's *World History: Continuity & Change* inserts Palestine freely where it is inappropriate in the following examples. "[Abraham] migrated with his family to Palestine." It should be Canaan in this case, in keeping with the text when it reads ". . . according to [biblical] accounts . . ." because the Hebrew Bible doesn't speak of "Palestine." "[Mid-1200s B.C. Moses] leads Hebrews to Palestine." "[By the 1100s B.C.] [t]he whole region soon became known as Philistia, or Palestine." The same error is repeated with respect to the Christian Scriptures. "At first the disciples worked mainly in the Jewish communities of Palestine."[25] The Gospels speak of Judea and Galilee, not Palestine.

Another publisher's offering, *Ancient World History* by McDougal Littell seems to want to force Palestine in wherever it can, especially in maps regardless of the time period—definitely the sign of a political agenda. Falsely root the present day Palestinians in ancient times and one enhances the legitimacy of that people's claim to (all of) the land of Israel. In covering early history, this textbook uses the appropriate label Canaan, which is apparently less threatening than Israel, in passages such as "Canaan was the ancient home of the Hebrews." Quickly, however, the textbook adopts such a direct use of Palestine that the reader is left wondering what version of history is being told. It injects Palestine into a discussion of the Phoenicians, who in fact referred to *themselves* as Canaanites. The Roman renaming is projected backward more than a thousand years.

> Setting the Stage. The Phoenicians lived in a region at the eastern end of the Mediterranean Sea that was later called Palestine. The Phoenicians were not the only ancient people to live in Palestine. The Romans had given the area that name after the Philistines, another people who lived in the region. Canaan was the ancient home of the Hebrews, later called the Jews, in this area. . . . In fact, Hebrews often used the word Canaan to refer to all of ancient Palestine.[26]

All the anachronistic land terminology in McGraw-Hill's *Traditions and Encounters* is supported by a map entitled "Israel and Phoenicia 1500–600 B.C.E." which features an inset of Israel, Judah and Phoenicia. The inset's largest font labels are "Palestine" and "Egypt." The Israelite examples are all the more surprising considering that the section following the Israelites, which describes the Phoenicians, highlights Canaan as Phoenician terminology. "North of the Israelites' kingdom in Palestine, the Phoenicians occupied a narrow coastal plain between the Mediterranean Sea and the Lebanon mountains. They spoke a Semitic language, referring to themselves as Canaanites and their land as Canaan. (The term Phoenician comes from early Greek references.)"[27] It seems that a double standard is at work here. The Phoenicians, a people who no longer exist, can call their land Canaan and themselves Canaanites. Yet their contemporaries, the Israelites, whose descendants the Jews founded a modern nation in the same area, are repeatedly described as residing in Palestine, a name they never used.

Similarly McGraw-Hill's *Glencoe World History* begins its discussion of the Phoenicians with "The Phoenicians lived in the area of Palestine along the Mediterranean coast . . ." despite the fact that the map shows their region *north* of what is labeled Palestine. In the following textbook section entitled "The 'Children of Israel'," it is noted "According to their history, the Israelites migrated from Mesopotamia to Palestine, which the Hebrews referred to as Canaan."[28]

These passages from three textbooks that discuss the Phoenicians display chronological contortion. Other textbooks do perfectly well calling the land "Canaan" "Israel" "Judah" or "Judea" until the Romans renamed it after the Jewish revolts. In addition, they incorrectly imply that the rest of the world called the land "Palestine" and the Hebrews were out of the mainstream to name it something quaint and unique. In passages that attempt to define the name of the land and discuss the concept of the naming of land and peoples, and their self-identification, these textbooks get it all wrong.

The mistakes in McDougal Littell's *Ancient World History* continue in a map entitled "Canaan, the Crossroads, 2000–600 B.C." The labeling of Canaan/Israel/Judah in the main section as "Palestine" is confusing and gratuitous. No map is shown of the united monarchy of Israel. Regarding the same time period covered by the map, the textbook reads "the kings of Assyria defeated Syria, Palestine and Babylonia." and an accompanying map of the Assyrian Empire labels the region simply as "Palestine."[29] This is especially egregious and anachronistic terminology for Israel and Judah.

The World and Its People by McGraw-Hill/Glencoe is also among those textbooks introducing confusing land nomenclature. "If Abraham moved to the land of Canaan (Palestine), he would be blessed . . ." The parenthetical adds nothing but confusion for Abraham's time period. Also, a teacher sidebar contrasts the name and concept "Modern Israel" with "Ancient Palestine" as if the biblical Israel never existed, does not serve as the foundation of modern Israel, and as if a Palestinian entity existed in ancient times from which today's Palestinians draw their roots. "Teach: Making Comparisons. Write 'Modern Israel' and 'Ancient Palestine' on the board. Have students examine the text and photographs in this section to find items that might be classified under each heading. Discuss ways that modern Israel reflects its ancient heritage."[30] The exercise should not use "Palestine." "Ancient Israel" would be the accurate term to describe the region during biblical times, but the textbook goes to unreasonable lengths to avoid this phrasing.

McGraw-Hill's *Glencoe World History*, overlays "Palestine" onto the labels Judah and Israel in a map entitled "Ancient Israel." The use of Palestine in the text body seems gratuitous and arbitrary when applied to the Israelites, and appears ideologically driven. "Although later [after King David] the Israelites would be conquered and scattered, Palestine remained the Promised Land in the minds of many Jews."[31] In the mind of Jews the Promised Land was Israel, not Palestine.

World Cultures and Geography: Eastern Hemisphere and Europe by McDougal Littell helpfully presents a summary of its relative view of the three major religions. A unit overview for the teacher summarizes "key ideas" for the section "Birthplace of Three Religions." "Judaism, Christianity, and Islam all share common traits. Judaism is a story of exile. Christians believe that Jesus was the promised Messiah. The Qur'an is the collection of God's revelations to Muhammad."[32] The reduction of Judaism to a series of exiles in this geography text covering Israel and the Palestinian territories is meant to reinforce the notion that Jews were displaced from the historical land of Israel long ago and to reduce the legitimacy of their contemporary residence in that land.

Another example from *Glencoe World History* shows the danger of conflating ancient conflicts erroneously to the present. In a section entitled "Connections Past to Present: Conflict in Palestine," the accompanying

illustration shows Israeli armored jeeps firing tear gas at Palestinian rioters. The caption reads

> Conflict in Palestine. Conflict in Southwest Asia has a long history.
> When the Israelites entered Palestine, around 1220 B.C., other peo-
> ples were already settled there. One of these peoples were the Philis-
> tines. For over two centuries, Israelites and Philistines fought for
> control. By 1020 B.C., the Israelites found themselves on the verge of
> being conquered by the Philistines. . . . David, the next king of the
> Israelites, defeated the Philistines and established control over all of
> Palestine.[33]

The erroneous parallels between the Israelite–Philistine conflict and
today's Israeli–Palestinian conflict are subtle but clear—the Israelites
(Israelis) took over Palestine. These are the same false parallels the Palestinians favor drawing between themselves and the Philistines, as if their
historical and genealogical roots lay in the Philistines and Philistia. In
fact, the Philistines were an Indo-European people unrelated to the
Semites, the ethnic group to which both Jews and Arabs belong.

Some Arab groups' materials posit the Palestinians as the only original inhabitants of Israel. A section on archaeology in AWAIR's *Arab World
Studies Notebook* discusses "Canaanite influence on the Hebrews," sug-
gesting that Canaanites "wrote down materials which appeared in the
Old Testament more than one thousand years later," and that "even the
names most closely associated with Hebrew traditions appear to have
been Canaanite in origin."[34]

Many of the same problems are found in McGraw-Hill's *Traditions and
Encounters: A Global Perspective on the Past*. Palestine is used exclusively for
its description of the history of the Israelites until the united monarchy.
Some examples follow. "Israelites formed a branch of Hebrews who settled in Palestine (modern-day Israel)." Again, the "Palestine" of ancient
times is contrasted with the modern nation called Israel. "[Abraham]
migrated to Palestine about 1850 B.C.E. . . ." "According to their scriptures,
some Hebrews migrated from Palestine to Egypt during the eighteenth
century B.C.E." "[T]his branch of the Hebrews departed under the leadership of Moses and went to Palestine. . . . [T]hese Hebrews, known as the
Israelites, fought bitterly with other inhabitants of Palestine and carved
out a territory for themselves."[35] The textbook emphasizes the theme of
the Israelites (Israelis) invading Palestine, battling the local population

and forcibly occupying the land because of the historical parallels it sees between the era of the Exodus and today's Israeli–Palestinian situation. Despite the continuous presence of some Israelites who remained behind in Canaan during the famine-induced migration to Egypt, the language used casts the returning Israelites as usurpers.

Finally, the expression "ancient Palestine," which the examples show is a red flag for inappropriate terminology, appears in a product by Thomson Wadsworth, *World Civilizations*. "When he died, a revolt against [Solomon's] successor split the Hebrew kingdom in two: Judea and Samaria, or, as they are sometimes called, Judah and Israel."[36] Only this and another Thomson text call the Hebrew kingdoms Judea and Samaria. The word "Israel" seems to be only grudgingly used, and nowhere in the text or map entitled "Ancient Palestine and the Jewish Kingdoms" is the word "Israel" present, even, as it should be, for the unified monarchy.

JESUS THE PALESTINIAN

The Arab narrative aims to remake Jesus, the Jew, into a Palestinian hero to the exclusion of his Jewish identity, rather than alongside it. In an era in which Christians move increasingly in the direction of emphasizing the Jewishness of Jesus, and many Jews look on approvingly, the Palestinian narrative is moving in the opposite direction. As reported in *Ha'aretz* in 2006, "It was only a decade ago that Yasser Arafat effectively made Bethlehem Christians into the very symbol of Palestine, by choosing the city's Church of the Nativity to declare that Jesus was a Palestinian. 'This is the birthplace of our Lord the Messiah, the Palestinian,' he stressed."[37]

Jesus' traditional birthplace in Bethlehem is within the territory of the Palestinian authority. A portion of the Palestinian population is Christian, although declining rapidly in recent years. Clearly, the notoriety of Jesus as a personage in history and religion is so great that the Palestinians' desire to lay claim to his legacy is natural and understandable. The image of Jesus as arising from poor origins to become a person of influence with a message of hope and optimism for the downtrodden and oppressed resonates strongly with the Palestinians, Muslim and Christian alike, given their history. However, the Palestinian narrative does not accommodate the reality of Jesus' Jewish identity coexisting with a newer Palestinian one. It is a binary situation for them: Jewish and Palestinian are mutually exclusive. Therein lies the fallacy of it. To admit Jesus' Jewish identity threatens their exclusive claim to his inheritance, key among them their claims to the land of his birth and ministry.

The denial of Jesus' Jewish identity and its replacement with a Palestinian one is a fabrication.[38] According to an Evangelical perspective, "In [Palestinian Liberation Theology], Jesus loses his Jewish identity to assume a Palestinian one. . . . For advocates of PLT, it's not a stretch to say that Jesus was a revolutionary Palestinian martyr."[39]

The concept results in some inaccurate terminology. *Human Heritage: A World History* by McGraw-Hill/Glencoe asserts that "[a]fter Jesus died, [his followers] tried to spread his gospel, or teachings, among the Jews in Palestine. They had little success, however. Most *Palestinian* Jews wanted a political messiah. They were not interested in a religious one." [emphasis added][40] The inaccurate term Palestinian Jews is one more example of many textbooks' confusing overuse of Palestine and overdrawn parallels between ancient history and the present Israeli–Palestinian situation.

Ancient World History adopts wholesale the myth of Jesus as a Palestinian developed by the Palestinian leadership. "Jesus was raised in the village of Nazareth in northern Palestine."[41] The Gospels speak of Nazareth as located in Galilee, not Palestine. They make no mention of Palestine because no one called it Palestine at that time, and Jesus was a Jew. Another offering by MacDougal Littell, *World Cultures and Geography: Eastern Hemisphere and Europe* also spins the "Jesus was a Palestinian" myth. "Sometime during the years 8 to 4 B.C., a Jewish boy named Jesus was born in Bethlehem, a small town in ancient Palestine."[42] *World Cultures: A Global Mosaic* by McGraw-Hill claims "Jesus, the founder of Christianity, was born in Palestine while it was under Roman rule."[43] The Gospels say Jesus was born in "Bethlehem of Judea." Then, regarding Jesus' youth, we are again transported to a mythical "northern Palestine" as if such a place existed then. The textbook declares, "According to the Gospels, Jesus grew up in Galilee, a region in northern Palestine."[44] One cannot correctly say "according to the Gospels" in this sentence. A better geographic orientation would be provided by simply saying "a region north of Jerusalem," since the section "Birthplace of the Three Major Religions" opens with a discussion of Jerusalem. *Glencoe World History* says about Jesus: "The Development of Christianity: Guide to Reading, Main Ideas. Jesus, a Jew from Palestine, began his public preaching."[45]

Although it is a middle-school level textbook with only a moderate level of historical detail, *The World*, published by Pearson/Scott Foresman offers a fascinating glimpse into the permeation of ideology into the textbook historical narrative in strange and inconsistent ways. Unlike many of its peer products, this textbook's discussion of the Hebrews does not make use of the term Palestine even once. Canaan, Israel, and Judah are used as appropriate for each historical period. However, when it comes to Christianity, the perspective radically changes. The insistence of the authors in situating Jesus in a fictitious "Roman province of Palestine" that did not exist until more than 100 years later, leads to the most egregious and bold statement, in a student chapter review no less, that Jesus was a Palestinian. It begins, "[Christianity] was started by Jesus, a Jewish man born in Judah, or Judea, the southern part of the Roman province of Palestine. Palestine included parts of the present-day countries of Israel and Jordan. " Then comes the most direct distortion. "Workbook Support: Workbook, p. 72. Q. T or F: Christianity was started by a young *Palestinian* named Jesus? A. T."[46] [emphasis added] The problematic workbook page appears again in teacher sidebar on a later page.

This textbook's explicit and unambiguous description of Jesus, a Jew in the Gospels and in most other textbooks, as he morphs completely into a Palestinian demonstrates the wholesale adoption of the Palestinian leadership's campaign to hijack Jesus as a symbol of Palestinian claims to the land and transform him into a hero of the Palestinian resistance to Israel. This is the boldest indictment of the anachronistic injection of the term Palestine into the account of Christian origins, taken to its logical conclusion. If students are required to answer "True" to the statement in the workbook's review questions, then Jesus must really have been a Palestinian.

Some textbooks carry the erroneous Palestine terminology so far as to remake Jesus the Jew into a Palestinian, and his Jewish listeners into Palestinians. Supplemental materials rewrite history to draw links of heritage between other ancient peoples of the region such as the Canaanites and Philistines and today's Palestinians to assert earlier roots in the land than those claimed by Jews.

CHAPTER SEVEN

THE FOUNDING OF ISRAEL: RIGHTS TO THE LAND, WAR AND REFUGEES

This chapter analyzes issues associated with Israel's founding in 1948. There are three major themes: 1) Israeli Jews, a majority of whom have roots in Middle Eastern countries, are called European colonists even though they are a multiethnic Semitic people with historical ties to Israel; 2) the longstanding Arab hostility to Israel that has been expressed in warfare against the Jewish state is soft pedaled; and 3) textbooks reference mainly Palestinian refugees and fail to mention the Jewish refugees from Arab lands that found new homes in Israel. Some supplemental materials are lacking in accuracy. They posit that Israeli Jews are white European colonialists in the same unsavory category as the imperialist European countries. Some textbooks obfuscate who started the wars waged on Israel by Arab countries and lay all the blame for the failures of the peace process on Israel. They claim that only Palestinian refugees suffered as a result of Israel's creation, and that Israel forcibly expelled all Palestinians.

ISRAELIS AS WHITE COLONIALISTS

The Middle East conflict increasingly reverberates within the politics of race: American and South African racial paradigms are inappropriately projected onto Israelis and Palestinians. Former President Jimmy Carter is the most notable proponent of this view. In his book *Palestine: Peace Not*

Apartheid, he writes "Utilizing their political and military dominance, [Israeli leaders] are imposing a system of partial withdrawal, encapsulation, and apartheid on the Muslim and Christian citizens of the occupied territories."[1] The questions the comparison raises are many. Who is white and who is brown? Who is colonial and who is indigenous?

The charge of anti-Semitism is made, but it is flipped around. Jews are anti-Semitic because they are white colonial oppressors. They are not Semites at all. Palestinians are the real Semites—brown, indigenous people. Therefore, Israelis are anti-Semitic.

Marc Dollinger, Richard and Rhonda Goldman Chair in Jewish Studies and Social Responsibility at San Francisco State University wrote, "Inaccurate comparisons between Israeli policy and South African apartheid, for example, seek to exploit American concerns about racism in the advance of anti-Zionist ideology. This is ironic, because on the American political scene, Jews have been in the forefront of the civil rights movement. . . ."[2]

In the Middle East, the racial and ethnic realities are often mischaracterized. It is important that textbooks communicate the following concepts.

- Jews have a historical and uninterrupted connection to the land of Israel.
- Jews are a Semitic people who have a legitimate right to dwell in that land.
- Jews worldwide and especially Israelis are perhaps the most ethnically diverse people in history.

In Every Tongue describes the multiethnic character of the Jewish people. "Jews have always been racially and ethnically diverse, intermarrying with the local peoples in whatever far flung lands they lived. In this way they came to resemble their non-Jewish neighbors."[3] The Jewish and Israeli experience harmonize well with the ethic of diversity and multiculturalism in the United States. Some textbooks do an intellectually honest job of presenting the multiethnic character of Israelis. Supplemental materials tend to discredit Jewish ties to the land of Israel.

Palestinians view the concept of Israel as a Jewish state as inherently discriminatory and racist. When the Zionist pioneers started purchasing tracts of land and building communities on a large scale, the Palestinians living there found their white European ways alien and un-Middle Eastern. They resented the cultural changes brought by the newcomers. As Israel developed as a Jewish state and opened its borders as a refuge for persecuted Jews from anywhere around the globe, the Palestinians felt excluded in their own land. The Palestinians believe that both institutionalized discrimination against Israeli Arabs in Israel itself and the Israeli administration of the West Bank and Gaza favor Jewish residents in all respects. They see a direct analogy between their situation and black citizens of South Africa under the former apartheid system. The dominant Muslim majority of the Palestinians feels, like many other Muslims, that Jerusalem from a religious point of view, should be exclusively Muslim.

The majority of today's Israeli population is of color, as highlighted, for example, in textbooks published by Holt. Ethiopian, Mizrahi, and Sephardic Jews outnumbered Jews of European origin before the last Russian migration. One could argue that Israeli culture has become increasingly Middle Eastern over time. The historical and religious ties of Jews to Jerusalem are accepted by historians. Except for brief periods free of Jewish presence imposed by various conquerors, Jerusalem has been home to significant numbers of Jews since the Jewish revolts of the first century.

Some Iranian leaders, among others, say that the Jews are really Europeans, not true Semites, and therefore have no basis for any rights to dwell in the land.[4] Iranian President Mahmoud Ahmadinejad said in December 2005,

> . . . The question is, where did those who rule today in Palestine, as an occupation regime, come from? Where were they born? Where did their parents live? They have no roots in Palestine . . . [O]ne of the important goals [of the Europeans in] creating the artificial regime "which occupies Jerusalem" and causes the Jews of Europe to emigrate there . . . was to expel the Jews from Europe . . . [and] build a Jewish camp in an Islamic region. . . .[5]

McDougal Littel's *World Geography* would disagree. In a map entitled "Ethnic Regions of Southwest Asia" both the Arab countries *and* Israel are shaded uniformly as "Semitic" with the labels "Arab" and "Jewish" superimposed.[6] This reference serves to illustrate the accurate description of Arabs and Jews as ethnically related, rather than consisting of separate racial groups.

Some textbooks write well about Jewish multiculturalism. In *World Geography Today*, published by Holt, the authors write, "Although most

Israelis practice Judaism, Israel is also multi-ethnic because Jews have emigrated there from all over the world." This point is reinforced with a review question, "Why is Israel's population so multi-ethnic?" The expected answer provided in the teacher's answer key reads, "[B]ecause Jews have immigrated there from all over the world and many Arabs still live there."[7] Holt's *World History: Continuity and Change* includes in its teacher's resources supplied with the text an audio clip of Israeli "ethno-pop" music showcasing Israel as multicultural and multiethnic.[8]

In McDougal Littell's *Ancient World History*, a student sidebar describes the relationship of Jews to the land in post-Roman exile history leading up to the founding of the state of Israel. "Global Impact: The Jewish Diaspora. Centuries of Jewish exile followed the . . . fall of Jerusalem in A.D. 70. . . . Jews fled to many parts of the world, including Europe. In the 1100s, many European Jews were expelled from their homes. Some moved to Turkey, Palestine and Syria. Others went to Poland and neighboring areas. The statelessness of the Jews did not end until the creation of Israel in 1948."[9] This textbook's treatment is probably the best of any we reviewed concerning the historical links between the Diaspora in Roman times and its reversal with the creation of Israel, and one of the few to discuss the expulsion of Jews from all major medieval western European countries.

On the other hand, Holt's *World History: The Human Journey* repeats the assertion of the Arab narrative that Israeli Jews are European colonialists. "Since the late 1800s, Jews from Europe had been establishing small colonies in Palestine."[10] The term "colonies" is a word the Arab narrative uses to describe Jews in the same terms as the European colonial powers that were in the process of being ousted during this era. "Colonies" means outsiders were coming into the region to exploit the land and people, rather than Jews who came to join their coreligionists who had lived in the land continuously since antiquity. To be more accurate, the wording should instead read "since the late 1800s, Jews were increasingly migrating to Ottoman and British mandatory Palestine to join existing Jewish communities."

McDougal Littell's *Modern World History: Patterns of Interaction* recommends a book for the teacher entitled *The New Intifada: Resisting Israel's Apartheid* edited by Roane Carey.[11] By this recommendation, the textbook expresses agreement with Carey and her contributors' inappropriate racial comparison between South Africa and Israel. "A solution that consigns the Palestinians to be Israel's wards in entities amounting, at most, to bantustans is no solution at all. As the system of apartheid is dismantled in South Africa, we must not stand by to see it erected in the West bank and Gaza Strip complete with the stamp of international legitimacy."[12]

AWAIR's *Arab World Studies Notebook* features an expansive section on colonialism, and uses the history of colonialism to delegitimize Israel. The section on "Colonial Legacy" features an Editors' Note that reads, "That colonialism lives can also be seen in lopsided U.S. support for anything Israel does. . . ."[13] In explaining the British Mandate period, the *Notebook* states, "The British had . . . promised Jewish colonists from Europe, who call themselves Zionists, the right to settle and create a homeland in Palestine. The colonization of Palestine led to increasing friction between the Zionists and the Arabs. . . ."[14]

In its section on Jerusalem, the *Notebook* asserts that Israelis in Jerusalem are "colonialists" and calls for an end to the "colonization" of Jerusalem. Reprinting from an Arab League publication, the *Notebook* states: "Other colonial suburbs were built by foreigners in Arab countries, but today no one suggests that Algiers, Tunis, Casablanca, etc., may be rightfully claimed by the Europeans who settled there during the colonial period of recent history. Only in the case of Jerusalem does the colonialist thinking still predominate."[15]

The *Notebook* charges that "since the 1967 war, Israeli settlement on confiscated Arab land in Jerusalem has proceeded quickly in order to establish a claim to the city."[16] It encourages teachers to present Jerusalem as "two cities:" the legitimate "city-shrine," which is "almost exclusively a home to . . . Palestinian Arabs," versus "the European-type colonial suburb-turned-city which foreign Jews built next to the historic religious city-shrine, even though they called it Jerusalem, too."[17] "[T]he 'Old City,' the Jerusalem that most people envisage when they think of the ancient city, is Arab," the materials state.[18]

The accusation that Israel is the remnant of the "colonial legacy" has no basis in historical fact. Israel is a state comprising primarily refugees from Europe, Ethiopia, Arab countries, and the former Soviet Union, and their descendants. In fact they were victims of the colonialist European powers making their escape from Europe rather than agents of the colonial powers. For the most part the major European colonial powers were rarely hospitable dwelling places for Jews. Relatively short periods of full acceptance and integration into European society were outweighed by the far more numerous eras of persecution and subjugation. The loyalty of Jews to their home countries was constantly under suspicion by national authorities and the common people alike. The mass movement of Jews to Poland from Western Europe, the expulsion from Spain, and the Holocaust were the most notable examples of the creation of large numbers of Jewish refugees in the history of the European colonial powers.

There are other, more historically accurate sources than those used by the *Notebook*. Authors Larry Collins and Dominique Lapierre write in *O Jerusalem*, "By the winter day in 1895 when Theodor Herzl witnessed the degradation of Alfred Dreyfus, thirty thousand of Jerusalem's fifty thousand inhabitants were already Jewish."[19] According to *The Statistical Yearbook of Jerusalem*, Jewish population in Jerusalem in 1922 numbered 33,900 while Arabs numbered 28,600.[20] Furthermore, British diplomatic sources wrote "The Mohammedans of Jerusalem are less fanatical than in many other places, owing to the circumstances of their numbers scarcely exceeding one quarter of the whole population,"[21] and by the late 1850s the Jews, "greatly exceed the Moslems in number."[22]

WARS AGAINST ISRAEL

One of the key concepts in the world of anti-Israel propaganda is the obfuscation of the hostility of Arab nations to the founding of the state of Israel in 1948, and thereafter as well. Many textbooks uncritically propagate the Arab narrative of the conflict between Israel and its neighboring countries. They suggest that Israel unilaterally started all the wars and through its own violence and warmongering imposed its will on the Arab nations and the Palestinians. A more complex and accurate presentation would neither by omission nor commission obscure the fact that the violence and formal warfare was initiated by Arab countries as a direct consequence of the adamant refusal to countenance an Israel of any size or shape. Arab states rejected the internationally sanctioned 1947 Partition Plan (approved by vote of the United Nations) and attacked Israel. Most observers would agree that had the Arab countries not attacked Israel in 1948, there would be an independent Palestine today along the lines of the partition plan.

The Arab and Palestinian perspective holds that the pre-1948 influx of Jews into their areas of residence, into a region they felt should belong to

Muslims, was in itself a hostile act. They believe the Jewish settlers' goal was to force them off their land. Therefore, they view the actions of Arab armies in 1948 in attacking Israel after it declared independence as a defensive act and not an act of aggression. Similarly, the participation of Arab armies and Palestinians in subsequent formal wars in 1956, 1967, 1973, and the Palestinian Intifadas were all seen as a response to Israeli aggression against both the Palestinians and Israel's Arab neighbors, to address their unequal power in the situation. Israel started the wars of 1956 and 1967 in order to seize more land for its expansion.

These are fundamental Arab and Palestinian beliefs about the armed conflicts with Israel. The best defense of their position is that Israel in fact did have superior technology supplied by the West in the conflicts after 1948. True, Israel did feel the need for pre-emptive strikes in the 1956 and 1967 wars. However, the Palestinian conclusions do not address the complexity of the region. Throughout its history, Israel has had to devise ways of protecting its civilian population with numerically inferior numbers of soldiers. A key tool in their strategy was to leverage technology to offset the numerical superiority of the military forces arrayed against it. Precisely because of its smaller population, Israel entered into armed conflicts, always with great reluctance and soul searching, because its potential casualties would be more than proportional. Israeli leaders' preference has always been to publicly and privately plead for Arabs and Palestinians to forgo hostilities, in spite of the fact that they foresaw the possibility of an outcome in 1948 and 1967 that would benefit Israel through an increase in the amount of territory under Israeli control.

A relatively small number of textbook titles offer an accurate perspective and can serve as worthy models for emulation. For example, *Harcourt Horizons World History* summarizes Israel's birth. "Jewish leaders announced the creation of Israel as an independent country. In an effort to destroy the new nation, Arab armies . . . attacked it."[23] This is a straightforward description of Arab reaction to partition, unfortunately rare in the textbooks.

World Geography Today, published by Holt, Rinehart and Winston, presents a balanced discussion of Israel's founding that acknowledges Arab attacks and the annexation of Gaza and West Bank by Egypt and Jordan respectively. "In 1947 the United Nations voted to divide Palestine into Jewish and Arab states. When the British withdrew from Palestine the next year, the Jewish leadership declared itself the independent state of Israel. Arab armies from Egypt, Iraq, Jordan (then called Transjordan), Lebanon, and Syria then invaded Israel. Israel pushed the Arab forces back and won more land. . . . At the same time, Jordan and Egypt took over the remaining Arab portions of Palestine."[24] The latter action by the Arab states is omitted by most textbooks.

In Holt's *World History: Continuity & Change*, the depth of the Arab hostility to the implementation of the Partition Plan and its implacable nature is made clear. "Immediately [upon declaring independence], the new Israeli state had to defend itself against invading Arab armies. 'This will be a war of extermination and a momentous massacre,' declared Azzam Pasha, the secretary general of the Arab League."[25] The same textbook reinforces this idea in a review exercise. "Writing to Explain. Write a short essay explaining the challenges Israel faced in its earliest days as a nation. A. Essays should mention invading Arab armies, the Six-Day War, attacks by the Palestine Liberation Organization, and the Yom Kippur War."[26]

The World, another Harcourt product, makes clear who started the 1973 Yom Kippur War. It suggests, in a teacher sidebar: "Discuss the strategic importance of Egypt's attack on Yom Kippur. . . . Point out that Yom Kippur is the Day of Atonement during which Jews ask God to forgive them for any wrongdoings, and it is marked by 24 hours of prayer and fasting."[27] This is one of the few texts to impart, albeit in a sidebar, the implications of the Arab aggression on the holiest day in the Jewish calendar.

On the other hand, many textbooks avoid such direct language about who started the wars. *World History: The Human Journey, Modern World*, by Holt features the following review question. "Q. Sequencing. . . . Use [the copied flowchart of Causes and Effects] to identify the events leading up to the Arab–Israeli war of 1948–1949. A. Causes: . . . Zionist groups waged terrorist campaign against British authorities, UN voted to partition Palestine, Arab countries moved against Israel. . . ."[28] The Jews waged a "terrorist campaign" yet Arab nations only "moved against" Israel. Why assume terrorism by Zionist groups?

World History: The Human Journey, blames Israel and implies Israeli aggression through a timeline entry: "1967. Global Events. Israel fights the Six-Day War *against* Arab neighbors." [emphasis added] The seemingly insignificant choice of *against* instead of *with* in the sentence casts Israel as the belligerent side in the conflict. A more accurate wording would be "Israel and its Arab neighbors fought the Six-Day War."[29]

Likewise McDougal Littell's *Modern World History: Patterns of Interaction*, describes the Arab–Israeli wars in terms that imply Israel started them. Israel is an aggressor that fights wars "against" its neighbors and captures Arab land. For example, "Main Ideas Q. What land did Israel gain from the wars *against* its Arab neighbors?"[30] [emphasis added] The textbook again implies, in a section on the Palestinians, that the Arab-Israel wars were started by the Israelis. "While the United Nations had granted the Palestinians their own homeland, the Israelis had *seized* much of that land, including the West Bank and Gaza Strip, during *its various* wars."[31] [emphasis added]

The wording using the possessive "its" coupled with "various" wars lumps them all inaccurately into the same category: Israel started them all and is aggressive and warlike. The 1948 and 1973 wars were quite different from the pivotal Six-Day War. The first two were initiated by Arab countries through invasion, the latter when Egypt closed Israeli shipping lanes. This is explained, in part, in earlier paragraphs in this text, but there is no proper tie-in to the wording of this key section about Palestinian nationalism. The term "seized" similarly portrays Israel as belligerent.

Modern World History reinforces its perspective on who was responsible for subsequent wars in the wording of a timeline entry. "1967. Israel wins Six-Day War and seizes more Palestinian land for what it calls security purposes."[32] The phrasing *"for what it calls* security purposes" is particularly pejorative—and inaccurate. The largest territory Israel captured was the Sinai from Egypt, which is not part of historic Palestine. The Sinai and the Suez canal formed a significant security buffer against Egypt's vastly more numerous military, the largest in the Arab world.

AWAIR'S *Arab World Studies Notebook* blames Israel alone for the wars in a way that says directly what the textbooks merely imply. In its explanation of "1948: The First Arab–Israeli War," the *Notebook* says, "As a result of Israel's declaration of independence and subsequent continued attempts to force the Palestinian Arab inhabitants out of their land, the neighboring Arab states vowed to come to the rescue of the Palestinian Arab civilian population."[33]

World History: The Human Journey, published by Holt, presents, in a chapter opening entitled, "Africa and the Middle East Since 1945," a time-line entry: "1948 Global Events. The state of Israel is declared; war *begins* with neighboring Arab states."[34] [emphasis added] Reinforcing the problematic phrasing is a review question. "Q. What happened immediately after the British withdrew from Palestine? A. The Zionists proclaimed the state of Israel there, and war *broke out* between Israel and the Arab states."[35] [emphasis added] It is misleading to say war spontaneously and passively "broke out." It should read instead "the Arab states attacked Israel."

Another textbook, by a different publisher, also soft pedals the Arab countries' role in initiating hostilities in 1948. McGraw-Hill/Glencoe's *The World and Its People* says "War soon *broke out* between Israel and its Arab neighbors."[36] [emphasis added]

In Scott Foresman's *The World* (Pearson) the attacks by the regular armies of several Arab nations are described in this manner: "Jews in Palestine celebrated, but Arab states opposed the division of Palestine and refused to recognize Israel. War then *broke out* between Arabs and Jews."[37] [emphasis added]

The systematic trend of hiding the Arab armies' invasion continues into a fourth publisher's product, *World History Since 1500: The Age of Global Integration* published by Thomson Wadsworth. "The Palestinians and the Arab nations refused to recognize the new state, and the first Arab–Israeli war began."[38] The language again hides the Arab countries invasion of Israel.

The following exercise from *World Cultures and Geography: Eastern Hemisphere and Europe* describes its view of the results of the partition plan. "Read and Take Notes. Reading Strategy; Identifying Problems and Solutions. . . . Arabs did not accept plan; Arab–Israeli wars began."[39]

A Prentice Hall offering, *World Cultures: A Global Mosaic* uses the same treatment for the Six-Day War. "In 1967, a third Arab–Israel war *occurred*. The fighting lasted six days."[40] [emphasis added]

Similarly McDougal Littell's *World Geography* summarizes the Arab–Israeli conflict in a timeline "Arab–Israeli Conflict. 1948, The state of Israel is created; war with Arabs *follows* immediately. 1967, Israel *takes control* of Jerusalem, West Bank, and Gaza Strip at the end of the Six-Day War."[41]

[emphasis added] The passage characterizes Israel as the aggressor in 1967 and by implication in 1948 as well.

AWAIR'S *Arab World Studies Notebook* misrepresents the causes of the 1967 Six-Day War and Israel's motivations in the war.

> 1967: The June War . . . Israeli shipping from [the southern port of Eilat] had to pass through Egypt's Straits of Tiran. The port handled a tiny percentage of Israeli shipping, but the closing of the straits during a time of tension between Egypt and Israel was portrayed in Western media as "a noose around Israel's neck." Although negotiations between the involved parties were beginning, Israel had established sufficient pretext for war and launched a "pre-emptive attack" on Egypt, Syria, and Jordan. By the end of this "pre-emptive attack" six days later, Israel had doubled its territory and lost fewer than seven hundred dead. The Arab dead numbered from ten to fifteen thousand.[42]

As the American Jewish Committee's critique of the *Notebook* points out, the claim that the Strait of Tiran was insignificant to Israeli shipping is inaccurate. By closing the strait, Egypt cut off all Israeli shipping bound for Eilat, Israel's chief oil port and its gateway to Africa and Asia, and through which passed 30 percent of the country's mineral exports. The *Notebook* views Israel's preemptive strike with derision (as indicated by the repeated use of quotation marks around "preemptive attack"). Israel had been suffering from ongoing attacks over several years prior to the war by terrorists on all its borders, with the active support of neighboring governments. On May 15, 1967, Egyptian and Syrian troops began deploying in large numbers on Israel's borders. Nasser continued his war-mongering rhetoric and closed the strait to Israeli shipping.

Notwithstanding the *Notebook*'s curt dismissal of the veracity of Western media reporting, there was clear evidence that war was imminent and that Israel's concerns about its survival were well founded. This background is essential in any study of the Six-Day War.

Finally, the *Notebook*'s claim about the magnitude of Israeli casualties is misleading. While Israel did lose considerably fewer lives than did the Arab armies in absolute terms, Israel, with a small population at the time, suffered losses of dead and wounded in six days proportional to its entire population on a par with the number of Americans lost in eight years of fighting in Vietnam. Moreover, the *Notebook* is cynical when it suggests that Israel's loss of life was insignificant because it gained so much territory. The largest portion of the territory gained in the war, the Sinai, was returned to Egypt in peace negotiations.[43]

ARABS WANT PEACE—ISRAEL DOES NOT

Arab hostility to Israel continued to play out even as attempts at peace-making unfolded in the years after Israel's founding. Some textbooks portray this accurately. *Modern World History*, published by McDougal Littell, makes plain that the Arab world looked upon Egyptian President Anwar Sadat's peace initiative, welcomed in the West and Israel, as a betrayal of their uniformly hostile stance against Israel's existence. The following appears in a teacher sidebar "Efforts at Peace: Critical Thinking. Q. Why do you think Sadat's peace initiative enraged Arabs? A. Possible answer: It offered to recognize Israel. Q. How are Yitzhak Rabin and Anwar Sadat similar? A. Possible answer: Both were courageous leaders who were killed for their willingness to compromise in the interest of peace."[44] The perspective of the passage is evenhanded and factual.

Palestinians argue that, although Israelis may publicly profess interest in peace and negotiations, it is only a cover for the Israelis' expansionist aims and the continuing subjugation of the Palestinians through the exercise of greater power. The Israelis did not and do not want peace, but the Arabs do. This is the Palestinians' belief. The best defense of their position is that Israel did not allow even the limited Palestinian self-rule called for in the Oslo accords. On the other hand, the Palestinian perspective does not take into account Israeli fears for the security of its civilian population against numerically superior Arab armies and terrorists alike. For example, after the 1967 war, Israelis thought that their victory would bring long sought recognition and peace in exchange for the return of the territories it captured. Instead, Arab countries responded with the Khartoum declaration: no recognition of Israel, no negotiations, no peace with it. Similarly, the Palestinian refusal to recognize and live in peace with the Israelis is well documented. Many Palestinians believed that the Oslo Accords had turned the PLO leadership into a tool of the Israeli state in suppressing their own people. Palestinian public opinion has been consistent in its support of violent tactics against the Israelis.

An accurate perspective requires acknowledgment that Sadat came to Israel in response to the Israeli government's invitation. *World History: The*

Human Experience by Glencoe says plainly that "[Sadat] accepted an invitation to visit Israel . . ."[45] The Glencoe text makes clear the mutuality of the peace moves, but some other books make Sadat the only hero.

For example, *World Cultures and Geography: Eastern Hemisphere and Europe* presents material designed for slower learners in another teacher sidebar. The exercise "Activity Options, Differentiating Instruction: Less Proficient Readers, Sequencing" requires students to construct the following timeline:

1947	UN divided Palestine
1948	Israel declared an independent state, First Arab–Israeli War won by Israel
1964	PLO formed
1967	Second Arab–Israeli War won by Israel
1973	Third Arab–Israeli War won by Israel
1977	Egypt sought peace with Israel
1993	Israel and the PLO signed agreement[46]

To say merely that Egypt "sought" peace with Israel implies that Egypt was peace loving prior to 1977. Since 1948 it had served as the most powerful frontline confrontation state in violent opposition to Israel, viewing itself as the standard bearer of Arab nationalism. Particularly after Gamal Abdel Nasser assumed the presidency in 1954, he identified military action against Israel as a means to assert Arab unity and power. In addition, the Intifadas, the Palestinian uprisings beginning in 1987, do not appear in the timeline at all, but they were as significant (and bloody) as the formal wars Israel fought with the armies of Arab countries. Israel did not "win" them. The first Intifada was an important prelude to the peace agreement with the PLO, and the second was the Palestinian response to the failed negotiations at Camp David.

Supplemental teaching materials depict Israel as responsible for the failure of the peace process rather than the hostility of the Arab states. The *Arab World Studies Notebook* states that "Israel rejected all peace offers."[47] The Arab Cultural Center's *Educational Guide* features an essay entitled, "The Peace Process as an Instrument of Oppression," which says,

> The reality on the ground is that Israel is using the peace process as a convenient cover for expanding settlements and tightening control. . . . For many years, Israel gave the impression that it has always been

genuinely seeking peace. . . . Today it is apparent to an increasing number of people that the Palestinians are the ones who are actively and unflinchingly endeavoring . . . for a permanent peace. . . .[48]

This is outright propaganda. Alan Dershowitz writes, "Israel has offered the Palestinians every reasonable opportunity to make peace, but the Palestinians have rejected every such offer, most recently at Camp David and Taba in 2000–2001."[49]

REFUGEES: PALESTINIAN AND JEWISH

The 1947 partition of British mandatory Palestine into two states, one for Jews and the other for Arabs, was internationally recognized and approved by the General Assembly of the United Nations. It followed the pattern of the contemporaneous partition of British-ruled India into Hindu-majority India and Muslim Pakistan, initiated by the British as the colonial ruler, when the two nations attained independence.

As Arab armies invaded Israel after the UN partition, boundaries moved and the Arab and Jewish populations shifted. The territory the military of each side was able to conquer and hold was not static. Battle lines did not necessarily follow the partition plan's boundaries for the Arab and Jewish states nor the pattern of Arab and Jewish residents. During the fighting, Arabs moved from Israeli held areas to the territory held by the Arab armies and Jews who lived in Arab held areas moved to the areas controlled by Israel. The shifting of populations and boundaries after Israel declared independence was much like in India, Africa, and the Balkans, and earlier in the twentieth century, Turkey and Greece. Joan Peters writes in *From Time Immemorial: Origins of the Arab–Jewish Conflict Over Palestine*, about the case of the Indian subcontinent. "The exchange between India and Pakistan in the 1950s was overwhelming in magnitude: 8,500,000 Sikhs and Hindus from Pakistan fled to India, and roughly 6,500,000 Muslims moved from India to Pakistan."[50]

Textbooks should accurately address all the complexities of the refugee problem, including Jewish refugees from Arab lands.

* The number of Arabs who fled their homes in 1948 from the land that became Israel as a result of its creation in 1948

- The number of Jews who fled Arab countries, also as a result of the creation of Israel in 1948
- Where did all the refugees settle, Jews and Arabs?
- Why did they resettle where they did?
- What solution was found for their resettlement?

The textbook treatment of the complex dimensions of this most sensitive Arab–Israeli issue is highly problematic in many cases. The use of loaded terminology and the complete omission of the Jewish refugees required for proper context are common.

THEMES OF PROBLEMS WITH
TREATMENT OF THE REFUGEE ISSUE

There are five problematic areas in the textbooks that deal with refugees. First, some textbooks and supplemental materials attempt to portray most or all of the Palestinian refugees as "expelled" by Israel. The reality is more complex. Some were expelled, some fled from war, some chose not to live with Jews.

Second, some textbooks imply it was Israel, not Arab countries, who put Palestinians in refugee camps, a claim that is historically unsound. There are 1.3 million Arab citizens of Israel who do not live in refugee camps and another 1.3 million who live in refugee camps created by Arab governments.[51]

Third, the language of the textbooks reflects the terminology of the Arab narrative. In fact the refugee "camps" have been in existence for nearly sixty years and feature permanent concrete-block housing and UN infrastructure.

Fourth, there is no textbook that deals directly with the Jewish refugees from Arab countries who fled as conditions became intolerable during the backlash after the creation of Israel. The fact that a refugee *exchange* occurred is not acknowledged at all. This is a major omission.

Fifth, some textbooks gloss over the Middle East origin of many Israeli immigrants and portray Jewish immigration as if it were exclusively from Europe.

FLIGHT OR EXPULSION?

Most texts and some supplemental materials repeat, or at a minimum support, the Palestinian point of view that Israel's pre-independence Jewish leadership and its official military forcibly expelled most or all of those Arab inhabitants who left what became Israel. Palestinians believe an organized campaign of ethnic cleansing was conducted by Israeli forces to erase the Palestinian presence from the land to make room for Jews to move in. The best defense of the Palestinian position is that cases of Palestinians being expelled did in fact occur. On the other hand, they represented only a partial picture. Most historians agree that the exodus was some combination of flight in response to various factors and expulsion by Jewish military forces.

The exodus of Arabs from Jewish-held areas, as much as the deliberate policies of the pre-independence Jews or Israelis after May 1948, was due to tremendous fear on the part of the Arabs in reaction to the departure of their leaders. Historian Howard Sachar writes,

> The most obvious reason for the mass exodus was the collapse of Palestine Arab political institutions that ensued upon the flight of the Arab leadership—at the very moment when that leadership was most needed. The departure of mukhtars, judges and cadis from Haifa and the New City of Jerusalem, from Jaffa, Safed and elsewhere, dealt a grave blow to the Arab population. The semifeudal character of Arab society rendered the illiterate fellah almost entirely dependent on the landlord and cadi, and once this elite was gone, the Arab peasant was terrified by the likelihood of remaining in an institutional and cultural void.[52]

McGraw-Hill's *Traditions and Encounters* achieves a balanced and complete picture in describing the Arab flight and the implications for Arab neighbors of Israel. "During and after the [War of Independence] fighting, hundreds of thousands of Palestinian Arabs fled, first from the war and then from the prospect of life under Jewish political control, and for the surrounding Arab states these refugees served as a symbol of the Arab's defeat in Palestine and as a spur to Arab nations' determination to rid their region of the hated presence of Israel."[53] This is good, factual, and contains a lack of distortion.

On the other hand, *World History: The Human Journey, Modern World*, published by Holt, incorrectly asserts all or most of the refugees were expelled by Israel. Then it inaccurately implies there were negotiations over the Palestinian refugees in which Israel refused Arab proposals for the refugees' return or the payment of compensation. "Hundreds of thousands of Palestinians who had been expelled from the land claimed by Israel were living as refugees in camps. The Israeli government would not allow the return of the Palestinians, nor would it pay the Palestinians for lands seized. Palestinian lands were given to Jewish immigrants."[54] In fact, Arab nations refused to recognize or negotiate with Israel in any way.

One high school level textbook, which has the space and audience adequate to convey a nuanced, accurate approach, gets it wrong. *World Civilizations*, published by Thomson Wadsworth, describes the exodus of Arabs as follows. "But the triumphant *Israelis* then expelled many hundreds of thousands of Palestinian Arabs from their ancestral lands, *creating* a reservoir of bitterness that guaranteed hostility for decades to come, with both Palestinian Arabs and Jews making mutually contradictory claims to a 'Right of Return.'"[55] [emphasis added] According to this text, Israelis solely created the problem.

AWAIR's *Arab World Studies Notebook* asserts that "[l]ong before May 15, 1948 . . . , armed Jewish groups had driven much of the Palestinian population from their homes, thus capturing most of the Palestinians' land . . ." The *Notebook* promotes a BBC Thames Television video entitled *Palestine: Abdication*. The synopsis reads in part: "In November 1947 the U.N., due to U.S. pressure, votes to partition; violence breaks out in full, as Jewish forces begin emptying Palestinian cities and villages. By April of 1948, 700,000 Arabs had been evicted or had fled."[56]

The following two items in *World History: The Human Experience* by Glencoe are its only coverage of the refugee issue and are found in two different textbook sections. The first passage reads "[a]s a result of partition, more than 700,000 Palestinians became homeless." The second, covering a later era, is headed by a picture captioned "Palestinian Arabs in Exile." The accompanying sidebar reads "The Storyteller. An Israeli observer records the expulsion of Arabs from Israeli-held territory: 'Masses of people marched on behind the next. . . . From close up it was sad to watch this trek of thousands going into exile...' —from *The People of Nowhere*, Danny Rubenstein, 1991."[57] The wording implies all of the refugees were expelled, and its lack of clarity as to whether the passage and picture describe 1948, 1967, or 1991, sows confusion in the minds of the reader. The picture appears to be a group of 400 Hamas men that Israel deported to Lebanon in 1992 in response to a series of attacks on Israeli soldiers and not related at all to the exodus of women and men described in the "Storyteller" text.

The refugee issue is also mishandled in *World Geography Today*, published by Harcourt/Holt. A graph entitled "Top Five Sources of Refugees (2002 Estimates)" shows 3,000,000 from "Palestine," the second highest after Afghanistan.[58] Compare this figure with the 726,000 at Israel's founding cited by United Nations sources. Such a high figure without a breakdown of its components is misleading. The vast majority of a figure of such magnitude must be descendants of those created in 1948. The failure to clarify these issues leads students to draw incorrect conclusions.

WHO PUT THE PALESTINIAN REFUGEES IN CAMPS?

Some of the textbooks strongly imply that Israel itself placed and kept Palestinian refugees in the camps, in agreement with Palestinian beliefs. This has no defensible logic.

The idea that Israel, surrounded by hostile Arab governments and devoid of any influence there, could affect the Arab states' refusal to integrate or resettle the Palestinians seems farfetched. These governments, with the exception of Jordan, carried out a deliberate, cynical, and remarkably inhumane policy of keeping the refugees in squalid camps on their territories so that the refugees would serve as political pawns in world opinion to pressure Israel.

World History: The Human Journey, Modern World, published by Holt correctly says "Most Arab countries refused to resettle the Palestinians, arguing that such a move would justify the seizure of their lands or lessen the pressure on Israel to return the lands."[59]

The World, by Pearson/Scott Foresman adds geographic confusion when it says, "[d]uring the war [of Israel's independence] hundreds of thousands of Palestinians had fled *Palestine* and settled in refugee camps in *Israel*."[60] Many of the refugee camps were in the West Bank and Gaza, ruled by Egypt and Jordan in 1948, or in other Arab countries. *Some* of the camps came under Israeli rule in 1967, some nineteen years later.

McDougal Littell's *World Geography* implies that it was Israel rather than the Arab countries who forced the Palestinian refugees into the squalid camps. "Caught in the middle of this turmoil were Palestinian

Arabs. . . . Many of these people had roots in Palestine that went back for centuries. They either fled their homes or were forced into UN-sponsored refugee camps just outside Israel's borders. The land designated for Palestinians on the West Bank and Gaza Strip is under Israeli control."[61]

Modern World History by McDougal Littell features a Palestinian writer's false claim that Israel rather than Arab governments placed the refugees in the camps. A prominent item in the student text, set off in a box, is entitled "Analyzing Primary Sources. The Palestinian View/The Israeli View." The "Palestinian View" was written by Fawaz Turki (attributed to *"The Arab–Israeli Conflict"*) and reads "these people [Israelis] . . . shoved us in refugee camps."[62]

WHY CALL A COMMUNITY IN EXISTENCE FOR 60 YEARS A "CAMP"?

The Palestinian narrative holds that the communities where Palestinian refugees settled in 1948 and 1967 were only temporary dwelling places that would be rapidly disbanded as their residents received redress through resettlement in their original homes. Their beliefs have remained unchanged in the intervening years, so they prefer to keep the camp terminology to reinforce the temporary nature of the communities.

The terminology of victimization used in the Arab narrative and repeated uncritically in the textbooks extends to the communities in which the original refugees and their descendants have lived for almost sixty years. Permanent housing and infrastructure make it difficult to imagine why, other than for pure propaganda purposes, these communities are called "camps."

The following passage in McDougal Littell's *World Geography* is typical. "Today, most of the Palestinians living in the *camps* were actually born there and have never been to the lands designated for the Palestinian state. The *camps* house upwards of 35,000 people and some as many as 50,000 people. The UN and other nations provide money for education and health care needs." [emphasis added] A student sidebar reads "Connect to the Issues: Population. Palestinian Refugee *Camps*. In 1949, the UN authorized the creation of 53 Palestinian refugee *camps*. The *camps* were supposed to be used only for a short time until the Palestinians were resettled. That was over 50 years ago."[63] [emphasis added]

The same textbook makes an egregious comparison of Palestinian refugees to Native Americans on reservations in the United States. A set of questions and answers in a teacher sidebar dovetails with a less detailed student sidebar. "Connect to the Issues, Population: Palestinian Refugee Camps. Have students compare and contrast the predicament of Palestinians in the Eastern Mediterranean to that of Native Americans in the United States. Teachers might wish to outline the history of the displacement of Native Americans by European settlers, and later, the creation of reservations by the U.S. government."[64]

The strong inference is that Israel created Palestinian refugee camps and forced the refugees to stay there to live in subjugation. The Arab nations took that action, not Israel.

OMISSION OF JEWISH REFUGEES

Most textbooks make no mention of what essentially became a refugee *exchange*: hundreds of thousands of Jews, residents of Arab countries for thousands of years, were expelled or chose to flee hostile anti-Semitic societies. Arab governments and their citizens alike, after Israel's repulsion of their invading armies, made life difficult or impossible for Jews living under their rule. No matter that Jews had lived in Iraq, for example, for millennia and that it was a cradle of Jewish civilization in biblical as well as post-biblical times, the site of the crafting of the Babylonian Talmud. Historian Howard Sachar writes "Even [in August 1948] the Damoclean sword of Moslem xenophobia was descending on the large and historic Jewish communities of North Africa and the Islamic Middle East. Between 1948 and 1957, as a consequence of government pressure, economic strangulations, and physical pogroms, some 467,000 Jews would be compelled to flee their ancestral homes in Moslem lands. The largest number of them would find asylum in Israel. . . ."[65]

An organization, JIMENA (Jews Indigenous to the Middle East and North Africa), was founded to remedy the lack of knowledge and recognition of these Jewish refugees. Its mission is "to advocate and educate about the history and plight of the Jews indigenous to the Middle East and North Africa. . . . To reestablish historical context [o]ur story must be returned to the narrative of the modern Middle East from which it has been erased."[66]

The Palestinians believe their circumstances have nothing to do with Jewish refugees from the Arab nations created at roughly the same time as they were, regardless of whether the Jewish refugees were resettled in Israel or sought refuge elsewhere. The best defense of their position is that they argue that actions of Arab governments were beyond their control and that they should not have to pay the price for the actions of those governments against Jews or anyone. Palestinians feel that to consider injustices done to other groups by the same actors would lessen the central position the Palestinians occupy in any solution to the conflict. On the other hand, Palestinians applaud those same Arab governments for their military action against Israel which produced the Palestinian refugee exodus. Had the Arab armies not attacked Israel a Palestinian state would have existed from 1948 on and any refugee displacement would have been significantly less.

World History: Continuity and Change by Holt, to its credit, does mention the Jewish refugee side of the refugee exchange, explaining the Middle Eastern origin of hundreds of thousands of Jews who were resettled in Israel. "Between 1949 and 1952, roughly 600,000 Jews, mostly refugees from Eastern Europe and the Arab states, made their homes in Israel,"[67] but even this description does not begin to describe the conditions in Arab countries that led these Jews to flee and seek refuge in Israel. Conditions of harassment, violence, financial and property confiscations, and governmental threats of expulsion reached a crescendo in countries such as Iraq when Israel was established in 1948. The establishment of Israel served both as a convenient excuse for despotic regimes to act upon centuries of hostility against the Jewish population as well as the impetus for harsher and renewed pogroms spurred by resentment at Israel's victory in the 1948 War of Independence.[68]

One textbook steers the discussion of the refugee issue away from Israelis of Middle Eastern origin and towards those with European origins. *World Cultures and Geography: Eastern Hemisphere and Europe*, published by McDougal Littell is especially egregious, offering the following exercise in a teacher sidebar:

> Activity Options, Multiple Learning Styles: Visual/Interpersonal. . . . Task. Tracing the movement of Jews and Palestinian Arabs to and from Palestine after World War II. Purpose. To understand the relationship between geography and history in the region . . . Activity.

> Have students work in pairs to trace the movements of Jews and Palestinians in the region after World War II. Have them draw arrows on the outline map from the various countries in Europe from which the Jews came to Palestine and also indicate on the map where Palestinians fled after the partition of Palestine. Have students write a summary of these events.[69]

Jewish immigrants' country of origin is restricted to Europe. Perhaps it is to avoid completely the discussion of the large number of Jews forced to leave their homes in Arab countries who found refuge in Israel. Nevertheless the inclusion of Jewish refugees from Arab countries is required for an accurate picture of the complex overall refugee question.

The treatment of the three issues related to Israel's founding in instructional materials that are covered in this chapter is troubling on several counts. A few textbooks include the ethnic diversity of Israeli Jews and their Middle Eastern roots, while on the other hand one textbook in particular teaches only about Israelis with origins in Europe. Some instructional materials associate the establishment of Israel with European colonialism, comparing Israelis to Europeans who settled in Arab lands during the heyday of European empires. In this view, Israelis are colonists who do not belong there.

Virtually everywhere else in the world refugees have been absorbed and resettled. But in the case of the Palestinians, they were not absorbed, even though the majority of them live in the area the UN designated for an Arab state. At the same time that some of the Palestinians became refugees, a violent backlash against Jews occurred in many Arab countries in retaliation for Israel's founding. Hundreds of thousands of Jews had to flee their homes and found refuge in Israel.

CHAPTER EIGHT

TERRORISM AND INTERNAL CONFLICT

Textbooks do not adequately explain the founding of Israel as a moral redressing from the United Nations for the injustice of the Holocaust and the need to fulfill the national aspirations of the Jewish people. Instead, its founding is reduced to the alleged selection of terrorism as a policy by Israeli forces. Violence occurred but was rejected by most Jews as a strategy, and most historians would agree it was the diplomatic and political efforts of Jewish and Gentile leaders that facilitated the establishment of a Jewish state. In contrast to their overemphasis on Jewish violence, many textbooks and some supplemental materials consistently reflect the Arab narrative that seeks to push the consistent and widespread use of terrorism by the Palestinians against Israel far into the background. The PLO, founded to destroy Israel as called for in its charter until its modification in the 1990s, is recast in a more benign light as merely an advocate for a Palestinian state.

Textbook lessons on the Palestinian Intifadas or uprisings against Israeli presence in the West Bank and Gaza are one dimensional presentations of a complex reality. A wide variety of often violent Palestinian actions are reduced to "civil disobedience." Textbook publishers often want to maximize the visual depiction of school age children, peers of their student readers, wherever possible. The result is an exaggeration of the role of children participating in the revolts.

TERRORISM

Textbooks often describe the founding of Israel as a successful Jewish terrorist campaign. They generally adopt a narrative that holds that both Arabs and Jews had their terrorists and both practiced violence in roughly the same proportion. In this view, neither side's practices are in the interests of long term peace or global stability. The attempt to be "even-handed" actually distorts history and contemporary reality.

The use of terrorism against Israeli civilians has been employed as a deliberate policy, first by Arab governments and later by the Palestine Liberation Organization, Hamas, and Hezbollah in an attempt to destroy Israel. There is no equivalent on the Israeli side. There was no parallel diversity of opinion nor open debate in the Arab world on this issue at the time, and in most quarters, there still is not. As in the case of other controversial aspects of the Arab–Israeli conflict, there are few textbooks that present any of this context for the student or the teacher.

The textbooks' and supplemental materials' discussion about terrorism makes extensive use of terminology which is not consistently applied. Our analysis shows that Arab violence and extremism is described in relatively benign terms while Israeli actions and reactions are cast in a largely negative light.

Virtually all textbooks describe the founding of the PLO in 1964. But, as is the case concerning the refugee issue, the years between Israel's founding in 1948 and the Six-Day War in 1967 are often glossed over to the point of confusion. More than one textbook implies that the PLO's founding three years prior to that war was actually in reaction to Israel's victory in the war three years later. Many textbooks also fail to mention the Arab rejection of the 1947 UN partition that would have created an Arab state and the actions by the Arab nations that prevented the establishment of an Arab state in the areas of mandatory Palestine that ended up in Arab hands in 1948.

Palestinian goals and tactics are clearly stated in the Palestine National Charter:

> Armed struggle is the only way to liberate Palestine. Thus it is the overall strategy, not merely a tactical phase. . . . Commando action constitutes the nucleus of the Palestinian popular liberation war. . . .

The liberation of Palestine, from an Arab viewpoint, is a national (qawmi) duty and it attempts to repel the Zionist and imperialist aggression against the Arab homeland, and aims at the elimination of Zionism in Palestine. . . . The partition of Palestine in 1947 and the establishment of the state of Israel are entirely illegal, regardless of the passage of time, . . . Since the liberation of Palestine will destroy the Zionist and imperialist presence. . . .[1]

Israel and the PLO agreed to recognize each other in negotiations during the early 1990s. PLO Chairman Yasser Arafat wrote in a letter to Israeli Prime Minister Rabin dated September 9, 1993, "[T]hose articles of the Palestinian Covenant which deny Israel's right to exist, and the provisions of the Covenant which are inconsistent with the commitments of this letter are now inoperative and no longer valid."[2]

The founding objective of the PLO is often characterized in the textbooks as advocacy for a Palestinian state, an objective that most nations in the world would endorse, including a majority of Israelis. However, as historian Howard Sachar documents and a few textbooks correctly recount, the 1964 goal was more violent and absolute: the destruction of all of Israel, without regard to the territories that Israel captured in 1967.

Actually, the decision had been made as early as the Arab summit meeting of January 1964, when the Palestinians were formally authorized "to carry out their role in liberating their homeland and determining their destiny." Several months later, an assembly of Palestine Arabs was convened in Hashemite [Jordanian] Jerusalem, and from its proceedings emerged the Palestine Liberation Organization. The PLO goal, baldly stated, was "to attain the objective of liquidating Israel," and for that purpose to establish a "Palestine Liberation army." To ensure his own tight control, . . . Nasser placed the Sinai and the Gaza Strip at the PLO's "disposal."[3]

Absent too, for the most part, is any openly stated linkage drawn between the long history of Arab terrorism and Israeli fears. Supplemental materials posit that terrorism against Israel is justifiable and deny links between radical Islam and terrorism. The reversal of the perceived Israeli and Arab roles as David and Goliath respectively that occurred as a result of Israel's victory in the Six-Day War forms the backdrop of the backward and forward recasting of all Israeli history.

DIFFERENT STANDARDS OF TERMINOLOGY

Before we examine the individual themes related to terrorism, it is useful to summarize the use of terminology which applies to all the themes. Table 8.1 summarizes the use of terminology describing violence by both sides in various textbooks.

The phrasing of passages describing Arabs studiously avoids words such as "terrorist" and "attack" in favor of the more benign, even romantic terms of a liberation movement. "Armed struggle" sounds less threatening and more honorable than "terrorist attacks on unarmed civilians." "Guerillas" is a romanticized term favored by Latin American "freedom fighters," for example. The U.S. civil rights movement made use of nonviolent "civil disobedience. " The Reverend Dr. Martin Luther King, Jr. did not advocate rock throwing, rioting, and firing of weapons. He certainly did not endorse violent stabbings, massacres, hijackings, or bombings targeting civilian airliners or athletes. The widespread extent of terrorism as a Palestinian policy and tactic is dismissed out of hand by the phrasing "a *few* fanatics."

On the other hand, language used to describe Jews exaggerates the scope of violent actions. The fringe elements of Jewish extremists in existence for a few years morphs into a boundless "terrorist campaign" which is given outsized significance. Israeli defensive measures in response to terrorist attacks by Palestinians are characterized in harsh terms. The words "settlers" and "colonists" to describe Israeli civilians are favored

---

Table 8.1: Comparison of the Terminology of Middle East Violence

Good Arabs / Bad Jews: A Political Glossary

Palestinians	Israelis
Armed Struggle	Terrorist campaign
Guerillas	Forceful bombings and assassinations
Rebels	Settlers/colonists
A few fanatics	Zionist assault
Civil disobedience	Repays violence with violence
Unarmed youth	Militarized

because they elicit unsympathetic images that Israeli Jews are European "colonialists."

The word "Zionist" is paired with "assault" which makes the subject of the phrase seem cruel. "Repays violence with violence" equates terrorism with self-defense and other forms of military action. "Militarized" also castigates Israelis, evoking thoughts about aggressive military states.

A considerable number of textbooks seem to wish away the history of Palestinian terrorism. Terrorism against Israelis is portrayed as somehow different, more excusable, and even as a justifiable tactic, especially in supplemental materials. Encouraging terrorism was an official policy to oppose Israel employed by the Arab nations during the first several decades of Israel's existence and certainly was the principal means employed by Palestinians and the PLO when it was formed in 1964 and for long afterwards. Terrorist attacks continue to this day.

ISRAEL'S FOUNDING AND JEWISH TERRORISM

The Palestinian perspective is that Israelis used terrorism as a policy against Arab civilians and British forces during the period before and after their declaration of independence. It is their belief that they were victims of this terrorism. In defense of their argument, there were rare acts of violence against civilians committed by Jewish forces, most notably the events at the village of Deir Yassin. On the other hand, the acts were committed by Jewish fringe groups. The Israeli leadership disavowed the acts of violence.

World History: The Human Journey, Modern World by Holt addresses the terrorism at Israel's founding of only the Jewish side in the conflict. "Meanwhile [after the Holocaust] extremist Zionist groups waged a terrorist campaign against British authorities. In 1946 a group called the Irgun, led by Menachem Begin . . . blew up the King David Hotel in Jerusalem. Eventually a virtual state of war existed between the British and the Zionists."[4] The King David bombing is important, especially since Menachem Begin later became prime minister. The hotel was the British military headquarters and a warning was telephoned in advance but these facts are omitted. There is no mention of Arab terrorism against Jews in the run up to the end of the mandate and in the decades before. For example, during the period August 23–28, 1929 Sachar reports, "the [Arab] mob attacked the Orthodox Jewish quarters [in Jerusalem] . . . Hebron . . . Haifa and Jaffa, even in Tel Aviv. Numerous Jewish agricultural villages were similarly attacked. . . . By [August 28] 133 Jews had been killed, 399 wounded."[5] The textbook avoids the word "terrorism" in its description of any Arab or Palestinian violence, until the mention of Hamas in the 1994-1995 time period, an odd omission.

Nor is there any mention that the Jewish leadership in Palestine was aghast at Begin's action at the King David Hotel. "In fact, the [Jewish] Agency was no less horrified than the British government by the King David bombing. Ben-Gurion, who had never brought himself totally to disavow earlier underground raids on British installations, now furiously anathemized the Etzel [the Irgun] and urged Palestine Jewry to turn its members in wherever they were discovered."[6] Tactics in the struggle against the Arabs were a source of debate and concern to the Jewish leadership. Jewish leader Chaim Weizmann, later to become Israel's first president, described in 1944 the tactics of the most extremist factions such as Lech'i as "'the tragic, futile, un-Jewish resort to terrorism.'" He and other Jewish leaders regarded these factions as ungovernable. In addition, the command of the Haganah, the mainstream Jewish military that would become the Israeli Army after statehood, immediately repudiated the attack, and then the Jewish government did likewise.[7] None of this essential background is reflected in the text, even in summary format. An accurate picture would require both a more honest appraisal of Arab terrorism and the rejection of terrorism by Jewish leaders.

World History: Continuity and Change, by Holt, uses loaded terminology. "Some [Zionist] extremists even formed terrorist groups . . . to drive the British out of Palestine."[8] Why not call the Zionist extremists "guerillas?" There is a double standard operative.

The same textbook tackles the significant and sensitive incident in Deir Yassin, but does not provide complete context, and thereby misleads.

> When the war ended in 1949 . . . over half a million Arab refugees had fled the country. Many Arabs fled as a result of the terror inspired by an Irgun assault on the Arab village of Deir Yassin, where men, women and children were massacred. Such actions frightened other Arabs into flight. The Irgun released statements intended to heighten Arab fears: "We intend to attack, conquer and keep [territory] until we have the whole of Palestine . . . in a greater Jewish state . . . We hope to improve our methods in future and make it possible to spare women and children." The ploy worked, but the fleeing Palestinians created another major refugee problem.[9]

While the text correctly identifies the Irgun as an "extremist organization," (another participant was Lech'i, the "Stern Gang," even more radical than the Irgun) the assault on Deir Yassin is controversial and this textbook does not treat the various aspects of the incident with the required care. Despite its earlier characterization of the Irgun as an extremist pre-independence force against the British, the sequence of the material in the text implies that the Deir Yassin incident happened after Israel was declared a state, with the further implication that the state of Israel committed the atrocity as a policy. In fact the incident occurred April 9, 1948, more than a month before the declaration of independence.

The Earth and Its Peoples by Houghton Mifflin adopts "evenhanded" but erroneous terminology in describing Arab and Jewish actions during the Mandate. "The Arabs unleashed a guerrilla uprising against the British in 1936, and Jewish groups turned to militant tactics a few years later."[10] However, unlike some of the other texts cited in this section, it does not use the word "terrorism" about one side and not the other.

Terminology used by *World Civilizations: The Global Experience* (Prentice Hall) is similar to other textbooks described previously in this section. Its language generates an unsympathetic reaction to Zionist actions. "The [pre-independence] Zionist assault [on the British in response to limitations on immigration] was spearheaded by a regular Zionist military force, the Haganah, and several underground terrorist organizations."[11] Similarly, language in describing Palestinian terrorism does not allow for explaining a full context of the Israeli response. "A wave of suicide bombings by Palestinians targeted Israeli civilians, while the Israeli government attacked Palestinian cities and refugee camps in turn."[12] Israeli military leaders avoided civilians wherever they could, given that Palestinian terrorists hid in Palestinian civilian population centers. Palestinian terrorists, on the other hand, specifically targeted civilians.

THE FOUNDING OF THE PLO AND ITS TRUE GOAL

Today's Palestinian perspective is that the Palestine Liberation Organization was founded for the purpose of achieving Palestinian self-determination in a state of their own. Their view is that the denial of Israel's right to exist outlined in the Palestinian Covenant and reflected in PLO policy to end any Israeli presence in all of mandatory Palestine are unimportant in the larger picture of the struggle for Palestinian independence.

PLO Chairman Yasser Arafat's statements during the Oslo negotiating process of the 1990s that these provisions of the covenant were null and void showed the lack of importance of the provisions. True, today's Palestinian leadership under Palestinian Authority President Mahmoud Abbas recognizes Israel and seeks a state in the West Bank Gaza and Jerusalem according to their borders that existed before the Six-Day War. On the other hand, the fundamental Palestinian opposition to Israel cannot be dismissed as unimportant or a relic of the past. For example, the position of the Hamas leadership, elected by Palestinians in 2005, has been quite consistent. The movement does not recognize Israel and has refused to renounce violence.

A few textbooks do get elements of this history correct. *World History: Continuity and Change* by Harcourt/Holt defines the PLO in a glossary entry in the following terms. "Palestine Liberation Organization. Umbrella organization for a variety of Palestinian nationalist groups opposed to the existence of Israel."[13] This direct and correct statement of the ultimate goal contrasts with other texts which instead say outright or imply that the PLO's goal was to obtain a Palestinian state limited to the *territories occupied by Israel in 1967.*

Even *World Cultures and Geography: Eastern Hemisphere and Europe* by McDougal Littell, whose poor content on many issues is prominent in this analysis, says openly "In 1964, some Palestinian people formed the Palestine Liberation Organization (PLO). The PLO refused to recognize Israel's right to exist."[14]

McGraw-Hill's *Glencoe World History* likewise states clearly the PLO's objective regarding the whole of Palestine. "In 1964, the Egyptians took the lead in forming the Palestine Liberation Organization (PLO) to represent the interests of the Palestinians. The PLO believed that only the Palestinian peoples had the right to create a state in Palestine." The passage continues with an unequivocal description of Palestinian terrorism: "At the same time, a guerilla movement called al-Fatah, headed by the PLO political leader Yasir Arafat, began to launch terrorist attacks on Israeli territory. Terrorist actions against Israel continued for decades."[15] Glencoe's *World History: The Human Experience,* supplies even better historical context when it mentions terrorist provocations from Egyptian territory as a motivation for the Israeli participation in the Sinai campaign. "[In the 1956 Suez Crisis] Israel wanted to end Egyptian guerrilla attacks on its borders."[16] The same textbook clearly states the liquidation of Israel was the intent of the PLO. "In their struggle for nationhood, the Palestinians in 1964 formed the Palestine Liberation Organization (PLO) to eliminate Israel and to create a Palestinian state."[17]

World History Since 1500: The Age of Global Integration published by Thomson Wadsworth records in a glossary entry: "Palestine Liberation Organization (PLO). An organization founded in the 1960s by Palestinians expelled from Israel; until 1994 it aimed at destruction of the state of Israel by any means."[18] However, the body of the text does not highlight the destruction of Israel like this entry does. Likewise, another volume by the same publisher, *World Civilizations* states "[The PLO's] single goal was the destruction of the state of Israel . . ."[19]

World History: The Human Journey published by Holt, makes the linkage between Israeli fears and policy clear. "[After the 1979 peace treaty with Egypt] Palestinian terrorist attacks and calls by its leadership for Israel's demise continued. As a result, Israelis resisted any idea of a Palestinian state."[20] This is an accurate and factual explanation for Israeli actions.

On the other hand, other textbooks are not as accurate as the examples above. *World Geography* by McDougal Littell recounts "In the 1960s, the Palestinian Liberation Organization (PLO) was formed to regain the land for Palestinian Arabs,"[21] not to destroy Israel and its timeframe is unhelpfully vague to properly place the PLO's founding several years prior to the 1967 war. It continues, using clouded terminology by omitting the word "terrorist" to describe PLO tactics and by employing the softer term "military." "Over the years the PLO has pursued political and military means to take possession of Arab land in Israel and allow the refugees to return to their homes."[22]

The World (Harcourt Horizons) obfuscates the true goal of the PLO. "In 1964, at a meeting of Arab leaders, a group called the Palestine Liberation Organization (PLO) was formed. The group's purpose was to organize the Palestinians in their struggle for a homeland."[23] On the other hand, it does note, in a teacher sidebar. "Civics and Government: Provide Means of Managing Conflict. Q. Why do you think the PLO was not included in the first peace talks with Israel? A. Accept reasonable answers, such as the terrorism of the PLO and the PLO's refusal to recognize Israel."[24] While this is much clearer on the true PLO goal, the additional information is for the teacher only and may not make it into the classroom discussion.

Like many other texts, *Modern World History* conveniently omits the PLO goal of eradicating Israel. In a glossary entry it defines the organization in this way: "PLO. n. The Palestine Liberation Organization—an organization dedicated to the establishment of an independent state for Palestinians . . . "[25] and not the more accurate "eradication of Israel from the Middle East."

In McDougal Littell's *World Cultures and Geography: Eastern Hemisphere and Europe*, a teacher sidebar repeats the softened definition of the PLO found in other texts. "Instruct: Objective, Conflict Over Palestine. . . . Q. What is the PLO? When and why was it formed? A. The Palestine Liberation Organization. It was formed in 1964 to oppose Israel and create a Palestinian state."[26] The softer terminology "oppose" sounds akin to advocacy limited to the diplomatic arena. More accurate wording would be "destroy" or "liquidate" according to its charter and actions.

Glencoe World History also misstates the true goal of the PLO. "In 1964, an Arab organization called the Palestine Liberation Organization was founded to bring about an independent Arab state of Palestine."[27] Likewise, McGraw-Hill's *Traditions & Encounters* omits the goal of bringing about Israel's demise. "The PLO, the political organization that served as a government in exile for Palestinians displaced from Israel, had been created in 1964 under the leadership of Yasser Arafat (1929–2004) to promote Palestinian rights."[28] The error is repeated and reinforced in a glossary entry: "Palestinian [sic] Liberation Organization (PLO). Organization created in 1964 under the leadership of Yasser Arafat to champion Palestinian rights."[29] This is only half the story. "Champion" is a term that romanticizes the organization and its goals in the tradition of less terrorist liberation movements in other parts of the world.

McDougal Littell's *Modern World History* uses soft language to describe PLO actions and harsher terms to portray Israel's deterrent responses for the purposes of avoidance of future terrorist attacks. "During the 1970s and 1980s, the military wing of the PLO intensified its armed struggle against Israel. Israel responded forcefully, bombing suspected rebel bases in Palestinian towns."[30] A more accurate passage might read ". . . the PLO intensified its terrorist campaign against Israeli civilians with bombings, armed attacks on schools, murder of Israeli Olympic athletes, and airplane hijackings. Israelis responded with military strikes targeting terrorist leaders."

A full page section entitled "The Fight for Peace in Southwest Asia: Road Map to Nowhere?" is found in *The World and Its People*, by McGraw-Hill/Glencoe. It frankly acknowledges that Palestinians want all of Israel's land. But the language about the violence reflects an attitude of a plague on both your houses that shortchanges student understanding of the positions of both sides. Expressions such as "a violent cycle of revenge-attack-revenge began," "the violence began again," "[t]he region's cycle of violence continues and it is not easy to stop," and "political disagreements in Israel, unrest in the Palestinian areas"[31] connote equivalence.

ARAB TERRORISM IS MINIMAL/
TERRORISM IS UNISLAMIC

The Palestinian position is that acts of terrorism should not define their national liberation movement. They believe they were forced to resort to violent acts because the world refused to pay attention to their plight. However, this view is overly simplistic.

World History: The Human Journey, Modern World, published by Holt, acknowledges that terrorism by the Hamas movement remains a problem and thoroughly explains that Israel has been the target of continued terrorist attacks. Therefore, it is especially egregious that the same textbook, in a special section on terrorism, goes out of its way to minimize the scope of Arab terrorism as beyond the Palestinian mainstream. "Terrorism in the Middle East. . . . The ongoing conflict between Israel and Palestine has been used by some to justify the horrendous acts of terrorism committed by a *few* fanatics."[32] [emphasis added] The language minimizes the official policy of the PLO, Hamas, and support from 70 percent of the population of the Palestinian territories for suicide bombings.[33]

Supplemental materials developed by Muslim advocacy organizations go even further than textbooks to deny the existence of terrorism. The Council on Islamic Education's curriculum asserts that the term "Islamic terrorism" is an "oxymoron"[34] and that "'Islamic fundamentalism' is a confusing misnomer, resulting in broad generalizations and misunderstanding."[35] The *Arab World Studies Notebook* explains: "The Western term, 'fundamentalism,' does not accurately describe the modern movements in Islamic countries to renew Islamic values. . . . Muslims prefer 'revivalism' as a more accurate description of this renewal. . . ."[36]

ISRAEL IS NOT A TERRORIST VICTIM/
TERRORISM AGAINST ISRAELIS IS JUSTIFIABLE

The Palestinians believe that acts of terrorism are legitimate means in their struggle for self-determination that are justified by the overwhelming power differential between themselves and the Israelis. Their belief is understandable in light of their history. However, terror attacks on civilians are not only morally wrong for any civilized society, throughout the history of the Israeli–Palestinian conflict Palestinian terror attacks have repeatedly set back the Palestinian aspirations for self-determination.

The Earth and Its Peoples by Houghton Mifflin, when discussing the PLO and Israel, puts Israeli defensive, deterrent actions on the same plane as terrorism by Arabs and paints Israel as militaristic. "The Palestine Liberation Organization (PLO), headed by Yasir Arafat, waged guerilla war against Israel, frequently engaging in acts of terrorism. The militarized Israelis were able to blunt or absorb these attacks and launch counterstrikes that likewise involved assassinations and bombings."[37] The use of the word "likewise" connotes symmetry. The word "blunt" implies that the attacks stopped, which they did not. Incredibly, Israeli civilians' ability to "absorb" terrorist attacks by suffering through them is in effect used to condemn Israel and its actions.

The World and Its People by McGraw-Hill/Glencoe is among those textbooks which conspicuously omit Israel as a victim of terrorism. "The Fight for Peace in Southwest Asia [i.e., the Middle East]. Review and Assess: . . . Beyond the Classroom . . . Research a Country such as Iraq, Northern Ireland, or Bosnia where people have suffered from terrorist attacks."[38] A unit specifically about the Middle East overlooks Israel as a victim of terrorism.

Some educational materials go beyond omission—they justify terrorism when it is directed toward Israel. The Council on Islamic Education curriculum makes this distinction: "While some Muslim extremists may perpetrate acts of terrorism, this does not diminish the legitimacy of righteous struggle against oppression and injustice experienced by Muslims in many parts of the world. . . ."[39] The Arab Cultural Center's *Educational Guide* also seems to support terrorist groups: "Hamas, Islamic Jihad, and Hizbullah are groups that emerged as a reaction to Israeli occupation of Palestine and Lebanon. These groups are military, political groups that oppose the displacement of Palestinian people."[40] By this definition, they are not terrorist at all.

AMERICAN COMPLICITY IN ISRAELI CRIMES:
U.S SUPPORT OF ISRAEL CAUSES TERRORISM

The Palestinian narrative holds that unquestioning U.S. support for Israeli policies gives the Israelis carte blanche to take whatever actions they desire against the Palestinians. They believe that America is working against their interests. True, U.S. diplomatic, financial, and economic support of Israel has been strong and consistent. On the other hand, the United States has not hesitated to confront the Israeli government on some issues, most notably construction of settlements. U.S. official policy against such unilateral actions by the Israelis that could prejudice negotiations puts its position closer to that of the Palestinians than the Israelis.

Sometimes America is criticized as well as Israel. *World Civilizations*, published by Thomson Wadsworth, portrays Israel as the unqualified aggressor and countenances no sympathy for its deterrent and defensive actions against terrorism. "For its part, as a besieged state, Israel used its well-disciplined and largely American-equipped armed forces to repay violence with violence and to continue occupying Palestinian lands."[41] The textbook portrays U.S. assistance to Israel as the root cause of the whole Middle East problem. Along the way, it also repeats a common stereotype and western media perspective that considers Israeli actions "eye-for-an-eye" retaliation.

Some instructional materials draw a direct connection between U.S. foreign policy in the Middle East and actions of terrorists, including the 9/11 attacks. The San Francisco based Arab Cultural Center's *Educational Guide to the Arab and Muslim World* states that the *Guide* is intended to "begin to answer the questions that arise . . . in the aftermath of the tragic events of September 11 [as] we witness an unprecedented focus . . . on Arabs and Muslims since September 11. . . ."[42]

The October 2001, issue of *Social Education*, the "official journal of the National Council for the Social Studies," carried articles advising teachers how to deal with the 9/11 attack in their classrooms. One of the articles, "At Risk of Prejudice, Teaching Tolerance about Muslim Americans," asked "What issues separate us from the Muslim world? Why does the United States so often seem to be unpopular among Muslims?" The author, Karima Alavi, Dar al Islam, allowed that, "there is no way that terrorist acts such as these can be justified . . . ," however, "those who commit them or sympathize with them often cite grievances against the United

States that are felt widely in the Islamic world." The two grievances she enumerates are 1) the U.S. policies in the Palestinian–Israeli conflict about which "there is a widespread sense in the Islamic world that its policies are unfair and lacking in evenhandedness" because "Muslims see the United States as standing against Muslim rights in Jerusalem . . ." and, 2) the U.S. supported embargo in Iraq that has resulted in the suffering of Iraqi civilians. Alavi goes on to observe, "In their relations with the Islamic world, the United States and its western allies frequently encounter fears and suspicions that were born in the long period of western colonization and imperialism."[43]

Zeina Azzam Seikaly, outreach coordinator at the Center for Contemporary Arab Studies at Georgetown University, wrote an article, also in the October 2001 *Social Education*, "At Risk of Prejudice: The Arab American Community." Shortly after the terrorist attacks of September 11, 2001, Seikaly writes: "As a result of the Arab–Israeli conflict and the United States' strong support of Israel, a politically charged atmosphere surrounds Arab Americans. Within the Arab American community, a strong perception exists that there is a bias toward Israel in American foreign policy and that the United States is not an impartial mediator in the conflict."[44] Seikaly refers teachers to the materials produced by AWAIR, CIE, Amideast, the National Council on U.S.–Arab Relations/High School Model Arab League, and other advocacy groups.

Finally, a textbook example that glosses over the full motivation of the 9/11 attackers is *Medieval Times to Today* (World Studies) published by Prentice Hall. In its entire discussion of 9/11 headed "Terrorism and War" it avoids completely the words "Muslim" or "Islam" or even "religious." The explanation offered is that "Al-Qaeda seeks to force the United States to withdraw its troops from the Middle East and end its support for Israel."[45] This assertion comes dangerously close to the supplemental materials' charge that Israel is responsible for causing 9/11. In addition, it is seriously misleading and lacking in historical context to focus only on the terrorists' desire to influence U.S. foreign policy. Al-Qaeda's vision, shared by some number of its coreligionists around the world, is an entire world where non-Muslims would submit to Muslim rule (the "Caliphate") to be governed according to Islamic law. This is exactly the goal of jihad as it was formulated in the earliest days of Islam. None of this material should be omitted from textbooks.

THE FIRST AND SECOND INTIFADAS

The first and second Intifidas (Intifada is Arabic for a "shaking" or a "shaking off"), violent uprisings staged by Palestinians against Israeli presence in the West Bank and Gaza, were watershed events in both the history of the Middle East conflict as well as the way the conflict was perceived in western media. The first Intifada began in December of 1987 and lasted until September 1993 with the signing of a peace accord between Israel and the Palestinians. The second began soon after Israeli opposition leader Ariel Sharon visited the disputed Temple Mount in Jerusalem (known in Arabic as the Haram As-Sharif, the Noble Sanctuary) in September 2000 and continues to the present. Textbooks treat as fact that Sharon's visit sparked the second Intifada, despite evidence that it was planned in advance as a response to the failed Camp David negotiations in summer of 2000. The first Intifada has been described as essentially "a war of attrition" between Israeli and Palestinian societies.[46]

As is true in most subject areas of the Middle East conflict, wording, terminology, and image are everything. Israeli commentator Nachman Shai wrote extensively about the interplay of the media and the military during the first Intifada. "In one sense, the Intifada can be seen as the war to win over Israeli and international public opinion. The Palestinians waged this war professionally and with great expertise. The objective of their public relations efforts was to manipulate the Israeli and international press in order to incite strong opposition to Israeli policies . . ."[47]

The Palestinian perspective holds that the Intifadas were spontaneous outpourings of rage from the Palestinian "street," especially Palestinian youth. Palestinians called their young people the "boys of the stones" to celebrate their role in the front lines of the revolt hurling rocks against the vastly superior Israeli military. They view the revolts as non-violent, just struggles against the Israeli presence in the West Bank and Gaza. The best defense of the Palestinian narrative is that some of the confrontations with the Israeli army did feature youths. The Palestinians did feel rage against the hopelessness of their situation in particular during the periods in which the revolts occurred. On the other hand, their argument is wrong because it overlooks the substantial armed violence and terrorism used by Palestinians against soldiers and civilians alike. Israeli restrictions such as curfews were put in place in the aftermath of acts of terrorism.

The portrayal of Palestinian behavior in the textbooks during these revolts is clearly reflective of the Palestinian narrative. Terms such as "civil disobedience" are used inaccurately by textbooks to excise Palestinian violence and terrorism. The term "civil disobedience" is used to describe the violent demonstrations in an effort to invoke American memory of the civil rights movement and Mohandas Gandhi's non-violent struggle to free India from British rule. Yet neither Gandhi nor Martin Luther King, Jr. would recognize Palestinian violence or terrorism as civil disobedience.

"The IDF, being a conventional army, had no expertise in handling violent civilian demonstrations," said Shai.[48] A few textbooks state clearly that the uprising was violent. However, the more violent acts committed by Palestinians such as the firing of arms at soldiers and civilians during demonstrations, not to mention terrorist bombings and other shootings targeting civilians, are omitted entirely to make the power equation between the two sides seem less equal. The use of weapons smuggled in from outside was common. For example, in 2005 Palestinian security funds manager Fuad Shubaki admitted that during the second Intifada in 2000 the Palestinian Authority itself was involved in smuggling weapons and producing weapons.[49]

As Shai wrote "The [first] Intifada was Israel's longest war. The IDF and Israeli society were in a continuous violent struggle with the Palestinians. It occurred during a period of continued terrorism that began with the Lebanon War and ended with the Gulf War, a time of crisis upon crisis."[50] There is no hint in textbooks that the uprisings had public relations motivations.

Some observers consider the first Intifada to be

> [t]he [r]ole [r]eversal of David and Goliath . . . The Palestinians were quick to recognize and capitalize on [a new, aggressive Israeli press]. They established an effective mechanism for providing information to the foreign press. As for their message, they were clever in reversing the classic David and Goliath roles, becoming David and portraying Israelis as Goliath. Mortimer B. Zuckerman said [in *U.S. News & World Report*] at the time that "The images of the Intifada have transformed the perception of Israel and of reality because the Arabs have succeeded brilliantly in shifting the ground of debate." [51]

Israel is presented as repressive and the Palestinians as heroic.

A fundamental principle of textbooks in general is the publishers' efforts to maximize their appeal to their target audience: students. This is a special challenge with respect to the "dry" subjects of history and geography, which school children love to hate. Wherever possible the effort to design educational products that engage students means a strong preference for featuring "peers" of student age on textbook covers, in pictures, illustrations, and in the student copy whenever possible over presenting adults in the same situations. If these children are other than Americans and can be portrayed as actors in history, textbook publishers will invariably frame a given historical subject from that angle.

The interests of textbook publishers in featuring school age youths to engage their student readers coincides with the goals of the Palestinian narrative in the erroneous representation of the Intifadas as a "children's revolt." The participation of young people in the uprisings has led textbooks to place exaggerated emphasis on the age of the rioters. For example, countless images of children facing off against soldiers and tanks were distributed to the media by the Palestinians. These images have found a welcome place in the textbooks. The overemphasis on the youth of Palestinian rioters feeds the images of the imbalance of power the Palestinian narrative seeks to propagate.

Moreover, as textbooks attempt to frame history by speaking the language students can understand, the offenses of rioters are described as violation of "curfew laws." To an American student this phrasing sounds as if rioters were staying away from their homes too late one night—a seemingly innocuous offense. In reality, attempts by the Israeli authorities to restore calm after violent demonstrations by adults and acts of terrorist violence can hardly be placed in the same category of curfew violations as understood by the typical American teenager.

The first Palestinian uprising is described in *Modern World History*, published by McDougal Littell, as "a widespread campaign of civil disobedience called the [I]ntifada, or 'uprising.' The Intifada took the form of boycotts, demonstrations, attacks on Israeli soldiers, and rock throwing by unarmed teenagers. . . . However, the civil disobedience affected world opinion, which, in turn, put pressure on Israel to seek negotiations with the Palestinians."[52] Besides the problematic focus on the age of the rioters, the loaded and inaccurate term "civil disobedience" appears twice in this passage. The passage also claims that Israel has refused to negotiate, which is inaccurate.

Modern World History includes a section highlighting five "developing nations." Notwithstanding the odd classification of Israel as "developing," it repeats passages from the earlier chapter about the nonviolent nature of the uprising. "First Intifada 1987 . . . was a widespread campaign of civil disobedience." A picture shows a lone boy with a slingshot facing an Israeli tank: exactly David against Goliath.[53]

Modern World History describes the second Intifada in terms much like the first. The textbook uses the "unarmed teenagers" expression, but without the "civil disobedience" label. "The Conflict Intensifies. The second Intifada began much like the first with demonstrations, attacks on Israeli soldiers, and rock throwing by unarmed teenagers. But this time the Palestinian militant groups began using a new weapon—suicide bombers."[54] The textbook prefers the romanticized "militants" over the more accurate term "terrorists." In addition, suicide bombings were not new in 2000, but a well-established pattern of Palestinian behavior. Major attacks occurred March 4, 1996 and September 4, July 30, March 21, 1997, to list a few.[55] Portraying them as new in 2000 is to ignore prior Palestinian terrorism.

The concept of civil disobedience was most notably articulated by Henry David Thoreau in his 1848 essay *Civil Disobedience* explaining his resistance to slavery and war with Mexico by nonviolent means that included the nonpayment of taxes. The concept was expanded by Mohandas Gandhi, who said, "pursuit of truth did not admit of violence being inflicted on one's opponent but that he must be weaned from error by patience and sympathy. . . . And patience means self-suffering. So the doctrine came to mean vindication of truth, not by infliction of suffering on the opponent, but on oneself."[56]

Martin Luther King, Jr. was impressed by Gandhi's philosophy and in his "Letter from a Birmingham Jail" called for nonviolent civil disobedience against unjust segregation laws.[57] The use of the term "civil disobedience" to describe violent acts committed during the uprising is a misuse of terminology that distorts the meaning of history.

YOUTH OF THE RIOTERS AND "CURFEW VIOLATIONS"

World History: The Human Journey, Modern World by Holt describes the first Intifada as follows. "In December 1987 [Palestinians in the occupied territories] began a violent uprising called the Intifada . . . Young Palestinians threw rocks, bottles, and homemade weapons at army patrols and other

Israeli authorities. The Israeli army responded with arms. In the first year alone, the Intifada claimed more than 300 Palestinian lives. Another 20,000 were wounded; almost 12,000 were imprisoned."[58] The textbook's use of the word "violent" is a step toward accuracy.

However, the overemphasis on youths to the exclusion of violence by adults and the description of the Palestinian actions are incomplete. Palestinian militants often fired arms at soldiers and civilians during demonstrations and protests, using the protesting youths as human shields. Their actions regularly went beyond the "homemade" weapons described in the textbook. Constant terrorism against Israeli civilians was the norm. Moreover, there are no references to parallel Israeli casualties.

The same perspective of omission of the participation by adults and the downplaying of violent Palestinian acts is adopted by *World History: Continuity & Change* by Harcourt/Holt. "[D]ay after day young Palestinians threw rocks, bottles or anything else they could lay their hands on at Israeli soldiers patrolling the [occupied] areas."[59] The emphasis is decidedly on youths—children. The theme of Palestinian powerlessness and desperation against the powerful Israeli military predominates.

World History: Connections to Today by Prentice Hall contains the following passage. "[Young Palestinians in the first Intifada] stoned Israeli troops and disobeyed curfew laws. . . ."[60] Rebellious American teenagers could readily empathize with the "disobedience" of their Palestinian counterparts when it is phrased in this manner.

At least *World Civilizations* by Thomson Wadsworth directly addresses the cynical propaganda purpose of the Intifada. A picture caption reads "Rock-throwing youth rioted in the streets in a persistent *intifada*, or uprising, which forced Israeli countermeasures and gave the Tel Aviv government a black eye in the world press."[61]

DISPROPORTIONATE VIOLENCE AND POWER

According to the Palestinian narrative, Israel's response to their largely peaceful protests was massive military repression resulting in the disproportionate deaths of many innocent and nonviolent Palestinians. They believe that the casualty figures illustrate the unequal power dynamic between themselves and the heavily armed Israeli military. The best defense of their argument lies in the civilian casualty counts in media reports, which would appear to make their point. However, an analysis of these figures reveals a more complex reality that does not support the conclusions of the Palestinian perspective.

McDougal Littell's *Modern World History: Patterns of Interaction* pushes the admission of Palestinian use of terrorism off the student page into a teacher sidebar. The sidebar connects a passage in the student text concerning the "civil disobedience" of the first Intifada with the following one about the second Intifada, which admits the Palestinians made free use of terrorism against Israeli civilians. "The Second Intifada. Palestine's militia and suicide bombers killed hundreds of Israelis, and Israeli forces responded with bombings that killed thousands of Palestinians."[62]

Moreover, the causalities reported are wrong. For example, an analysis by the International Policy Institute for Counter-Terrorism reports that

> the usual fatality count quoted in news articles presents an inaccurate and distorted picture of the al-Aqsa conflict, exaggerating Israel's responsibility for the death of noncombatant civilians. . . . [S]uch numbers hide as much as they reveal: They lump combatants in with noncombatants, suicide bombers with innocent civilians, and report Palestinian "collaborators" murdered by their own compatriots as if they had been killed by Israel. Correcting for such distortions, we can arrive at a figure of 617 Palestinian noncombatants killed by Israel, compared to 471 Israeli noncombatants killed by Palestinians[63]

through September 2002.

A product by a different publisher, Thomson Wadsworth, *World History Since 1500: The Age of Global Integration* repeats the theme of greater Israeli power. "Meanwhile, the Palestinians in the Occupied Territories began a campaign of civil disobedience, attacking Israelis with stones and sticks in 1987. The Intifada, or uprising, continued unabated in the face of massive repression by the Israelis."[64] The expression "massive repression" indicts Israel as practicing disproportionate violence. The phrasing "civil disobedience" and "stones and sticks" does not wash in this situation.

SHARON'S VISIT TO JERUSALEM'S TEMPLE MOUNT

The Palestinian narrative views former Prime Minister Ariel Sharon as the ultimate enemy of Palestinians, particularly as a result of Sharon's conduct of the first Lebanon War in the 1980s and his alleged role in the Sabra and Shatila massacres against Palestinians committed by Christian militiamen allied with the Israeli military. They believe it was natural for the spontaneous ire of Palestinian Muslims to be aroused by the visit of their enemy to their holy place it seemed Sharon was claiming as Israeli territory. In defense of the Palestinian argument, Sharon did plan his visit with the intention of asserting Israeli rights. On the other hand, Palestinian sources disclosed that the second Intifada broke out as part of a deliberate political strategy as a response to the failed Camp David peace negotiations.

The *Educational Guide to the Arab and Muslim World* makes no reference to terrorism or suicide bombings in its discussion of the fall 2000 Palestinian Intifada. Instead, it assigns the blame for the 2000 Intifada to then-Israeli Prime Minister Ariel Sharon: "Sharon's [visit to the disputed site Muslims call Noble Sanctuary] provoked large Palestinian protests in Jerusalem. . . . As in the previous Intifada . . . , Israeli soldiers responded to unarmed Palestinians . . . with rubber-coated steel bullets and live ammunition. . . . The Israeli military forces are continuing to attack Palestinian installations. . . ."[65]

Modern World History: Patterns of Interaction by McDougal Littell makes multiple references to Israeli politician Ariel Sharon's visit to the disputed Temple Mount in Jerusalem's Old City. A timeline entry reads "2000 Visit by Israeli leader Ariel Sharon to holy Arab site launches second Intifada and years of violence."[66] The text body on the following page states, "an Israeli political leader, Ariel Sharon, visited a Jewish holy place . . . in Jerusalem . . . , also the location of one of the most holy places for Muslims. . . . Sharon's visit to the vicinity of such a revered Muslim site outraged Palestinians. Riots broke out and a second Intifada was launched." A third reference is in a teacher review question, "Q. Why do you think Sharon's visit to the Temple Mount so angered Palestinians? A. Possible Answer: His presence suggested that it belonged to Israel or the Jews."[67] The textbook framing of this incident is consistent: a senior Israeli politician committed a violation of religion, a condemnable flaunting of the sensibilities of Muslims worldwide. The holiness of the site is contrasted with the corrupt politician Sharon. The demonizing of Sharon as an enemy of holiness and religion makes it difficult to objectively understand the incident or its implications.

Textbooks teach that that the Intifada was an unplanned Palestinian expression of frustration. Records show that Palestinian leaders were planning this action from the time of the failed Camp David peace negotiations or earlier. Senior Palestinian leader Marwan Barghouti said "'The

explosion would have happened anyway. It was necessary in order to pro-
tect Palestinian rights. But Sharon provided a good excuse. He is a hated
man.'"[68] Palestinian Communications Minister Imad Faluji, in a speech in
Southern Lebanon reported March 9, 2001, said "Whoever thinks that the
Intifada broke out because of the despised Sharon's visit to the Al-Aqsa
Mosque, is wrong, even if his visit was the straw that broke the back of the
Palestinian people. This Intifada was planned in advance, ever since President Arafat's return from the Camp David negotiations. . . ."[69] (Sharon did
not enter any mosque as he visited the Jewish holy site.)

WHY IS IT SO CHALLENGING TO
BE ACCURATE ON THE MIDDLE EAST?

If teaching of religion is inherently problematic because it is personal
and because the requirements of good pedagogy may clash with the belief
system of the religious tradition being taught, then why are lessons about
the Middle East often so flawed? True, the topic is complicated, and cause-
and-effect is not always clear, but the same could be said of any number of
lessons on world cultures and politics that do not seem to suffer as much
from the same systemic ills as the lessons about the Middle East. This can
include the struggles between Israel and Palestine, the war in Iraq, and
the price of gasoline at our local service stations. For example, teaching
students that Arab countries did not attack Israel or implying by omission
that Palestinian terrorism began with the founding of the PLO in 1964 is
just plain wrong.

Concerns that the Arab narrative has dominated many textbooks' versions of the Arab–Israeli dispute have been voiced since at least the early
1990s, in studies such as Mitchell Bard's 1993 *Rewriting History in Textbooks*.
Historical revisionists and their anti-Western, anti-American and pro-
Palestinian perspectives have found their way into textbook content and are
largely consonant with the Arab narrative. (Some textbooks enthusiasti-
cally recommend their works to students.[70]) University Middle East studies
centers, which house many of the scholarly experts to whom teachers turn
for expertise on the Middle East, are sources of historical inaccuracy. *The
UnCivil University*, concludes that "[p]oor scholarship, both due to errors
of commission and omission, plague the work of Middle East Studies faculty, including revisionism in rewriting the history of Israel and Jews."[71]

When world problems become local, people can feel threatened and fearful. The narrative in the textbooks can reflect that fear. Groups such as the Council on Islamic Education, founded in 1990, surmised that after the 9/11 attacks, Muslims in America could be blamed and threatened.[72] They, and other organizations advocating for Muslims in public schools, stepped up their longstanding efforts to attempt to shape the portrayal of Islam and of the politics and history of the Middle East (from which Islam is an inextricable part) in teaching materials. They recognized that these topics would receive even greater attention for a variety of reasons: some people wanted to understand more about Islam to defend Muslims from stereotyping and worse; some looked to the tenets of Islam and the role of the foreign policy of the United States in the Middle East to understand the motivations of the attacks; and some looked at these subjects to condemn the Muslim world.

It should surprise no one that among the thousands of theories and opinions about the troubled relationship between the West and Islam, both supporters and critics cite the unwavering alliance between Israel and the United States as a key factor in any discussion about safety and security within our own borders. (Those who are critical want to blame Israel for any number of alleged ills and often couch those complaints in erroneous historical facts; those who are supportive point out that Israel is the only democracy in the Middle East and thus our most reliable ally in a region where we need allies.) The ongoing fight against terrorism and the wars in Iraq and Afghanistan have linked every one of us, no matter our religion or ethnic background, to the Fertile Crescent and the religious, political, and cultural battles of the Middle East. Explaining the history and analyzing the current state of those faraway places in the textbooks has become a critical part of forming students' opinions. That essential function, combined with the general ignorance of most Americans of the complex and difficult history of the Middle East, has created a volatile mix. In an effort to be responsive to the sensitivities of Muslims, many publishers have bent over backwards to portray violent acts as benignly as possible, opting for sensitivity over accuracy. It is ironic that in a time when we must care more than ever about disseminating accurate information about the Middle East, many publishers, educators, and even academics have deferred to politics and propaganda disguised as scholarship.[73]

CHAPTER NINE

CONCLUSION

Historian Bernard Lewis notes the impact of the forces that can bend historical facts to fit a specific narrative. "We live in a time when great efforts have been made, and continue to be made, to falsify the record of the past and to make history a tool of propaganda; when governments, religious movements, political parties, and sectional groups of every kind are busy rewriting history as they would wish it to have been, as they would like their followers to believe that it was."[1] The *Economist* describes ideology in the history curriculum in a report on Slovakia and Hungary. "History textbooks are a test of a country's tolerance. . . . [D]o they see other countries' point of view?"[2]

Textbooks around the world are blatantly used as tools for propaganda, particularly when governments have an interest in covering up atrocities or molding a national identity based on a change in political ideology. For example, in June of 2005, Chinese and Korean protesters took to the streets to condemn a new set of Japanese junior high school texts because they failed to mention "comfort women," the approximately 200,000 females—mostly from Korea and China—whom the Japanese forced into sexual bondage during World War II.[3] In 1979, monarchy rule in Iran was replaced by Islamic theocracy, leading the new government to revise textbooks to promote a new identity based on Shi'a Islam and Iranian nationalism. Following the Spanish Civil War, Francisco Franco introduced fascist ideology into elementary schools to control political discourse. In May 2003, a team of U.S.-appointed Iraqi educators edited and revised hundreds of texts to omit references to Saddam Hussein, the Ba'ath party, and other topics related to the previous regime.[4] Textbooks throughout the Arab world and Iran are notoriously anti-Semitic.[5] Palestinian textbooks exhibit a ". . . consistent, long-standing negative attitude of the Palestinian curriculum towards the State of Israel, the Zionist movement, and the Jewish people."[6] It is shocking to discover that history and geography textbooks widely used in America's elementary and secondary classrooms contain some of the very same inaccuracies about Jews, Judaism, and Israel.

The problematic passages about Jews, Judaism, and the Middle East we uncovered in our analysis should evoke considerable concern on the part of American Jews because their history, theology, social structure, and ethical system are not being accurately represented in America's schools, both public and private. The history of Israel reflects too many elements of the Arab narrative without respect to historical accuracy.

Various critics and scholars have blamed the textbook publishing industry and found it deeply at fault for its seeming inability to convey the important lessons in a way that satisfies all educators and parents. It would be naïve and wrong to place the trouble with textbooks solely at the doorstep of textbook publishers. In our critique of their product, we do not see the publishers as motivated by any ill will or anti-Semitism toward Jews or by anti-Israel attitudes. They are not actors in a conspiracy to systematically slant textbook content across the subject areas covered by this analysis. In putting out flawed books the publishers have not been malicious, but unable to successfully navigate the economic, political, and cultural pressures brought to bear on the content of their books. Improving social studies texts requires evolution not revolution.

ALL INTEREST GROUPS ARE NOT CREATED EQUAL

The close examination of the treatment of Jews, Judaism, and the Middle East in textbooks and supplemental materials provides universal lessons. We could have chosen other racial, religious, or ethnic groups as the subject of our case study and still arrived at this point: the textbooks used in American schools reflect political perspectives. This should not be a surprise because educational materials the world over represent various political perspectives. This reality is not confined to the telling of history, although points of view are clearly involved in the writing of history. Other subjects are highly influenced by different points of view as well, whether they are pedagogical, value driven, or religious. The "reading wars," the "math wars," and the "science wars" are heated disputes about how these subjects should be taught. In these wars, interest groups play significant roles in promoting their methodology or belief systems and curriculum decision-makers at the state or local levels decide which approach they endorse and choose textbooks accordingly. It should not be a surprise that when it comes to history and social studies, various interest groups are also involved. Such involvement is not *a priori* a negative influence on the quality of textbooks. It becomes problematic when some groups are represented in the discussion while others are not and when the groups involved are more committed to promoting a particular agenda than to promoting accurate historical information.

Unfortunately, this has been the situation in recent years as the pendulum has swung from an almost universally positive treatment of American history and society in American textbooks to one in which the shortcomings of America have received more attention than America's virtues. Those who are more critical of America have been able to exert greater influence in the textbook arena, in part by taking advantage of the trend toward multiculturalism and away from a Eurocentric view of history. Similarly, interest groups that promote a pro-Arab, pro-Islam perspective have influenced the content of textbooks, often to the detriment of historical accuracy, while those with a different perspective were not involved in the process. The educational system's increased interest in Muslims and Islam in the aftermath of 9/11 and the Afghanistan and Iraq wars further opened the door to greater influence by Muslim advocacy groups. In addition, many of these groups working directly with the publishers during the development of the textbooks are the same people who also place supplemental materials in the classrooms to advance their particular point of view.

Both publishers and educators need to be able to better distinguish between advocacy groups that work for historical accuracy such as the American Jewish Committee and the Institute for Curriculum Services (ICS) on the one hand, and groups promoting a particular agenda such as the

Council on Islamic Education (CIE) or Arab World and Islamic Resources (AWAIR) on the other. ICS was created in 2005 to address the issue of bias in textbooks. Every publishing house whose books we examined has indicated by its actions a willingness to improve its products to meet the needs or concerns of their consumers—the states—and school districts.

The wide influence of organizations like the Council on Islamic Education and Arab World and Islamic Resources in classrooms is problematic in several ways. They attempt to whitewash and glorify all things Islamic and promote Islam as a religion in a way no organization representing any other religion would dare. The organizations promote a pro-Arab, pro-Palestinian agenda in textbook's lessons on the Middle East augmented by unregulated supplemental materials. For example, CIE has weighed in during the adoption process to oppose the direct and unconditional use of the term "Israel" for the Israelite monarchy in textbooks, lest anyone make the connection between modern Israel and the kingdom that existed in the same location 3,000 years ago.[7]

CIE not only seeks to control the narrative about Islam and Muslims and their history, it even considers itself an authority on the relationship between Jesus and his fellow Jews. It is surprising that a Muslim organization would support retaining emphasis in textbooks of the purported high level of antagonism between Jesus and his fellow Jews: the Pharisees, Jewish religious leaders, and "the Jews" as a whole. Just such overemphasis on this supposed antagonism has led to centuries of anti-Semitism, which Christian leaders have repudiated.[8]

During the course of this study, we have noticed a pronounced shift in how CIE presents itself. The organization's current website stresses its mission to ". . . support and strengthen American public education as the foundation for a vibrant democracy, a healthy civil society, and a nationally and globally literate citizenry." It invokes inclusive and lofty First Amendment ideals. "By championing the establishment clause of the First Amendment of the U.S. Constitution, emphasizing access to contemporary academic scholarship about world history, world religions, world cultures and related topics, and promoting the cultivation of critical thinking skills, we seek to empower students to understand the world and America's unique and important role in global affairs."[9] In 2004, CIE started a new organization called the Institute on Religion and Civic Values with a mission ". . . to strengthen civil society by exploring issues at the intersection of faith, citizenship, and pluralism and to serve as a catalyst to align public policymaking with our nation's core values."[10] The IRCV website refers to the organization's "previous incarnation as the Council on Islamic Education" which may indicate a further shift away from open advocacy of Islam toward activities that sound more religiously neutral.

AWAIR's activities based on teacher training and dissemination of the *Arab World Studies Notebook* and the *Notebook*'s promotion as a widely-used resource for teachers are particularly cause for concern. In the words of the American Jewish Committee's critique of the Notebook, it

> purports to be a vehicle for elementary, middle, and high school teachers to learn about Arab and Muslim cultures from a benign perspective, to overcome stereotypes and promote understanding at the precollegiate level. Instead, it presents a heavy-handed, propagandistic view of the role of Islam in world history and current politics and of the Arab-Israeli dispute. With regard to the latter topic, it consistently distorts facts, applies the inappropriate and invidious paradigm of "colonialism," and brings emotion-laden poetry and short stories of victimization as the predominant voice of Palestinian culture. . . . [A]s the single source for teachers' understanding of Islam to be conveyed to a precollegiate audience, it is an unacceptable polemic.[11]

The widespread penetration of the *Notebook* into classrooms is symptomatic of the larger problem of supplemental materials in general. Our analysis of interest group–produced supplemental materials found that the alternatives to textbooks, however problematic the books may be, are often no better, and in many cases, they are much worse. Supplemental materials and other online resources are not subject to the same kind of, even if flawed, outside scholarly review as textbooks. They are often not vetted by an outside source, be it a curriculum review board as in the adoption states or a local committee of educators and administrators as occurs in some non-adoption states. They dispense with the appearance of impartiality or of an academic seal-of-approval in favor of advancing a particular point of view. While they may offer perspectives for discussion in the hands of a skilled and informed teacher, they cannot substitute for the depth and breadth of a well-constructed textbook.

UNTROUBLING THE TEXTBOOK

The tens of millions of public and private school students represent every possible cultural, linguistic, religious, and socioeconomic group in

America. Accurate textbooks that tell the same well-researched material on world cultures, history, geography, and civics are the most efficient tools to unite an otherwise unimaginably diverse nation under the broad set of shared values that make us a nation.

The adoption process, for all of its problems, is an attempt to ensure that the materials our students use are pedagogically sound and historically accurate. Neither textbooks nor the adoption process are as good as they could be and ought to be, but they are the best options at this time. Any remedies for problems in the adoption process cannot be proposed on a one size fits all basis. Each unique state adoption process has its advantages and drawbacks with respect to achieving historical accuracy in textbooks.

Untroubling the textbook requires change in two major areas: in the adoption and materials evaluation processes and at the publishing houses. States and school districts must improve their vetting process for supplemental materials produced by advocacy groups. In order to gain entry into the classroom, should not these materials conform to the same state standards and curricular guidelines required of textbooks?

Publishers must be willing to re-dedicate themselves to putting out a higher quality product. Many publishers currently call on academics to advise them either on an ad hoc basis or at such a removed level of involvement that the actual words on the page do not pass through a rigorous scholarly review in-house. But a remedy calling for increased involvement by scholars is no guarantee of neutrality, objectivity, or accuracy, at least regarding the history of Israel. *The UnCivil University*, points out that "[t]he field of Middle East studies has become dominated by a specific political outlook that situates the world, and everyone in it, according to a narrow agenda. . . . Certainly not all professors in Middle East studies are anti-Israel, nor have all those who have criticized Israel done so inappropriately. But anti-Israelists have successfully silenced many dissenters and dominate the field."[12]

Publishers need to make more effective use of the in-house fact checkers that they all employ. When historical inaccuracies are pointed out by representatives of organizations devoted to ensuring historical accuracy, these fact checkers are able to verify and correct the problems. Publishers need to institute better systems for uncovering and fixing inaccuracies in their material on their own.

The same internal fact checking review process should apply to the work of the development houses as to those lessons or chapters created by the publishers' own staff developers and writers. We found in our research that in some cases oversight of the development agencies consisted of ensuring that the textbooks contained the required minimum number of demonstrable points to fulfill the standards requirements of the states, without additional or extensive quality checks. Publishers need to follow a consistent and exigent oversight process for any person or agency contributing content to their products.

Publishers should work more with organizations trying to promote accuracy and honesty in classroom materials. As some non-governmental advocacy groups have discovered, it is a much more successful strategy to work with publishers out of the public eye in the earlier stages of the development of a social studies textbook.

The Jewish community, until now, has been largely absent from this aspect of textbook publishing, as the analysis in this volume can attest. How else would so many egregious textbook entries exist about Jews, Judaism, and Israel? True, there may be Jewish scholars on the editorial boards of the publishing houses. Jewish writers and academics certainly contribute to the body of the books themselves, and Jewish community groups have occasionally spoken up during public evaluations of textbooks in key states. Hadassah, for example, a national Jewish women's organization, has a volunteer-based Curriculum Watch that looks for mistakes about Judaism and Israel in textbooks usually *after* they have been published. The American Jewish Committee published an extensive critique of the *Arab World Studies Notebook*.[13] However, these examples represent specific and limited efforts by a subgroup of an organization that has a different fundamental focus. The problem is large and its solution requires an organization whose funding and mission are dedicated solely to solving it.

To achieve true reform, the Jewish community and others who are not currently represented need a seat at the table with the publishing houses. The publishers have already demonstrated with the Muslim community and others that they are willing and happy to accommodate such requests because they know that they benefit from creating allies among those who might otherwise become their critics. In 2005, the San Francisco Jewish Community Relations Council, based on its identification of serious bias in public school texts, created the national Institute for Curriculum Services (ICS), "dedicated to promoting accurate and unbiased instructional material on Jews, Judaism, and Israel."[14] ICS had considerable success improving the content by making over 400 edits during the 2005–2006 California social studies adoption, and the organization has now embarked on a national strategy to replicate its model of scholarly analysis, effective advocacy with departments of education, and thoughtful dialogue throughout the United States. In January 2007, the Jewish Council for Public Affairs (JCPA), the umbrella organization that represents 125 Jewish Community Relations Councils and fourteen national organizations, became the co-sponsor of ICS. ICS differs from the other Jewish organizations mentioned above because it is devoted to the single purpose of involvement in school curriculum matters and has a strategic national approach to addressing the problems with textbooks.

ICS assists and collaborates with Jewish organizations nationwide, works with publishers on textbooks that are in development, helps publishers correct materials now in print, creates relevant curricula for distribution, communicates with education officials, and provides teacher training. In 2006–2007, ICS and the Jewish Community Federation of Louisville participated in Kentucky's statewide textbook adoption, successfully bringing about over 600 edits that improve the accuracy of textbook content regarding Jews, Judaism, and Israel. Work with publishers on additional edits is underway while ICS moves to assist other Jewish communities throughout the country with their state adoptions. An increasing number of publishers consult with ICS during the pre-publication phase of textbook development. By skillfully developing relationships and offering itself as a community-based resource and sounding board for all content related to Jews, Judaism, and Israel, ICS has demonstrated its ability to work successfully with the major publishers. The publishers have been glad to find a scholarly organization with whom to collaborate. ICS has, in its short existence, made progress in addressing the problems detailed in this book.

The Jewish community is slowly becoming aware of the importance of these efforts since 50 million students in American public schools and millions more in private schools, both religious and secular, take what they learn about Jews, Judaism, and Israel with them to college and for the rest of their lives. ICS, as the prominent voice representing Jewish NGOs, is best positioned for this task. The work has only begun, and it will take considerable time, energy, and financial resources to fix all that has been documented in this book and prevent future problems.

Nevertheless, the problems that we have encountered in this analysis are not Jewish community problems. They are American problems, because they speak to the difficulty of representing the full breadth and depth of American multiculturalism in our public schools. At the most basic level, the trouble with textbooks, given the critical role that textbooks play as molders of civic values and conveyors of truth, should be the concern of all citizens if any group—ethnic, racial, religious, or political—is misrepresented in their children's education. The poor scholarship so prevalent in the sections on Jews, Judaism, and the Middle East represents only a small sample of the thousands upon thousands of pages of social studies, history, and geography textbooks being thumbed through by American students at this very moment. What else is misrepresented? What other aspects of American culture, history, and values are being distorted? How is it that a country that cherishes its multicultural heritage and legislates to protect it has not figured out a way to teach about it more consistently?

When so much debate in America revolves around the U.S. role in the Middle East, and especially the relationship between U.S. foreign policy toward Israel and the larger struggles of the West with the Islamic world, discovering in our schools a pervasive set of erroneous beliefs about such a vital topic should alarm every taxpayer, every parent, and every citizen. In our increasingly interconnected world and at a time when global conflicts are drawn along religious, ethnic, and cultural lines, rather than by national boundaries, the United States has an undeniable moral responsibility to create an informed citizenry. We wield a power unequal to any other nation in the history of the planet, yet our citizens know surprisingly little about other peoples and not that much more about themselves. And, as we have seen, what they do learn may be wrong.

Public schools are our streets, our towns, our countryside. They are our civic institutions and our community halls. They are America. To allow bad textbooks and outright propaganda in supplemental materials into the schools is to pervert the very purpose of public education. The careful (and sometimes careless) selection of certain facts and omission of others, the explicit or implicit support for one set of values over another, is more than merely an intellectual exercise, a difference of opinion among well-intentioned people. These choices reveal our deep and conflicted political, religious, and ethical convictions, the beating, often divided heart of our American community. No wonder the battle for control of the textbooks is fought so vigorously.

CHAPTER TEN

METHODOLOGY

AREAS OF INQUIRY

The Institute for Jewish & Community Research conducted research on K–12 education in American public schools from 2004–2007. We focused on three main areas: 1) analyzing the content of social studies, history, and geography textbooks; 2) the distribution and usage of twenty-eight of the most widely used textbooks; and 3) the content and usage of supplemental materials in classrooms.

RESEARCH METHODS

We employed four methods to conduct our research: 1) content analysis; 2) survey research; 3) personal interviews; and 4) participant observation.

CONTENT ANALYSIS

Content analysis refers to the systematic study of *content* rather than *structure* of to determine meaning. In our case, we performed a detailed content analysis of student materials, including student textbooks, websites, and handouts, and of teacher materials, including teacher's editions of textbooks, curricula, lesson plans, teacher training materials, websites, and more. The content analysis of the textbooks focused on four subject areas:

- Jewish history, theology, and religion
- The relationship between Judaism and Christianity
- The relationship between Judaism and Islam
- The history, geography, and politics of the Middle East.

We analyzed twenty-eight textbooks. Nine of those textbooks were student editions; nineteen were teacher's editions. Teacher's editions contain all of the content of the student versions, plus unit overviews, teaching guidelines, background information, glossaries, gazetteers, suggested further readings for teachers and students, and answers to chapter review questions. We included in our analysis all elements available in the teacher's editions.

The content analysis consisted of several steps: 1) Using indices and tables of contents, we identified all units, chapters, and pages that contained mention of any of our subject areas. 2) A team of scholars read each page identified in step 1 and created a compendium of quotes from the textbooks about the subjects detailed above, including commentary on what the text should say and background information supporting their evaluation. 3) A peer review of the evaluations was conducted, with each scholar reviewing and commenting on the findings of the fellow scholars. Each scholar indicated agreement or disagreement with his or her peers and provided support for the conclusions. 4) The findings of the initial analysis and peer reviews were compiled.

The peer review process included:

- Rabbi Shlomo Zarchi[1] has expertise in Jewish theology, scripture, religion, and ancient Jewish history.
- Dr. Ephraim Isaac[2] is an academic, author, and expert in ancient Jewish history; the origins of Christianity, including non-canonical early Christian scriptures; the relationship of Judaism and Islam; and comparative religion.

SUPPLEMENTAL MATERIALS, CURRICULA, AND OTHER CONTENT ANALYSIS

We evaluated non-textbook materials, including DVDs, CDs, websites, curricula, handouts, teacher trainings, workshops, and so on, based on the same criteria as our analysis of the textbooks. In addition, we also analyzed these materials based on published statements of their authors, including mission statements available on their websites, public pronouncements of the leaders of workshops and trainings, and personal interviews.

SELECTION OF TEXTBOOKS

We examined grade levels 5–12 textbooks, including some advanced placement editions. Our survey of school districts confirmed that our list of twenty-eight textbooks represented a broad sample of social studies, history, and geography textbooks in use in American public schools.

Textbooks were selected in the following areas:

- Ancient and Modern Civilizations (2)
- World History (18)
- International Geography (4)
- World Cultures (4)

SURVEY OF SCHOOL DISTRICTS

We conducted a survey of textbook distribution in all fifty states and the District of Columbia to determine whether our initial list of twenty-eight textbooks represented widely used social studies, geography, and history textbooks in the United States.

The study used two complementary techniques. In the twenty-one adoption states, including the District of Columbia,[3] textbook lists were culled from state Department of Education websites. District representatives were contacted by phone or e-mail for additional information or assistance with data collection.

For the twenty-nine non-adoption states, we constructed a stratified survey of individual districts, for a total of sixty-seven districts. Our trained interviewers conducted a national telephone survey of the two or three largest enrollment school districts within each state, including at least one urban and one suburban district.

The telephone survey was conducted between January–November 2006. The survey instrument took 20–30 minutes to administer. Follow-up was done through fax and e-mail. In most cases, researchers obtained only initial contact information by telephone. Follow-up was completed through e-mail or additional telephone contacts. The results of the survey are presented in Appendix C.

PERSONAL INTERVIEWS

We conducted over fifty personal interviews with educators, administrators, textbook repositories, providers of teacher trainings, among others. The interviews provided background information, context regarding textbook and supplemental material usage, the workings of the textbook industry, and related subjects. In a few cases, the interviews were conducted with individuals that requested confidentiality.

PARTICIPANT OBSERVATION

We attended classes, trainings, conferences, and workshops to record our observations and gather distributed materials. Additionally, at workshops and conferences where materials were available either for purchase or as complimentary samples, we collected, catalogued, and analyzed those materials, noting their origins as well as their content. We did not observe K–12 classes in progress.

TEXTBOOKS REVIEWED BY PUBLISHER PARENT COMPANY

Education Media and Publishing Group Limited (Houghton Mifflin Harcourt)

1. Arreola, Daniel. D., Marci Smith Deal, James F. Peterson, and Rickie Sanders. *World Geography*. California teacher's ed. Evanston, IL: McDougal Littell, 2006.

2. Beck, Roger B., Linda Black, Larry S. Krieger, Phillip C. Naylor, and Dahia Ibo Shabaka. *Modern World History: Patterns of Interaction*. Teacher's ed. Evanston, IL: McDougal Littell, 2005.

3. Beck, Roger B., Linda Black, Larry S. Krieger, Phillip C. Naylor, and Dahia Ibo Shabaka. *Ancient World History: Patterns of Interaction*. Teacher's ed. Evanston, IL: McDougal Littell, 2005.

4. Beck, Roger B., Linda Black, Larry S. Krieger, Phillip C. Naylor, and Dahia Ibo Shabaka. *World History: Patterns of Interaction*. Student ed. Evanston, IL: McDougal Littell, 2003.

5. Bednarz, Sarah W., Ines M. Miyares, Mark C. Schug, and Charles S. White. *World Cultures and Geography: Eastern Hemisphere and Europe*. Teacher's ed. Evanston, IL: McDougal Littell, 2005.

6. Berson, Michael J., ed. *World History*. (Harcourt Horizons). Teacher's ed. Orlando: Harcourt, 2005.

7. Boehm, Richard G., Claudia Hoone, Thomas M. McGowan, Mabel C. McKinney-Browning, Ofelia B. Miramontes, and Priscilla H. Porter *Ancient Civilizations*. (Harcourt Brace Social Studies). Teacher's ed. Orlando: Harcourt Brace, 2002.

8. Bulliet, Richard W., Pamela Kyle Crossley, Daniel R. Headrick, Steven W. Hirsch, Lyman L. Johnson, and David Northrup. *The Earth and Its Peoples: A Global History.* Advanced placement ed. Boston: Houghton Mifflin Company, 2005.

9. Carrington, Laurel, Mattie P. Collins, Kira Iriye, Rudy J. Martinez, and Peter N. Stearns, eds. *World History: The Human Journey.* Student ed. Austin: Holt, Rinehart and Winston, 2003.

10. Carrington, Laurel, Mattie P. Collins, Kira Iriye, Rudy J. Martinez, and Peter N. Stearns, eds. *World History: The Human Journey, Modern World.* Teacher's ed. Austin: Holt, Rinehart and Winston, 2005.

11. Hanes, William T. III, ed. *World History: Continuity & Change.* Annotated teacher's ed. Austin: Holt, Rinehart and Winston, 1999.

12. Harcourt Horizons, ed., *The World.* (Harcourt Horizons). Teacher's ed. Orlando: Harcourt, 2003.

13. Helgren, David M., Robert J. Sager, and Alison S. Brooks. *People, Places, and Change.* Teacher's ed. Austin: Holt, Rinehart and Winston, 2005.

14. Sager, Robert J., and David M. Helgren. *World Geography Today.* Teacher's ed. Austin: Holt, Rinehart and Winston, 2005.

McGraw-Hill

15. Bentley, Jerry H. and Herbert F. Ziegler. *Traditions and Encounters: A Global Perspective on the Past.* Boston: McGraw-Hill, 2006.

16. Boehm, Richard G., David G. Armstrong, Francis P. Hunkins, Dennis Reinhartz, and Merry Lobrecht. *The World and Its People.* Teacher's ed. New York: McGraw-Hill/Glencoe, 2005.

17. Farah, Mounir A., and Andrea Berens Karls. *World History: The Human Experience.* Student ed. New York: McGraw-Hill/Glencoe, 2001.

18. Greenblatt, Miriam and Peter S. Lemmo. *Human Heritage: A World History.* Teacher's ed. New York: McGraw-Hill/Glencoe, 2006.

19. Lamm, Robert C. *The Humanities in Western Culture.* Boston: McGraw-Hill, 1996.

20. Spielvogel, Jackson J. *Glencoe World History.* Teacher's ed. New York: McGraw-Hill/Glencoe, 2005.

Pearson Education

21. Ahmad, Iftikhar, Herbert Brodsky, Marylee Susan Crofts, and Elisabeth Gaynor Ellis. *World Cultures: A Global Mosaic.* Teacher's ed. Upper Saddle River, NJ: Pearson/Prentice Hall, 2004.

22. Boyd, Candy D., Geneva Gay, Rita Geiger, James B. Kracht, Valerie O. Pang, C. Frederick Risinger, Sara M. Sanchez. *The World.* (Scott Foresman Social Studies). Teacher's ed. Glenview, IL: Pearson/Scott Foresman, 2005.

23. Ellis, Elisabeth G., and Anthony Esler. *World History: Connections to Today.* Student ed. Upper Saddle River, NJ: Prentice Hall, 2001.

24. Jacob, Heidi H., and Michal L. LeVasseur. *Medieval Times to Today* (World Studies). Teacher's ed. Upper Saddle River, NJ: Pearson/Prentice Hall, 2005.

25. Jacob, Heidi H., and Michal L. LeVasseur. *The Ancient World.* (World Studies). Teacher's ed. Upper Saddle River, NJ: Pearson/Prentice Hall, 2005.

26. Stearns, Peter N., Michael Adas, Stuart B. Schwartz, and Marc Jason Gilbert. *World Civilizations: The Global Experience.* 4th ed., Advanced placement ed. New York: Pearson/Longman, 2006.

Thomson

27. Adler, Philip J., and Randall L. Pouwels. *World Civilizations.* 4th ed., Instructor's ed. Belmont, CA: Wadsworth/Thomson, 2006.

28. Upshur, Jiu-Hwa L., Janice J. Terry, James P. Holoka, Richard D. Goff, and George H. Cassar. *World History Since 1500: The Age of Global Integration.* vol. 2. Belmont, CA: Wadsworth/Thomson Learning, 2002.

IMPRINTS OF MAJOR TEXTBOOK PUBLISHING CORPORATIONS

Pearson Education	Houghton Mifflin Harcourt Publishing	McGraw-Hill
Elementary	**Houghton Mifflin Company**	**McGraw-Hill Education**
Pearson/Scott Foresman	School Division	McGraw-Hill/ Glencoe
Secondary	McDougal Littell	Macmillan/ McGraw-Hill
Pearson Prentice Hall	College Division	SRA/McGraw-Hill
Higher Education	**Harcourt Education**	McGraw-Hill Higher Education
Pearson Addison-Wesley	Harcourt School Publishers (K–6)	
Pearson Longman	Holt, Rinehart and Winston (6–12)	
Pearson Allyn & Bacon	Harcourt Assessment	
Pearson Prentice Hall		

Source: Corporate Websites

Textbook Usage Survey: Extent of Usage by Publisher Parent Company

Reviewed Textbook Title	Usage*	Number of Adoption States	Number of Sample Districts in Non-Adoption States	Two Biggest Adoption States: California and Texas
Houghton Mifflin Harcourt				
World History: Patterns of Interaction. McDougal Littell	Wide	13	18	Texas
The World. (Harcourt Horizons). Harcourt	Wide	17	7	Texas California
Ancient Civilizations. (Harcourt Brace Social Studies). Harcourt Brace	Wide	10	10	Texas California
World Geography Today. Holt, Rinehart and Winston	Wide	10	10	Texas
People, Places, and Change. Holt, Rinehart and Winston	Wide	11	7	Texas
Modern World History: Patterns of Interaction, McDougal Littell	Moderate–Wide	11	5	No
World History: The Human Journey. Holt, Rinehart and Winston	Moderate	9	4	Texas
World Geography. McDougal Littell	Moderate	7	4	Texas
World History: The Human Journey, Modern World. Holt, Rinehart and Winston	Moderate	7	3	No

*The rating scale is derived by summing the number of adoption states plus the number of sampled districts in non-adoption states in which each textbook is in use.

Scale: 0 None
          1–3 Minimal
          4–13 Moderate
          14–17 Moderate–Wide
          18–31 Wide

Reviewed Textbook Title	Usage*	Number of Adoption States	Number of Sample Districts in Non-Adoption States	Two Biggest Adoption States: California and Texas
Houghton Mifflin Harcourt (cont.)				
Ancient World History: Patterns of Interaction. McDougal Littell	Moderate	6	1	No
The Earth and Its Peoples: A Global History. (Advanced Placement Edition). Houghton Mifflin.	Moderate	6	0	Texas
World Cultures and Geography: Eastern Hemisphere and Europe. McDougal Littell	Moderate	4	1	No
World History: Continuity & Change. Holt, Rinehart and Winston	Minimal	1	2	No
World History. (Harcourt Horizons). Harcourt	Minimal	0	1	No
McGraw-Hill				
The World and Its People. McGraw-Hill/Glencoe	Wide	13	13	No
Human Heritage: A World History. McGraw-Hill/Glencoe	Moderate	6	7	No
World History: The Human Experience. McGraw-Hill/Glencoe	Moderate	6	6	No
Glencoe World History. McGraw-Hill/Glencoe	Moderate	6	5	Texas
Traditions and Encounters: A Global Perspective on the Past. McGraw-Hill	Minimal	1	1	Texas
The Humanities in Western Culture. vol. 1, McGraw-Hill	Minimal	1	0	No

*The rating scale is derived by summing the number of adoption states plus the number of sampled districts in non-adoption states in which each textbook is in use.

Scale: 0 None
          1–3 Minimal
          4–13 Moderate
          14–17 Moderate–Wide
          18–31 Wide

Reviewed Textbook Title	Usage*	Number of Adoption States	Number of Sample Districts in Non-Adoption States	Two Biggest Adoption States: California and Texas
Pearson				
World History: Connections to Today. Prentice Hall	Wide	13	15	Texas
World Cultures: A Global Mosaic. Pearson/Prentice Hall	Moderate	8	5	No
Medieval Times to Today. (World Studies). Pearson/Prentice Hall	Moderate	4	8	California
The Ancient World. (World Studies). Pearson/Prentice Hall	Moderate	2	9	No
The World. (Scott Foresman Social Studies). Pearson/ Scott Foresman	Moderate	3	5	California
World Civilizations: The Global Experience. (Advanced Placement Edition). Pearson/Longman	Moderate	5	2	Texas
Thomson				
World Civilizations. Thomson Wadsworth	Minimal	3	0	No
World History Since 1500: The Age of Global Integration. vol. 2. Wadsworth/Thomson Learning	None	0	0	No

*The rating scale is derived by summing the number of adoption states plus the number of sampled districts in non-adoption states in which each textbook is in use.
Scale: 0 None
         1–3 Minimal
         4–13 Moderate
         14–17 Moderate–Wide
         18–31 Wide

APPENDIX D

OUTLINE OF THE ARAB NARRATIVE

Ancient History and Palestinian Origins

- The roots of the Palestinians extend back into ancient times, to the Canaanites and the Philistines, for whom Palestine was named. These original inhabitants of the land lived there before any Hebrews arrived from outside of the area, so Palestinian claims to the land predate any by Jews.

- The Jews may or may not have had a connection to the land during the time of their ancient kingdoms, but whatever ties they had to the land were severed by a series of exiles: first to Babylon and then after the two revolts against the Romans. The Jews disappeared from the land and no longer have any claim to it.

- All people who lived in Ancient Palestine were Palestinians, including Jews.

- Jerusalem is more holy to Muslims than to Jews. In fact, Jews have no religious ties to Jerusalem.

Zionism and the Founding of Israel: "The Catastrophe"

- Under Muslim rule, Jews and other minorities had lived in harmony for centuries. Zionism intruded upon this harmony by asserting Jewish dominance that the Palestinian people refused to accept.

- The arrival of the European Jews to Palestine under Zionism was part of the colonialist movement by Europeans that drove the establishment of global empires. As Europeans, they do not belong in the Middle East.

- The Jews established their state by terrorism against both British soldiers and Arab civilians. Israeli state terrorism against Palestinians continues today.

- The Israelis massacred and exiled Palestinian civilians and forced them to live in squalid conditions in refugee camps.

- The idea of Israel as a Jewish state is inherently racist and discriminatory against its substantial numbers of Arab citizens.

Israeli Behavior Toward the Palestinians

- Israel started wars in 1956 and 1967 to grab additional land for its expansion.

- Israel built settlements in the occupied territories for its expanding population, taking the best land and displacing more Palestinians from their homes and farms.

- The Israelis do not want peace. They only use the peace process as a means to continue their control of Palestinian land.

- Israel intentionally provokes Palestinians into violence in the name of self defense so Israel will not have to make peace.

Palestinian Resistance to Israeli Oppression

- The Palestine Liberation Organization was founded to achieve Palestinian self-determination. It turned to violence as a legitimate means to resist when all other avenues of achieving justice for the Palestinians were closed off by overwhelming Israeli power.

- Desperate Palestinians launched two uprisings, the Intifadas, spontaneous outpourings of rage from the Palestinian "street." Israel used massive military might against unarmed civilians and youth to crush the rebellion.

- The 9/11 attacks were a result of U.S. support for Israel.

NOTES

One: Textbooks Are in Trouble

1. For more on this research, see D. Alverman (1987), "The Role of Textbooks in Teachers Interactive Decision Making," *Reading Research and Instruction 26*, 115–127; D. Alverman, "Teacher–Student Mediation of Content Area Texts," *Theory into Practice 27* (1989): 142–147; K. Hinchman (1987), "The Textbook and Those Content-Area Teachers," *Reading Research and Instruction 26*, 247–263, and J. Zahorik, "Teaching Style and Textbooks," *Teaching and Teacher Education 7*, 2 (1991): 185–196.

2. Kevin Laws and Mike Horsley, "Educational Equity? Textbooks in New South Wales Secondary Schools," *School of Teaching and Curriculum Studies,* The University of Sydney, http://alex.edfac.usyd.edu.au/Year1/cases/Case%2014/Textbooks_in_Secondary_Sch.html#The%20Role%20of%20Textbooks%20in%20Sch (accessed January 11, 2008).

3. Chester E. Finn, "Today's Textbooks Offer an Unhealthy Diet of History," *USA Today*, March 25, 2004, p. 15A. (accessed July 23, 2007).

4. William Bennetta, *The Textbook League*, www.textbookleague.org (accessed November 22, 2005).

5. According to Stephen Driesler, an executive with the Association of American Publishers, schools in the U.S. typically try to replace books every five to eight years to keep up with developments and changing standards. But the scarcity of funds in poorer districts extends their use much longer. See "Aging Textbooks Fail Illinois Kids," *Chicago Tribune*, April 16, 2006 found at http://www.texastextbooks.org/pdfs/Illinoistextbooks.pdf (accessed May 20, 2008).

6. The sum is the 2006 actual total for the "ELHI" category less supplementals. Peter Appert, "Making the Grade—2007: Economic Outlook for the Educational Publishing Industry" (presentation, Association of American Publishers School Division 2007 Annual Meeting, Austin, TX, February 8–9, 2007), 20, http://www.publishers.org/SchoolDiv/documents/PeterAppert.pdf (accessed April 18, 2007).

7. Interview with author, May 1, 2007.

8. Gilbert T. Sewall, *World History Textbooks: A Review* (New York: The American Textbook Council, 2004), 15.

9. Kyle Ward, *History in the Making* (New York: New Press, 2006); Frances Fitzgerald, *America Revised: History schoolbooks in the Twentieth Century* (Boston: Little, Brown and Company, 1979).

10. "Publishers," Council on Islamic Education, http://www.cie.org/Audiences.aspx?id=pb (accessed January 10, 2008).

11. A.E. Winship, "Textbooks," *Department of Superintendence,* Cincinnati: N.E.A., February 24, 1915: quoted in Frank A. Jensen, *Current Procedure in Selecting Textbooks* (Philadelphia, PA: J.B. Lippincott Company, 1931), 7 and William Marsden, *The School Textbook: Geography, History and Social Studies* (London: Woburn Press, 2001), 31.

12. Appert, "Making the Grade—2007" (accessed March 20, 2007). Textbook sales excludes the "supplemental" category.

13. A trade book is any book intended for a general audience, including fiction, history, science, biography, and so on. This category includes both cloth- and paperbound, as well as both juvenile and adult titles. In other words, most non-specialty books in the local bookstore.

14. "American Association of Publishers 2006 S1 Report: Estimated Book Publishing Industry Net Sales 2002–2006," *Management Practice Inc.,* http://www.publishers.org/main/PressCenter/documents/S12006FINAL.pdf (accessed January 10, 2008).

15. The Learning Source Ltd., "About Us," www.learningsourceltd.com/TLS_pages/About_Us.htm (accessed July 31, 2006).

16. John Kander and Fredd Ebb, "New York, New York," 1977.

17. Tamim Ansary, "The Muddle Machine: Confessions of a Textbook Editor," *Edutopia,* November 10, 2004, http://www.edutopia.org/magazine/nov04 (accessed July 23, 2007).

18. Mel and Norma Gabler, "Mission Statement," The Mel Gablers' Educational Research Analysts, http://www.textbookreviews.org/index.html?content=http%3A//www.textbookreviews.org/about.htm (accessed April 15, 2007).

19. Joe Holley, "Textbook Activist Mel Gabler, 89," *Washington Post,* December 23, 2004, p. B08.

20. Thomas B. Fordham Institute, *The Mad, Mad World of Textbook Adoption* (Washington, D.C.: Thomas B. Fordham Institute, 2004), 9.

21. The adoption states are Alabama, Arkansas, California, Florida, Georgia, Idaho, Indiana, Kentucky, Louisiana, Mississippi, Nevada, New Mexico, North Carolina, Oklahoma, Oregon, South Carolina, Tennessee, Texas, Utah, Virginia, and West Virginia. Although Washington D.C. and Hawaii are not officially considered adoption states, we consider them de facto adoption states because in each case there is only one district which does review and recommend textbooks. See "AAP School Division NASTA Adoption Schedule," *American Association of Publishers School Division,* 2006. http://www.publishers.org/SchoolDiv/TextBooks/documents/AdoptionChartAAP06.pdf (accessed August 1, 2007).

22. Fordham Institute, *Mad, Mad World.*

23. Personal interview with author.

24. For example, in Texas an environmental science textbook submitted for adoption was the subject of "detailed objections . . . lodged by 'an advocacy group whose members have strong ties to the oil and gas industry,' said Adele Kimmel, a staff attor-

ney for Trial Lawyers for Public Justice who is representing the plaintiffs [in a lawsuit against the Texas Board of Education for rejecting the textbook]. . . . A different work did pass muster, however. 'The book that got approved without any editing was something underwritten by the oil and gas industry,' says Kimmel." See Melissa Ezarik, "The Textbook Adoption Mess–And What Reformers Are Doing to Fix It," District Administration, March 2005, http://www.districtadministration.com/page.cfm?p=1022 (accessed September 20, 2007).

25. Melissa N. Matusevich, "Strange Bedfellows: Censorship and History Textbooks," *Social Studies Research and Practice* 1, no. 3 (Winter 2006):361.

26. Sewall, *World History Textbooks*, 11.

27. Diane Ravitch, *The Language Police: How Pressure Groups Restrict What Students Learn* (New York: Alfred A. Knopf, 2003), 34.

28. Ravitch, *Language Police*, 142.

29. U.S. Department of Education, National Center for Educational Statistics, "Digest of Educational Statistics, 2005 NCES 2006-030, Table 3," http://nces.ed.gov/fastfacts/display.asp?id=65 (accessed August 13, 2007).

30. Frances FitzGerald, *America Revised: History Schoolbooks in the Twentieth Century* (Boston: Little, Brown and Company, 1979), 35-36.

31. Keith C. Barton and Linda Levstik, "Why Don't More History Teachers Engage Students in Interpretation?" *Social Education* (2003):358.

32. Ravitch, *Language Police*, 134.

Two: When the Textbook Is Not Enough:
Supplemental Materials, Teacher Trainings, and More

1. Sandra Koehler, "Ten Commandments for School Backpack Packing," *Associated Content*, October 2, 2005, http://www.associatedcontent.com/article/10067/ten_commandments_for_school_backpack.html (accessed April 4, 2007).

2. "Nutrition Assistance Programs," *United States Department of Agriculture Food and Nutrition Service*, www.fns.usda.gov (accessed July 11, 2007).

3. "The Four Food Groups, Old and New," *Jewish Vegetarianism*, www.jewishveg.com/schwartz/ffgroups.html (accessed July 11, 2007).

4. "Social Studies: The Heart of the Curriculum," *85th Annual Conference of National Council for the Social Studies*. Kansas City, Missouri. November 17–20, 2005.

5. Craig D. Jerald and Richard M. Ingersoll, *All Talk, No Action: Putting an End to Out-of-Field Teaching* (Washington, D.C.: The Education Trust, 2002), 5–6.

6. *Council for Islamic Education*, www.cie.org (accessed May 3, 2005).

7. "Comments from K–12 Textbook Publishers," *Council on Islamic Education*, http://www.cie.org/ItemDetail.aspx?id=N&m_id=80&item_id=181&cat_id=118 (accessed February 7, 2006).

8. Gilbert T. Sewall, "Islam and the Textbooks," *The American Textbook Council*, New York, 2003, http://www.historytextbooks.org/islamreport.pdf, 24–25.

9. Diane Ravitch, *The Language Police: How Pressure Groups Restrict What Students Learn* (New York: Alfred A. Knopf, 2003), 147.

10. Nick Schou, "Pulling His Cheney," *OC (Orange County) Weekly*, October 25, 2001, http://www.ocweekly.com/news/news/pulling-his-cheney/22330, p. 1.

11. American Jewish Committee, *Propaganda, Proselytizing, and Public Education: A Critique of the Arab World Studies Notebook* (New York: American Jewish Committee, February 2005), 1–2.

12. Ellen Mansoor Collier, "Taking the Mystery Out of the Middle East," *Saudi Aramco World*, January–February 2002, http://www.saudiaramcoworld.com/issue/200201/taking.the.mystery.out.of.the.middle.east.htm (accessed July 31, 2006), 2.

13. "About AWAIR," *Arab World and Islamic Resources Online*, http://www.awaironline.org/aboutus.htm (accessed April 30, 2008), p. 3

14. "Conferences: 1st Annual Boston Conference 2003, Panels and Speeches," *Harvard Arab Alumni*, http://www.harvardarabalumni.org/openconference22.php (accessed February 2, 2006), p. 3.

15. "Local Muslim Accepted To Area Textbook Review Committee," *CAIR-DFW* www.cairdfw.org/newsbriefs2.sthml (accessed July 31, 2006).

16. Elaine Gale, "O.C. Religion; Believers Enlightening Students; Muslim's Non-profit Business Seeks to Correct Misconceptions in Textbooks," *Los Angeles Times*, January 8, 2000, p. 12.

17. Adam Daifallah, "Saudi P.R. Move: Islamic Books in U.S. Libraries," *New York Sun*, November 20, 2002, www.nysun.com (BO quality checked 4/25/07)

18. Michael Isikoff and Mark Hosenball, "CAIR Play?" *Newsweek*. December 29, 2006.

19. Home page, *Middle East Policy Council*, www.mepc.org (accessed April 15, 2007).

20. "Who We Are," *Amideast*, http://www.amideast.org/about/who.htm (accessed April 5, 2008).

21. "Arab Heritage Fund," *Amideast*, www.amideast.org/about/arab_heritage_fund/default.htm (accessed April 25, 2007).

22. *Amideast*, http://www.amideast.org/pubs_one/ (accessed April 25, 2007).

23. "About Us," *Amideast*, http://www.amideast.org/about/annual_reports/2006/contributions.htm (accessed March 7, 2008).

24. *Islam America*, http://www.IslamAmerica.org (accessed April 25, 2007).

25. Edward Said, "What Happens After Survival," *Al Ahram Weekly Online*, April 4–10, 2002, issue no. 580, http://www.islamamerica.org/articles.cfm/article_id/64 (accessed April 25, 2007).

26. *Islamic Networks Group*, http://www.ing.org/ (accessed April 25, 2007).

27. "ING & Schools," *Islamic Networks Group*, http://www.ing.org/ (accessed April 25, 2007).

28. *Islamic Networks Group*, http://www.ing.org/about/page.asp?num=4 (accessed April 25, 2007).

29. Charley Able, "Model Arab League Helps Students Gain a World View," *Rocky Mountain News*, March 22, 1998, p. 25A.

30. Drew Atkins, "Students Participate in Model Arab League," *The Daily Nexus*, April 22, 2003, www.dailynexus.com/news/2003/5021.html (accessed April 25, 2007).

31. "ADC and Education," American-Arab Anti-Discrimination Committee, http://www.adc.org/ (accessed April 30, 2007).

32. "ADC and Education," American-Arab Anti-Discrimination.

33. "ADC and Education," American-Arab Anti-Discrimination.

34. Alternate Focus, http://www.alternatefocus.org/ (accessed April 30, 2007).

35. Alternate Focus, http://alternatefocus.org/index.php?c=shows (accessed April 30, 2007).

36. Middle East Cultural and Information Center, http://www.mecic.org/ (accessed April 30, 2007).

37. *Facing History and Ourselves*, http://www.facinghistory.org/ (accessed April 30, 2007).

38. Adam Strom. "The Armenian Genocide," *Facing History and Ourselves*, http://www.facinghistory.org/ (accessed April 30, 2007).

39. Jodi Tharan, e-mail message to author, March 13, 2007.

40. *Muslim Hope*, February, 2005, http://www.muslimhope.com/ (accessed April 30, 2007).

41. "Teaching About Islam, The Middle East," *Education World*, http://www.education-world.com/a_curr/profdev009.shtml, (accessed April 30, 2007).

42. IslamiCity, http://www.islamicity.com/ (accessed April 30, 2007).

43. History in the News: The Middle East, http://www.albany.edu/history/middle-east/ (accessed April 30, 2007).

44. Islamic Resistance, http://www.moqawama.org/english/index.php (accessed April 30, 2007).

45. "Teachers Institute: A Summer Institute on Islam," *Dar al Islam*, http://www.daralislam.org/Programs/CurrentActivities/Teachersinstitute.aspx, (accessed April 30, 2007).

46. Yitzhak Santis, "Middle East Nationalism: Arab–Israeli Conflict Analysis and Update" (presentation, California Council for the Social Studies Annual Conference, Oakland, CA, March 2–4, 2007).

Three: Learning about Jewish Origins: Stereotypes of Jews

1. Philip J. Adler and Randall L. Pouwels, *World Civilizations*, 4th ed., instructor's ed. (Belmont, CA: Wadsworth/Thomson, 2006), 47.

2. Michael J. Berson, ed. *World History*, (Harcourt Horizons), teacher's ed. (Orlando: Harcourt, 2005), 182.

3. Jerry Bentley and Herb Ziegler, *Traditions & Encounters: A Global Perspective on the Past* (Boston: McGraw-Hill, 2006), 45, 281.

4. William Travis Hanes III, ed., *World History: Continuity & Change*, annotated teacher's ed. (Austin: Holt, Rinehart and Winston, 1999), 48.

5. James L. Kugel, *How to Read the Bible: A Guide to Scripture, Then and Now* (New York: Free Press, 2007), 680.

6. Roger B. Beck, Linda Black, Larry S. Krieger, et al., *Ancient World History: Patterns of Interaction*, teacher's ed. (Evanston: McDougal Littell, 2005), 115.

7. Robert C. Lamm, *The Humanities in Western Culture* (Boston: McGraw-Hill, 1996), 22.

8. Richard W. Bulliet, Pamela Kyle Crossley, Daniel R. Headrick, et al., *The Earth and Its Peoples: A Global History*, advanced placement ed. (Boston: Houghton Mifflin Company, 2005), 80.

9. Adler and Pouwels, *World Civilizations*, 45.

10. Adler and Pouwels, *World Civilizations*, 47.

11. Bulliet, Crossley, Headrick, *Earth and Its Peoples*, 75.

12. Adler and Pouwels, *World Civilizations*, 48.

13. Peter N. Stearns, Michael Adas, Stuart B. Schwartz, et al., *World Civilizations: The Global Experience*, 4th ed., advanced placement ed. (New York: Pearson Education, 2006), 106.

14. Laurel Carrington, Mattie P. Collins, Kira Iriye, et al., eds. *World History: The Human Journey*, student ed. (Austin: Holt, Rinehart and Winston, 2003), 169.

15. John Bright, *A History of Israel* (Louisville, KY: Westminster John Knox Press, 2000), 442, 445, 446.

16. *Webster's Third International Dictionary of the English Language Unabridged* (Springfield, MA: Merriam-Webster, 2002), 1821.

17. Matthew 23:15 (New American)

18. Rodney Stark, *The Rise of Christianity: How the Obscure, Marginal Jesus Movement Became the Dominant Religious Force in the Western World in a Few Centuries* (San Francisco: HarperCollins, 1996).

19. Miriam Gleenblatt and Peter S. Lemmo, *Human Heritage: A World History*, teacher's ed. (New York: McGraw-Hill, 2006), 248.

20. John D. Durand, "Historical Estimates of World Population: An Evaluation," *University of Pennsylvania, Population Center, Analytical and Technical Reports*, http://www.census.gov/ipc/www/worldhis.html (accessed September 9, 2007).

21. Acts 2:5, 11 (New American)

22. Stearns, Adas, Schwartz, *The Global Experience*, 27.

23. Beck, Black, Krieger, *Ancient World History*, 170.

24. Beck, Black, Krieger, *Ancient World History*, 170.

25. Isaiah 42:6 (Jewish Publication Society)

26. Amos 3:2 (Jewish Publication Society)

27. Richard G. Boehm, David G. Armstrong, Francis P. Hunkins, et al., *The World and Its People*, teacher's ed. (New York: McGraw-Hill/Glencoe, 2005), 473–474.

28. Iftikhar Ahmad, Herbert Brodsky, Marylee Susan Crofts, et al., *World Cultures: A Global Mosaic*, teacher's ed. (Upper Saddle River, NJ: Prentice Hall, 2004), 563.

29. Adler and Pouwels, *World Civilizations*, 47.

30. Jackson J. Spielvogel, *Glencoe World History*, teacher's ed. (New York: McGraw-Hill, 2005), 56, 59–60.

31. Hanes III, *Continuity & Change*, 47, 49.

32. Carrington, Collins, Iriye, *Human Journey, Modern World*, 65.

33. Beck, Black, Krieger, *Ancient World History*, 12–13.

34. Berson, *World History*, 181.

Four: Judaism and Christianity

1. Peter N. Stearns, Michael Adas, Stuart B. Schwartz, et al., *World Civilizations: The Global Experience*, 4th ed., advanced placement ed. (New York: Pearson Education, 2006), 107.

2. *The New American Bible*, St. Joseph personal size ed. (New York: Catholic Book Publishing Company, 1992), footnote page 183.

3. Pope John Paul II, "Address at the Great Synagogue of Rome: April 13, 1986," *Boston College Center for Christian–Jewish Learning, Christian–Jewish Relations Library*, http://www.bc.edu/research/cjl/meta-elements/texts/cjrelations/resources/documents/catholic/johnpaulii/romesynagogue.htm (accessed January 10, 2008).

4. Richard W. Bulliet, Pamela Kyle Crossley, Daniel R. Headrick, et al., *The Earth and Its Peoples: A Global History*, advanced placement ed. (Boston: Houghton Mifflin Company, 2005), 360–2.

5. Padraic O'Hare, *The Enduring Covenant: The Education of Christians and the End of Antisemitism* (Valley Forge, PA: Trinity Press International, 1997), 7.

6. James L. Kugel, *How to Read the Bible: A Guide to Scripture, Then and Now* (New York: Free Press, 2007), 366.

7. Peter D. Hocken, "Repentance for Sin Against the Jewish People," *The Jerusalem Connection*, July–August 2006, 22.

8. "Nostra Aetate: Declaration on the Relation of the Church to Non-Christian Religions," *The Vatican*, October 28, 1965, http://www.vatican.va/archive/hist_councils/ii_vatican_council/documents/vat-ii_decl_19651028_nostra-aetate_en.html (accessed September 10, 2007).

9. "Building New Bridges in Hope, Jewish–Christian Dialogue," *United Methodist Church*, http://web.umcom.org/interior_print.asp?ptid=4&mid=3301 (accessed October 5, 2007).

10. The 199th General Assembly, Presbyterian Church (U.S.A.), *A Theological Understanding of the Relationship between Christians and Jews*, (Louisville, KY: The 199th General Assembly, Presbyterian Church (U.S.A.), 1987), 4.

11. Stephen P. McCutchan, "Replacement Theology: The Heresy That Will Not Die," *Jerusalem Connection*, July–August 2007, 22.

12. Mounir A. Farah and Andrea Berens Karls, *World History: The Human Experience*, student ed. (New York: McGraw-Hill/Glencoe, 2001), 307.

13. Elisabeth G. Ellis, and Anthony Esler, *World History: Connections to Today*, student ed. (Upper Saddle River, NJ: Prentice Hall, 2001), 142.

14. Michael J. Berson, ed., *World History* (Harcourt Horizons), teacher's ed. (Orlando: Harcourt, 2005), 301.

15. Robert C. Lamm, *The Humanities in Western Culture* (Boston: McGraw-Hill, 1996), 307.

16. Lamm, *Humanities*, 311.

17. Philip J. Adler and Randall L. Pouwels, *World Civilizations*, 4th ed., instructor's ed. (Belmont, CA: Wadsworth/Thomson, 2006), 49.

18. Adler and Pouwels, *World Civilizations*, 137.

19. Adler and Pouwels, *World Civilizations*, 139.

20. David M. Helgren, Robert J. Sager and Alison S. Brooks, *People, Places, and Change*, teacher's ed. (Austin: Holt, Rinehart and Winston, 2005), 384.

21. Bulliet, Crossley, Headrick, *Earth and Its Peoples*, 134.

22. Adler and Pouwels, *World Civilizations*, 136–137.

23. James Carroll, *Constantine's Sword: The Church and the Jews* (Boston: Houghton Mifflin Company, 2001), 110.

24. Berson, ed., *World History*, 301.

25. Harcourt Horizons, ed., *The World* (Harcourt Horizons), teacher's ed. (Orlando: Harcourt, 2003), 301.

26. William Travis Hanes III, ed., *World History: Continuity & Change*, annotated teacher's ed. (Austin: Holt, Rinehart and Winston, 1999), 132.

27. Adler and Pouwels, *World Civilizations*, 138.

28. Council on Islamic Education, "Assessment of Programs Submitted for 2005 California History–Social Science Adoption & Assessment of CRP/IMAP Findings," (submitted to Tom Adams, California Curriculum Commission, August 26, 2005), page 10 of the section entitled "Assessment of the CRP/IMAP Findings (Advisory Recommendations)."

29. Etgar Lefkovits, "Priests: Remove Anti-Semitic Liturgy," *Jerusalem Post*, April 20, 2007, http://www.jpost.com/servlet/Satellite?cid=1176152838943&pagename=JPost%2FJPArticle%2FShowFull (accessed January 30, 2008).

30. "Nostra Aetate," *The Vatican* (accessed September 10, 2007).

31. Hanes III, *Continuity & Change*, 132.

32. Bulliet, Crossley, Headrick, *Earth and Its Peoples*, 134.

186 THE TROUBLE WITH TEXTBOOKS

33. Candy D. Boyd, Geneva Gay, Rita Geiger, et al., *The World* (Scott Foresman Social Studies), teacher's ed. (Glenview, IL: Pearson/Scott Foresman, 2005), 296.

34. Adler and Pouwels, *World Civilizations*, 137–138.

35. *World History: Ancient Civilizations* (Boston: Houghton Mifflin, 2006), 470-471.

36. Instructional Materials Advisory Panel, appointed by California State Board of Education, "CRP/IMAP Advisory Recommendations, 2005 History–Social Science Adoption," 2005, item 31–33.

37. Council on Islamic Education, "Assessment of Programs," page 10 of the section entitled "Assessment of the CRP/IMAP Findings (Advisory Recommendations)."

38. "Nostra Aetate," *The Vatican* (accessed September 10, 2007).

39. Acts 2:36 (Revised English Version)

40. John 1:11 (Revised English Version)

41. Roger B. Beck, Linda Black, Larry S. Krieger, et al., *Ancient World History: Patterns of Interaction*, teacher's ed. (Evanston, IL: McDougal Littell, 2005), 169.

42. Mark 12:28–32 (New English Version)

43. Roger B. Beck, Linda Black, Larry S. Krieger, et al., *Modern World History: Patterns of Interaction*, teacher's ed. (Evanston, IL: McDougal Littell, 2005), 14.

44. Hanes III, *Continuity & Change*, 132.

45. One Christian observer writes, "Israel's faith had always had an eschatological orientation in that it looked forward to the triumph of [God's] purpose and rule." See John Bright, *A History of Israel* (Louisville, KY: Westminster John Knox Press, 2000), 452.

46. Berson, *World History*, 301.

47. Beck, Black, Kriesger, *Modern World History*, 14.

48. Bulliet, *Earth and Its Peoples*, 134.

49. Adler and Pouwels, *World Civilizations*, 49.

50. This is not to say that anti-Semitism is no longer a problem in the United States. Rather, the number of people professing such feelings has declined 3% since 2002, and the trend seems to favor continued philo-Semitism, given that younger people were more likely to have favorable attitudes toward Jews than people over 65. Anti-Defamation League, "ADL Survey: Anti-Semitism Declines Slightly in America," *ADL: Fighting Anti-Semitism, Bigotry and Extremism*, http://www.adl.org/PresRele/ASUS_12/4680_12.htm (accessed February 6, 2006). See also Anti-Defamation League, "American Attitudes towards Jews in America," *ADL: Fighting Anti-Semitism, Bigotry and Extremism*, March 2005, http://www.adl.org/anti_semitism/anti_semitic_attitudes.pdf, 21 (accessed February 6, 2006).

Five: Double Standards in Teaching about Judaism Compared to Islam

1. Iftikhar Ahmad, Herbert Brodsky, Marylee Susan Crofts, et al., *World Cultures: A Global Mosaic*, teacher's ed. (Upper Saddle River, NJ: Prentice Hall, 2004), 582.

2. Gilbert T. Sewall, *Islam In The Classroom: What The Textbooks Tell Us* (New York: American Textbook Council, 2008).

3. *2005 Public Omnibus Survey* (San Francisco: Institute for Jewish & Community Research). See also http://www.pollingreport.com/religion.htm for a CBS news poll dated April 6–9, 2006.

4. This Supreme Court decision in 1963 allowed for teaching about religion in public schools. The decision did not center on the teaching of religion, but rather around Bible reading. It pitted a high school student who was a member of a Unitarian church

against the school district of Abington Township in Pennsylvania. At issue was the constitutionality of a state law requiring that "[a]t least ten verses from the Holy Bible shall be read, without comment, at the opening of each public school on each school day." The Supreme Court found the Pennsylvania law unconstitutional as a violation of the "Establishment Clause" of the First Amendment, which specifically prohibits the government's establishment of a religion. (Later decisions clarified the Court's position, differentiating between a private person's reasonable expression of religious belief, even on school grounds, and how the "state"—in this case, represented by the school district—must demonstrate neutrality toward a particular religion or toward religion in general.) Writing for the majority, Justice Tom C. Clark mandated neutrality with respect to all "religious opinions and sects" and added "[t]he government is neutral, and while protecting all, it prefers none, and it disparages none." Text of the Supreme Court decision is found at "School Prayer: Abington v. Schempp (1963)," *National Center for Public Policy Research*, http://www.nationalcenter.org/scot63.htm.

5. Gallup Survey, *The Gallup Poll*, January 15-18, 2007, http://www.galluppoll.com/content/default.aspx?ci=1690 (accessed August 13, 2007).

6. Edward Said, *Orientalism* (New York: Vintage Books, 1978).

7. "The Qur'an and Qur'anic Interpretation (tafsir)," *The University of Georgia*, www.uga.edu/islam/quran.html (accessed August 13, 2007).

8. Carrie Kilman, "One Nation, Many Gods," *Teaching Tolerance*, Fall 2007, 42.

9. Carrie Kilman, "One Nation, Many Gods," *Teaching Tolerance*, Fall 2007, 44.

10. "Toolbox: 10 Tips for Starting a World Religions Curriculum," *Teaching Tolerance*, Fall 2007, 44.

11. Candy D. Boyd, Geneva Gay, Rita Geiger, et al., *The World* (Scott Foresman Social Studies), teacher's ed. (Glenview, IL: Pearson/Scott Foresman, 2005), 331.

12. Boyd, Gay, Geiger, *The World*, 57.

13. William Travis Hanes III, ed., *World History: Continuity & Change*, annotated teacher's ed. (Austin: Holt, Rinehart and Winston, 1999), 883.

14. Hanes III, *Continuity & Change*, 885.

15. Peter N. Stearns, Michael Adas, Stuart B. Schwartz, et al., *World Civilizations: The Global Experience*, 4th ed., advanced placement ed. (New York: Pearson Education, Inc., 2006), G-11, G-15.

16. Roger B. Beck, Linda Black, Larry S. Krieger, et al., *Modern World History: Patterns of Interaction*, teacher's ed. (Evanston, IL: McDougal Littell, 2005), 15.

17. Beck, Black, Krieger, *Modern World History*, 14–15.

18. Sarah W. Bednarz, Ines M. Miyares, Mark C. Schug, et al., *World Cultures and Geography: Eastern Hemisphere and Europe*, teacher's ed. (Evanston, IL: McDougal Littell, 2005), 209a.

19. Richard W. Bulliet, Pamela Kyle Crossley, Daniel R. Headrick, et al., *The Earth and Its Peoples: A Global History*, advanced placement ed. (Boston: Houghton Mifflin Company, 2005), 199.

20. John Sabini, *Islam: A Primer*, 6th ed. (Washington, D.C.: Amideast, 2001), 1.

21. Sabini, *Islam*, 7.

22. "Glossary of Terms Associated with Islam and Muslim History," *Council on Islamic Education*, http://cie.org/ItemDetail.aspx?id=N&m_id=52&cat_id=101&item_id=110 (accessed September 21, 2007).

23. *The American Heritage Dictionary of the English Language* (Boston: Houghton Mifflin Company, 2000), 1822.

24. Audrey Shabbas, ed., *Arab World Studies Notebook* (Berkeley: AWAIR and MEPC, 1998), 17.

25. Shabbas, *Notebook*, 17.

26. Shabbas, *Notebook*, 18.

27. Shabbas, *Notebook*, 18.

28. *Teaching About Islam and Muslims in the Public School Classroom*, 3rd ed. (Fountain Valley, CA: Council on Islamic Education, 1995), 48–49.

29. *Teaching About Islam*, Council on Islamic Education, 48.

30. *Understanding Islam*, Ministry of Education, Kingdom of Saudi Arabia, http://www.moe.gov.sa/openshare/EnglishCon/About-Saud/Religion4.htm_cvt.html (accessed December 4, 2007).

31. Shabbas, *Notebook*, 4.

32. "Dhimmitude in History," *Dhimmitude*, www.dhimmitude.org/d_history_dhimmitude.html (accessed September 17, 2007).

33. Shabbas, *Notebook*, 4.

34. Edward Rothstein, "Was the Islam of Old Spain Truly Tolerant?," *New York Times*, September 28, 2003.

35. "Maimonides/Rambam 1135–1204," *Jewish Virtual Library*, www.us-israel.org/jsource/biography/Maimonides.html (accessed September 17, 2007).

36. Rothstein, "Islam of Old Spain."

Six: The Ancient History of Israel

1. Laurel Carrington, Mattie P. Collins, Kira Iriye, et al., ed., *World History: The Human Journey, Modern World*, teacher's ed. (Austin: Holt, Rinehart and Winston, 2005), 706.

2. For an excellent summary of proper terminology for the land in various time periods of history see "Guide for Accurate Depictions of Jews, Judaism and Israel in Textbooks," (reference guide, Institute for Curriculum Services: National Resources Center for Accurate Jewish Content in Schools, June 2007).

3. Council on Islamic Education, "Assessment of Programs Submitted for 2005 California History-Social Science Adoption & Assessment of CRP/IMAP Findings," (submitted to Tom Adams, California Curriculum Commission, August 26, 2005), page 4 of the section entitled "Assessment of the CRP/IMAP Findings (Advisory Recommendations)."

4. Bernard Lewis, *The Middle East: A Brief History of the Last 2,000 Years* (New York: Touchstone, 1995), 31.

5. Kings 14:19 (Jewish Publication Society)

6. James L. Kugel, *How to Read the Bible: A Guide to Scripture, Then and Now* (New York: Free Press, 2007), 381.

7. *The New American Bible* (New York: Catholic Book Publishing, 1992), 103 [footnote].

8. Luke 3:1–2 (New American Bible)

9. Matthew 2:1 (New American Bible)

10. Acts 1:6 (New American Bible)

11. Acts 10:36–37 (New American Bible)

12. Michael J. Berson, ed., *World History* (Harcourt Horizons), teacher's ed. (Orlando: Harcourt, 2005), 184, 178E.

13. Harcourt Horizons, ed., *The World* (Harcourt Horizons), teacher's ed. (Orlando: Harcourt, 2003), 86, 662.

14. Iftikhar Ahmad, Herbert Brodsky, Marylee Susan Crofts, et al., *World Cultures: A Global Mosaic*, teacher's ed. (Upper Saddle River, NJ: Prentice Hall, 2004), 587.

15. William Travis Hanes III, ed., *World History: Continuity & Change*, annotated teacher's ed. (Austin: Holt, Rinehart and Winston, 1999), 666.

16. Mounir A. Farah and Andrea Berens Karls, *World History: The Human Experience*, student ed. (New York: McGraw-Hill, 2001), 798.

17. Laurel Carrington, Mattie P. Collins, Kira Iriye, et. al., eds., *World History: The Human Journey*, student ed. (Austin: Holt, Rinehart and Winston, 2003), 44–45.

18. Richard W. Bulliet, Pamela Kyle Crossley, Daniel R. Headrick, et al., *The Earth and Its Peoples: A Global History*, advanced placement ed. (Boston: Houghton Mifflin Company, 2005), 74.

19. Miriam Gleenblatt and Peter S. Lemmo, *Human Heritage: A World History*, teacher's ed. (New York: McGraw-Hill/Glencoe, 2006), 107, 114–115.

20. Farah and Karls, *Human Experience*, 83–84.

21. Peter N. Stearns, Michael Adas, Stuart B. Schwartz, et al., *World Civilizations: The Global Experience*, 4th ed., advanced placement ed. (New York: Pearson/Longman, 2006), 106.

22. Carrington, Collins, Iriye, *Human Journey, Modern World*, 4, 6.

23. David M. Helgren, Robert J. Sager and Alison S. Brooks, *People, Places, and Change*, teacher's ed. (Austin: Holt, Rinehart and Winston, 2005), 384.

24. Robert J. Sager, and David M. Helgren, *World Geography Today*, teacher's ed. (Austin: Holt, Rinehart and Winston, 2005), 452.

25. Hanes III, *Continuity & Change*, 29I–29J, 46–47, 132.

26. Roger B. Beck, Linda Black, Larry S. Krieger, et al., *Ancient World History: Patterns of Interaction*, teacher's ed. (Evanston, IL: McDougal Littell, 2005), 77.

27. Jerry Bentley and Herbert Ziegler, *Traditions & Encounters: A Global Perspective on the Past*, teacher's ed. (Boston: McGraw-Hill, 2006), 45–48.

28. Jackson J. Spielvogel, *Glencoe World History*, teacher's ed. (New York: McGraw-Hill/Glencoe, 2005), 55–56.

29. Beck, Black, Krieger, *Ancient World History*, 78, 96.

30. Richard G. Boehm, David G. Armstrong, Francis P. Hunkins, et al., *The World and Its People*, teacher's ed. (New York: McGraw-Hill/Glencoe, 2005), 473, 509.

31. Spielvogel, *Glencoe World History*, 56.

32. Sarah W. Bednarz, Ines M. Miyares, Mark C. Schug, et al., *World Cultures and Geography: Eastern Hemisphere and Europe*, teacher's ed. (Evanston, IL: McDougal Littell, 2005), 209a.

33. Spielvogel, *Glencoe World History*, 57.

34. Audrey Shabbas, ed., *Arab World Studies Notebook*. (Berkeley, AWAIR and MEPC, 1998), 263.

35. Bentley and Ziegler, *Traditions & Encounters*, 45–48.

36. Philip J. Adler and Randall L. Pouwels, *World Civilizations*, 4th ed., instructor's ed. (Belmont, CA: Wadsworth/Thomson, 2006), 44.

37. Bradley Burston, "Christmas 2006: Is Jesus still a Palestinian?," *Ha'aretz*, December 14, 2006, http://www.haaretz.com/hasen/spages/800092.html (accessed April 19, 2007).

38. Supplemental materials provided by Arab and Muslim interest groups are strong advocates of the idea of a Christianity rooted in Palestinian identity and connecting it to alleged Israeli persecution of Christians. An excerpt from the discussion of "The First Christians" in AWAIR's Arab World Studies Notebook quotes Palestin-

ian leader Hannan Ashrawi: "I keep reminding people that Christianity started in Palestine," yet she mentions nothing of the Jewish connection to the land, and ignores Christianity's roots in and connection to Judaism. Ashwari asserts that "Muslims are guardians of holy places, of Christian places, as Christians can be guardians of Muslim holy places." Audrey Shabbas, ed., "The First Christians," *Arab World Studies Notebook* (Berkeley: AWAIR and MEPC, 1998), 102.

The *Notebook* describes Christianity's beginning without mentioning Jews, Judaism, or Israel. The materials claim that while Arab Muslims and Arab Christians are "indigenous" to "Palestine," Jews are at best interlopers in the region, and, at worst, colonialist oppressors committed to ethnic cleansing of Christians:

> In less than 30 years (since the Israeli occupation of Jerusalem in 1967) . . . the number of Christians in the faith's geographical heart, Jerusalem, has dropped . . . The drain of Christians from the Holy Land . . . is part of a general exodus of Palestinian Arabs from a homeland they have found hostile and unpromising. Beginning in 1948, when the new State of Israel occupied vast areas of Palestinian land and began imposing harsh conditions on its Arab inhabitants, steady emigration has scattered the Holy Land's Christian families throughout the earth.

Shabbas, "First Christians," *Notebook*, 103.

Elias Rishmawi, an Arab Christian community leader is quoted in the Notebook accusing Israel of ethnic cleansing: "Israelis have targeted the Palestinian Christian community for extinction. We are an endangered species . . ." Shabbas, *Notebook*, 84. In reality, Christians gradually became a minority in the Holy Land during the first hundred years of the rule of Islam, and in the modern Middle East, Israeli Arab Christians form proportionally one of the largest Christian minorities within Arab populations. Daphne Tsimhoni, "Israel and the Territories—Disappearance: Disappearing Christians of the Middle East," *Middle East Quarterly*, Winter 2001, www.meforum.org/article/15.

Furthermore, Walid Phares, professor of Middle East studies at Florida Atlantic University, writes of "large-scale oppression of Middle East Christians" throughout the "Arab Middle East." Phares reports on the arrest, torture, and imprisonment of Lebanese Christians under Syrian occupation; the targeting of south Sudanese Christians by Islamist forces; the routine raids of Christian villages in Egypt; and the fact that there are no Christian citizens of Saudi Arabia, since by law only a Muslim can be a Saudi citizen. Walid Phares, "Middle East Christians: The Captive Nations," in Malka Hillel Shulewitz, ed., *Forgotten Millions: The Modern Jewish Exodus from Arab Lands* (Continuum: London, 1999), 15–32.

39. Sheeley Neese, "Palestinian Liberation Theology," *The Jerusalem Connection*, March–April 2007, 23.

40. Greenblatt and Lemmo, *Human Heritage*, 249.

41. Beck, Black, Krieger, *Ancient World History*, 168.

42. Bednarz, Miyares, Schug, *World Cultures: Eastern Hemisphere*, 230.

43. Ahmad, Brodsky, Crofts, *Global Mosaic*, 565.

44. Bednarz, Miyares, Schug, *World Cultures: Eastern Hemisphere*, 230.

45. Spielvogel, *Glencoe World History*, 169.

46. Candy D. Boyd, Geneva Gay, Rita Geiger, et al., *The World* (Scott Foresman Social Studies), teacher's ed. (Glenview, IL: Pearson/Scott Foresman, 2005), 295, 274d, 297.

Seven: The Founding of Israel: Rights to the Land, War and Refugees

1. Jimmy Carter, *Palestine: Peace Not Apartheid* (New York: Simon and Schuster, 2007), 189.
2. Marc Dollinger, "Anti-Israel Boycott Movement is Misplaced," *San Francisco Chronicle*, August 17, 2007.
3. Diane Tobin, Gary Tobin, and Scott Rubin, *In Every Tongue: The Racial and Ethnic Diversity of the Jewish People* (San Francisco: Institute for Jewish & Community Research, 2005).
4. Columbia University Professor George Saliba was reported to have told one of his Jewish students, "See you have green eyes. You're not a Semite. [. . .] You have no claim to the Land of Israel." *Columbia Unbecoming*, DVD, directed by Avi Goldwasser (Boston: David Project, 2004). See the discussion in Gary A. Tobin, Aryeh K. Weinberg, and Jenna Ferer, *The UnCivil University* (San Francisco: Institute for Jewish & Community Research, 2005), 107.
5. "Special Report No. 39, Iranian Leaders: Statements and Positions (Part I)," *Middle East Media Reporting Research Institute*, January 5, 2006, http://memri.org/bin/articles.cgi?Page=countries&Area=iran&ID=SR3906 (accessed March 21, 2008).
6. Daniel D. Arreola, Marci Smith Deal, James F. Peterson, et al., *World Geography*, California teacher's ed. (Evanston, IL: McDougal Littell, 2006), 482.
7. Robert J. Sager, and David M. Helgren, *World Geography Today*, teacher's ed. (Austin: Holt, Rinehart and Winston, 2005), 458.
8. William Travis Hanes III, ed., *World History: Continuity & Change*, annotated teacher's ed. (Austin: Holt, Rinehart and Winston, 1999), 769E.
9. Roger B. Beck, Linda Black, Larry S. Krieger, et al., *Ancient World History: Patterns of Interaction*, teacher's ed. (Evanston, IL: McDougal Littell, 2005), 170.
10. Laurel Carrington, Mattie P. Collins, Kira Iriye, et al., eds., *World History: The Human Journey*, student ed. (Austin: Holt, Rinehart and Winston, 2003), 760.
11. Roger B. Beck, Linda Black, Larry S. Krieger, et al., *Modern World History: Patterns of Interaction*, teacher's ed. (Evanston, IL: McDougal Littell, 2005), 667.
12. Roane Carey, ed., *The New Intifada: Resisting Israel's Apartheid* (London: Verso, 2001), 334. Contributor Nancy Murray quotes herself from Breaking the Siege, the newsletter of the Middle East Justice Network, October-November 1993. Accessed May 1, 2008 at http://books.google.com/books?id=B7hZCPEYzysC&printsec=frontcover #PPA334,M1.
13. Audrey Shabbas, ed., *The Arab World Studies Notebook* (Berkeley: AWAIR and MEPC, 1998), 315.
14. Shabbas, *Notebook*, 318.
15. Shabbas, *Notebook*, 84.
16. Shabbas, *Notebook*, 83.
17. Shabbas, *Notebook*, 83–84.
18. Shabbas, *Notebook*, 84.
19. Larry Collins and Dominique Lapierre, *O Jerusalem!: Day by Day and Minute by Minute The Historic Struggle For Jerusalem and the Birth of Israel* (New York: Simon & Schuster, 1972), 22.
20. Maya Choshen, ed., "Population of Israel and Jerusalem, by Population Group, 1922–2005, " *Statistical Yearbook of Jerusalem, 2006*, http://www.jiis.org.il/imageBank/File/shnaton_2006/shnaton_C0105.pdf (accessed September 23, 2007).

21. British Consul James Finn to Earl of Clarendon, Jerusalem, January 1, 1858. From A.H. Hyamson, ed., *The British Consulate in Jerusalem in Relation to the Jews in Palestine, 1838–1914* (London: Edward Goldston Ltd., 1939–1941), 257, quoted in Joan Peters, *From Time Immemorial: The Origins of the Arab Jewish Conflict Over Palestine* (Chicago: JKAP Publications, 1984), 198.

22. British Consul James Finn to the Earl of Clarendon, January 17, 1856, from Hyamson, Consulate, 239, quoted in Peters, *Time Immemorial*, 199.

23. Michael J. Berson, ed., *World History.* (Harcourt Horizons), teacher's ed. (Orlando: Harcourt, 2005), 647.

24. Sager and Helgren, *World Geography Today*, 456.

25. Hanes III, *Continuity & Change*, 779.

26. Hanes III, *Continuity & Change*, 782.

27. Harcourt Horizons, ed., *The World* (Harcourt Horizons), teacher's ed. (Orlando: Harcourt, 2003), 666.

28. Laurel Carrington, Mattie P. Collins, Kira Iriye, et al., eds., *World History: The Human Journey, Modern World*, teacher's ed. (Austin: Holt, Rinehart and Winston, 2005), 705.

29. Carrington, Collins, Iriye, *The Human Journey*, student ed., 876.

30. Beck, Black, Krieger, *Modern World History*, 589.

31. Beck, Black, Krieger, *Modern World History*, 585.

32. Beck, Black, Krieger, *Modern World History*, 587.

33. Shabbas, *Notebook*, 373.

34. Carrington, Collins, Iriye, *The Human Journey*, student ed., 876.

35. Hanes III, *Continuity & Change*, 782.

36. Richard G. Boehm, David G. Armstrong, Francis P. Hunkins, et al., *The World and Its People*, teacher's ed. (New York: McGraw-Hill/Glencoe, 2005), 511.

37. Candy D. Boyd, Geneva Gay, Rita Geiger, et al., *The World* (Scott Foresman Social Studies), teacher's ed. (Glenview, IL: Pearson/Scott Foresman, 2005), 615.

38. Jiu-Hwa L. Upshur, Janice J. Terry, James P. Holoka, et al., *World History Since 1500: The Age of Global Integration*, vol. 2 (Belmont, CA: Wadsworth/Thomson Learning, 2002), 753.

39. Sarah W. Bednarz, Ines M. Miyares, Mark C. Schug, et al., *World Cultures and Geography: Eastern Hemisphere and Europe*, teacher's ed. (Evanston, IL: McDougal Littell, 2005), 242.

40. Iftikhar Ahmad, Herbert Brodsky, Marylee Susan Crofts, et al., *World Cultures: A Global Mosaic*, teacher's ed. (Upper Saddle River, NJ: Pearson/Prentice Hall, 2004), 617.

41. Arreola, Deal, Peterson, *World Geography*, 532.

42. Shabbas, *Notebook*, 374.

43. American Jewish Committee, *Propaganda, Proselytizing, and Public Education: A Critique of the Arab World Studies Notebook* (New York: American Jewish Committee, February 2005), 23.

44. Beck, Black, Krieger, *Modern World History*, 586.

45. Mounir A. Farah, and Andrea Berens Karls, *World History: The Human Experience*, student ed. (New York: McGraw-Hill/Glencoe, 2001), 955.

46. Bednarz, Miyares, Schug, *World Cultures: Eastern Hemisphere*, 245.

47. Shabbas, *Notebook*, 247.

48. *Educational Guide to the Arab and Muslim World* (San Francisco: Arab Cultural Center, no date), 59–60.

49. Alan Dershowitz, *The Case for Israel* (New Jersey: John Wiley & Sons, Inc., 2003), 105.

50. Peters, *Time Immemorial*, 26.

51. "Where Do the Refugees Live?," *United Nations Relief and Works Agency for Palestine Refugees in the Near East,* http://www.un.org/unrwa/refugees/wheredo.html (accessed May 1, 2008).

52. Howard Sachar, *A History of Israel: From the Rise of Zionism to Our Time,* 2nd ed. (New York: Alfred A. Knopf, 2006), 333.

53. Jerry Bentley and Herbert Ziegler, *Traditions & Encounters: A Global Perspective on the Past,* teacher's ed. (Boston: McGraw-Hill, 2006), 1105.

54. Carrington, Collins, Iriye, *Human Journey, Modern World,* teacher's ed., 701.

55. Philip J. Adler and Randall L. Pouwels, *World Civilizations,* 4th ed., instructor's ed. (Belmont, CA: Wadsworth/Thomson, 2006), 718.

56. Shabbas, *Notebook,* 373, 395.

57. Farah and Karls, *Human Experience,* 951, 962.

58. Sager and Helgren, *World Geography Today,* 111.

59. Carrington, Collins, Iriye, *Human Journey, Modern World,* teacher's ed., 701.

60. Boyd, Gay, Geiger, *The World,* (Scott Foresman), 615.

61. Arreola, Deal, Peterson, *World Geography,* 513.

62. Beck, Black, Krieger, *Modern World History,* 586.

63. Arreola, Deal, Peterson, *World Geography,* 513.

64. Arreola, Deal, Peterson, *World Geography,* 513.

65. Sachar, *History of Israel,* 335–336.

66. "Mission Statement," *JIMENA, Jews Indigenous to the Middle East and North Africa,* http://www.jimena.org/mission.htm (accessed September 24, 2007).

67. Hanes III, *Continuity & Change,* 779.

68. Ya'akov Meron, "Why Jews Fled the Arab Countries," *Middle East Quarterly,* September 1995, http://www.meforum.org/article/263.

69. Bednarz, Miyares, Schug, *World Cultures: Eastern Hemisphere,* 244.

Eight: Terrorism and Internal Conflict

1. "The Palestine National Charter: Resolutions of the Palestine National Council July 1–17, 1968," *The Avalon Project,* http://www.yale.edu/lawweb/avalon/mideast/plocov.htm (accessed November 2, 2007).

2. "Israel–PLO Recognition: Exchange of Letters Between PM Rabin and Chairman Arafat," *U.S Department of State,* September 9, 1993, http://www.state.gov/p/nea/rls/22579.htm (accessed November 2, 2007).

3. Howard Sachar, *A History of Israel: From the Rise of Zionism to Our Time,* 2nd ed. (New York: Alfred A. Knopf, 2006), 619

4. Laurel Carrington, Mattie P. Collins, Kira Iriye, et al., eds., *World History: The Human Journey, Modern World,* teacher's ed. (Austin: Holt, Rinehart and Winston, 2005), 701.

5. Sachar, *History of Israel,* 174.

6. Sachar, *History of Israel,* 267.

7. Sachar, *History of Israel,* 247, 333.

8. William Travis Hanes III, ed., *World History: Continuity & Change,* annotated teacher's ed. (Austin: Holt, Rinehart and Winston, 1999), 667, see also 779.

9. Hanes III, *Continuity & Change,* 779.

10. Richard W. Bulliet, Pamela Kyle Crossley, Daniel R. Headrick, et al., *The Earth and Its Peoples: A Global History*, advanced placement ed. (Boston: Houghton Mifflin Company, 2005), 842.

11. Peter N. Stearns, Michael Adas, Stuart B. Schwartz, et al., *World Civilizations: The Global Experience*, 4th ed., advanced placement ed. (New York: Pearson/Longman, 2006), 774.

12. Stearns, Adas, Schwartz, *The Global Experience*, 905.

13. Hanes III, *Continuity & Change*, 882.

14. Sarah Witham Bednarz, Ines M. Miyares, Mark C. Schug, et al., *World Cultures and Geography: Eastern Hemisphere and Europe*, teacher's ed. (Evanston, IL: McDougal Littell, 2005), 245.

15. Jackson Spielvogel, *Glencoe World History*, teacher's ed., (New York: McGraw-Hill/Glencoe), 932.

16. Mounir A. Farah, and Andrea Berens Karls, *World History: The Human Experience*, student ed. (New York: McGraw-Hill/Glencoe, 2001), 952.

17. Farah and Karls, *Human Experience*, 954.

18. Jiu-Hwa L. Upshur, Janice J. Terry, James P. Holoka, et al., *World History Since 1500: The Age of Global Integration*, vol. 2 (Belmont, CA: Wadsworth/Thomson Learning, 2002), 786.

19. Philip J. Adler and Randall L. Pouwels, *World Civilizations*, 4th ed., instructor's ed. (Belmont, CA: Wadsworth/Thomson, 2006), 718.

20. Laurel Carrington, Mattie P. Collins, Kira Iriye, eds., *World History: The Human Journey*, student ed. (Austin: Holt, Rinehart and Winston, 2003), 899.

21. Daniel D. Arreola, Marci Smith Deal, James F. Peterson, et al., *World Geography*, California teacher's ed. (Evanston, IL: McDougal Littell, 2006), 513.

22. Arreola, Deal, Peterson, *World Geography*, 513.

23. Harcourt Horizons, ed., *The World* (Harcourt Horizons), teacher's ed. (Orlando: Harcourt, 2003), 666.

24. Harcourt Horizons, *The World*, 667.

25. Roger B. Beck, Linda Black, Larry S. Krieger, et al., *Modern World History: Patterns of Interaction*, teacher's ed. (Evanston, IL: McDougal Littell, 2005), R83.

26. Bednarz, Miyares, Schug, *World Cultures: Eastern Hemisphere*, 244.

27. Spielvogel, *Glencoe World History*, 57.

28. Jerry Bentley and Herb Ziegler, *Traditions & Encounters: A Global Perspective on the Past*, teacher's ed. (Boston: McGraw-Hill, 2006), 1117.

29. Bentley and Ziegler, *Traditions & Encounters*, G-6.

30. Beck, Black, Krieger, *Modern World History*, 587.

31. Richard G. Boehm, David G. Armstrong, Francis P. Hunkins, et al., *The World and Its People*, teacher's ed. (New York: McGraw-Hill/Glencoe, 2005), 525.

32. Carrington, Collins, Iriye, *Human Journey, Modern World*, teacher's ed., 808.

33. "A Rising Tide Lifts Mood in the Developing World: Sharp Decline in Support for Suicide Bombing in Muslim Countries," Pew Research Center, July 2007, http://pewglobal.org/reports/display.php?ReportID=257, accessed November 7, 2007).

34. *Teaching About Islam and Muslims in the Public School Classroom*, 3rd ed. (Fountain Valley, CA: Council on Islamic Education, 1995), 50.

35. *Teaching About Islam*, 50.

36. Audrey Shabbas, ed., *Arab World Studies Notebook* (Berkeley: AWAIR and MEPC, 1998), 3–4.

37. Bulliet, Crossley, Headrick, *Earth and Its Peoples*, 842.

38. Boehm, Armstrong, Hunkins, *World and Its People*, 527.

39. *Teaching About Islam*, 50.

40. *Educational Guide to the Arab and Muslim World* (San Francisco: Arab Cultural Center, no date), 35.

41. Adler and Pouwels, *World Civilizations*, 718.

42. *Educational Guide*, ii.

43. Karima Alavi, "At Risk of Prejudice: Teaching Tolerance About Muslim Americans," *Social Education* 65, no. 6 (2001).

44. Zeina Azzam Seikaly, "At Risk of Prejudice: The Arab American Community," *Social Education* 65, no. 6 (October, 2001):349–351.

45. Heidi H. Jacob and Michal L. LeVasseur. *Medieval Times to Today* (World Studies), teacher's ed. (Upper Saddle River, NJ: Pearson/Prentice Hall, 2005), 242.

46. Nachman Shai, *The Spokesperson—In the Crossfire: A Decade of Israeli Defense Crises from an Official Spokesperson's Perspective* (Cambridge, MA: Joan Shorenstein Center: Press, Politics, Public Policy, Harvard University, 1998), 7.

47. Shai, *Spokesperson*, 7.

48. Shai, *Spokesperson*, 7.

49. Efrat Weiss, "Former Arafat Aide: He Purchased Arms with Israeli Money," *Ynetnews*, http://www.ynetnews.com/articles/0,7340,L-3251982,00.html (accessed August 23, 2007).

50. Shai, *Spokesperson*, 9.

51. Shai, *Spokesperson*, 9.

52. Beck, Black, Krieger, *Modern World History*, 587.

53. Beck, Black, Krieger, *Modern World History*, 667.

54. Beck, Black, Krieger, *Modern World History*, 588.

55. "Suicide and Other Bombing Attacks in Israel Since the Declaration of Principles, Sept 1993," *Israel Ministry of Foreign Affairs*, http://www.mfa.gov.il/MFA/Terrorism+Obstacle+to+Peace/Palestinian+terror+since+2000/Suicide+and+Other+Bombing+Attacks+in+Israel+Since.htm (accessed July 16, 2007).

56. M.K.Gandhi, "Satyagraha," *Wikipedia, the Free Encylopedia*, http://en.wikipedia.org/wiki/Satyagraha#Origins_of_Satyagraha (accessed May 8, 2008).

57. Martin Luther King, Jr., "Letter from Birmingham Jail," *The Martin Luther King, Jr., Research and Education Institute*, http://www.stanford.edu/group/King/popular_requests/frequentdocs/birmingham.pdf (accessed September 17, 2007).

58. Carrington, Collins, Iriye, *Human Journey, Modern World*, teacher's ed., 707–708.

59. Hanes III, *Continuity & Change*, 782.

60. Elisabeth G. Ellis and Anthony Esler, *World History: Connections to Today* (Upper Saddle River, NJ: Prentice Hall, 2001), 900.

61. Adler and Pouwels, *World Civilizations*, 716.

62. Beck, Black, Krieger, *Modern World History*, 667.

63. Don Radlauer, "An Engineered Tragedy: Statistical Analysis of Casualties in the Palestinian–Israeli Conflict, September 2000–September 2002," *International Policy Institute for Counter-Terrorism*, http://212.150.54.123/articles/articledet.cfm?articleid=439 (accessed July 3, 2007).

64. Upshur, Terry, Holoka, *World History Since 1500*, 755.

65. *Educational Guide*, 58.

66. Beck, Black, Krieger, *Modern World History*, 587.

67. Beck, Black, Krieger, *Modern World History*, 588.

68. Jeffrey Goldberg, "Arafat's Gift," *New Yorker*, January 29, 2001.

69. "PA Minister: The Intifada Was Planned from the Day Arafat Returned from Camp David," *The Middle East Media Research Institute, Special Dispatch Series Number 194,* March 9, 2001, http://memri.org/bin/articles.cgi?Page=archives&Area=sd&ID=SP19401#_edn1 (accessed September 24, 2007).

70. For example, Prentice Hall's *World Civilizations: The Global Experience* offers the following "Further Readings" at the end of the chapter on Israel's founding: "The period of the partition and the first Arab-Israeli conflict have been the subject of much revisionist scholarship in recent years. Some of *the best* of this is included in *important* books by Benny Morris, Walid Khalidi, Ilan Pappe, and Tom Segev." [emphasis added] Stearns, Adas, Schwartz, *The Global Experience,* 776.

71. Gary A. Tobin, Aryeh K. Weinberg, and Jenna Ferer, *The UnCivil University* (San Francisco: Institute for Jewish & Community Research, 2005), 152.

72. Some Muslims believe that they have been turned into scapegoats: A recent poll showed that 30 percent of Muslim Americans do not believe that Arabs/Muslims committed the attacks of 9/11. See "Muslim Americans: Middle Class and Mostly Mainstream," *Pew Research Center,* May 22, 2007, p. 57.

73. For more about this topic, see Tobin, Weinberg, Ferer, *UnCivil University.*

Nine: Conclusion

1. Bernard Lewis, *Islam and the West* (New York: Oxford University Press, 1993), 130.

2. "Slovakia's History: Textbook Wars," *The Economist,* March 29, 2008, 67.

3. Jonathan Zimmerman, "In Criticizing Japan's History Textbooks, Americans Should Think Twice," *Christian Science Monitor,* http://www.csmonitor.com/2005/0504/p09s01-coop.html (accessed August 13, 2007). For further reading about Japanese history textbooks, see Keith Crawford, "Culture Wars: Japanese History Textbooks and the Construction of Official Memory" in *What Shall We Teach the Children? International Perspectives on School History Textbooks,* ed. Stuart J. Foster and Keith A. Crawford (Greenwich, CT: Information Age, 2006), 49–68.

4. Khodadad (Khodi) Kaviani, "Theocratic Education: Understanding the Islamic Republic of Iran by Analyzing Its Textbooks," *Social Studies Research and Practice 1,* no. 3 (Winter 2006):374–375.

5. Hassan Fattah, "Don't Be Friends with Christians or Jews, Saudi Textbooks Say," *New York Times,* May 24, 2006, www.nytimes.com (accessed November 20, 2006).

6. Noa Meridor, "An examination of Palestinian fifth and tenth-grade textbooks for the 2004-2005 school year," *The Intelligence and Terrorism Information Center at the Israel Intelligence Heritage and Commemoration Center,* http://www.terrorism-info.org.il/malam_multimedia/English/eng_n/pdf/as_nm_e.pdf (accessed September 11, 2007).

7. Council on Islamic Education, "Assessment of Programs Submitted for 2005 California History-Social Science Adoption & Assessment of CRP/IMAP Findings," (submitted to Tom Adams, California Curriculum Commission, August 26, 2005), pages 4, 6 of the section entitled "Assessment of the CRP/IMAP Findings (Advisory Recommendations).

8. See the discussion of the Christian reassessment of its attitudes toward Jews in Chapter Four which includes excerpts of statements on Jews by major Christian denominations.

9. "Our Mission, Philosophy, and Approach," *Council on Islamic Education,* http://www.cie.org/ItemDetail.aspx?id=N&m_id=80&item_id=170&cat_id=114 (accessed March 31, 2008).

10. "About Us," Institute on Religion and Civic Values, http://www.ircv.org/index. php?option=com_content&task=view&id=5&Itemid=32 (accessed March 31, 2008).

11. American Jewish Committee, *Propaganda, Proselytizing, and Public Education: A Critique of the Arab World Studies Notebook* (New York: American Jewish Committee, February 2005), 29.

12. Gary A. Tobin, Aryeh K. Weinberg, and Jenna Ferer, *The UnCivil University* (San Francisco: Institute for Jewish & Community Research, 2005), 152.

13. American Jewish Committee, *Propaganda*.

14. *Institute for Curriculum Services*, www.icsresources.org (accessed August 13, 2007).

Ten: Methodology

1. Rabbi Shlomo Zarchi is a research fellow at the Institute for Jewish & Community Research. He received his rabbinic ordination from the Rabbinical Academy in Jerusalem and New York. Rabbi Zarchi is the rabbi of Congregation Chevra Thilim, the oldest Orthodox synagogue in San Francisco.

Rabbi Zarchi comes from a Hasidic family of rabbis that goes back six generations. Growing up in Brooklyn he learned Hebrew and Aramaic as soon as he was able to read. He began studying Kabbalah, shortly thereafter, at the age of five. He has studied under some of the great Hassidic and Kabbalistic masters. He is one of the foremost experts on the Kabbalah on the West Coast and is a frequent lecturer. Rabbi Zarchi currently teaches classes at the Jewish Community Center of San Francisco.

Rabbi Zarchi presently serves on the Vaad Hakashrus of Northern California.

2. Dr. Ephraim Isaac is the director, Institute of Semitic Studies, Princeton, NJ; Fellow of Butler College, Princeton University (1994-). Fellow, The Dead Sea Scrolls Foundation.

Born in Ethiopia where he got his early education, Dr. Isaac holds a B.A. degree in Philosophy, Chemistry, & Music (Concordia College); an M. Div. (Harvard Divinity School); a Ph.D. in Near Eastern Languages (Harvard University); and a D.H.L. (honorary, John Jay /CUNY). He was Professor at Harvard (1968 - 1977). The first professor hired in Afro-American Studies at Harvard, he was voted the best teacher each year by the students and the Department. In addition to Harvard (that endowed the "Ephraim Isaac Prize" in African Studies in 1998), Dr. Isaac has lectured at Hebrew U (Ancient Semitic Languages), Princeton U (Near Eastern Studies, Religion; V. Prof. (Religion & African American Studies 1995-01) & U of Pennsylvania (Religion, Semitic Languages), Howard U (Divinity School), Lehigh U (Religion), Bard College (Religion, History), and other institutions of higher learning. His subjects range from those mentioned above to Biblical Hebrew, Rabbinic Literature, Ethiopian History, Concept and History of Slavery, and Ancient African Civilizations. He has been a Fellow, National Endowment for the Humanities and the Institute for Advanced Studies. He has received many awards and honors including an honorary D. H. L. (John Jay College, CUNY), the "2002 Peacemaker Award" of the Rabbi Tanenbaum Center for Interreligious Understanding.

Dr. Isaac is author of numerous articles and books on (Late Second Temple) Jewish and (Ancient Ethiopic) Ge'ez literatures. Three of his recent works pertain to the oldest known manuscripts of The Book of Enoch (Doubleday, 1983) and An Ethiopic History of Joseph (Sheffield Press, 1990), and Proceedings of Second International Congress of Yemenite Jewish Studies (ISS & Univ. of Haifa, 1999). An expanded definitive version of his The Ethiopian Orthodox Church is in press (Africa World Press, 2001). He is currently working on a new edition of the "Dead Sea Scrolls Fragments of

The Book of Enoch" (Princeton Theological Seminary); "A History of Religions in Africa;" and "A Cultural History of Ethiopian Jews." He is on editorial boards of two international scholarly journals on Afroasiatic Languages and Second Temple Jewish Literature respectively.

3. An adoption state is one that has a formal textbook adoption process at the state level, while other states leave textbook adoption up to local districts. Adoption states develop a list of recommended textbooks from which local districts make their selection.

Index

About the Authors

DR. GARY A. TOBIN is the president of the Institute for Jewish & Community Research, San Francisco. He is also a senior fellow with the Baylor Institute for Studies of Religion. He earned his Ph.D. in city and regional planning from the University of California, Berkeley. Dr. Tobin has written books and monographs on anti-Semitism, including *Jewish Perceptions of Anti-Semitism* and *Anti-Semitic Beliefs in the United States*. His writings on prejudice in America's education systems include *The UnCivil University: Politics and Propaganda in American Education, A Profile of American College Faculty vol. 1: Political Beliefs & Behavior,* and *A Profile of American College Faculty vol. 2: Religious Beliefs & Behavior.*

Dr. Tobin's Jewish demography and Jewish identity texts include *Ethnic and Racial Diversity in the Jewish Community, Rabbis Talk About Intermarriage,* and *Opening the Gates: How Proactive Conversion Can Revitalize the Jewish Community.* He also writes about organized religion in America, having completed two works, *Church and Synagogue Affiliation* and *The Decline of Religious Identity in the United States.*

DENNIS R. YBARRA is a research associate at the Institute for Jewish & Community Research. He is the manager of the initiative on anti-Israelism and anti-Semitism in America's K–12 education system. Ybarra obtained a B.S. in business administration from University of California Berkeley, accompanied by substantial work in modern and biblical Hebrew. He earned an M.B.A. from the Wharton School of the University of Pennsylvania. He served as liaison to the Jewish community on behalf of the Catholic bishop of Sacramento, CA, 1990–2000, for whom he provided testimony in California History-Social Science adoptions. In 1994, the Sacramento City Council honored him for his work strengthening the ties between the city's Jewish and Catholic communities.